Spring's Edge 80

Aerial view of the DM Ranch. Photo by Joe Klobucar-Denco.

SPRING'S EDGE

A Ranch Wife's Chronicles

LAURIE WAGNER BUYER

UNIVERSITY OF NEW MEXICO PRESS ❧ ALBUQUERQUE

Library of Congress Cataloging-in-Publication Data
Buyer, Laurie Wagner, 1954–
Spring's edge : a ranch wife's chronicles / Laurie Wagner Buyer.
p. cm.
ISBN 978-0-8263-4391-8 (PBK. : ALK. PAPER)
1. Buyer, Laurie Wagner, 1954– —Homes and haunts—Colorado.
2. Colorado—Intellectual life—20th century.
3. Poets, American—20th century—Biography.
4. Colorado—Social life and customs.
5. Ranchers—Colorado—Biography.
6. Ranch life—Colorado. I. Title.
PS3552.U8944Z474   2008
811'.54—dc22
[B]
2007040976

Book and jacket design and type composition by Kathleen Sparkes.
This book was typeset using Minion OT 11/14.5, 26P6.
Display type is Engravers LT Standard Bold and Baka Too.

In memory of Bill Murray,

my angel in disguise,

and for his wife, Jo, my lady

leaning toward the wild side.

FEBRUARY 1997

⏀

A fallow time. Unable to write, I suffered. Poetry eluded me and I could not muster any enthusiasm to submit freelance work. Our six-hundred-acre ranch ten miles south of Fairplay, Colorado, and four miles up the county road toward Weston Pass, lay quiet and undisturbed under the snow as an unusually cold South Park winter dragged on interminably. Then, on the 15th, my husband, Mick, sold his main cow herd to a neighbor. I decided, on the spur of the moment, to write about the day's painful events to a friend. Sitting down in the evening with a yellow legal pad and a pen became a habit for me. Even if my scribbling amounted to nothing more than journal entries penned during the long nights in a room warmed by the wood stove after the day's chores were done, writing eased my spirit.

The DM cowherd summer of 1996. Mick sold these cows to Monte Innis in February 1997. Photo by Laurie Wagner Buyer.

Saturday, February 15th

Mick coaxes the main cow herd into the largest corral with a couple of bales balanced on a homemade buggy pulled behind the four-wheeler. He sorts off a three-year-old cow that never bred and one that slunk her fetus last week—an odd occurrence as Broken Toe is eight and this would have been her sixth calving. The calf, about seven months along, was out of the red Angus bull. Who knows why these things happen? The hay quality isn't good this year and the lack of necessary protein may have caused the spontaneous abortion. Broken Toe might have slipped on the ice, or she may have eaten pine needles up on the ridge. A sad day. The decision to sell the cows was tough, but with costs for hay sky-high and cattle prices rock-bottom, Mick couldn't afford to feed them.

Our neighbor to the east, Monte Innes, arrives at 6:30 a.m. with his truck and trailer to get the first load. A fierce west wind roars off the peaks and makes the twenty-degree temperature feel much colder. At times we can barely stand. We all spit dirt. Caked with dust, the cows' eyes run. Monte and I help Mick feed his yearling heifers. Monte praises the calves, saying they are grown out good and look well-cared for. The hay we feed, bales that Mick put up last summer, has remained green because it was barn stored. Monte hauls hay in addition to his full-time job and running his own cattle. Mick's hay is the nicest he's seen. "Want to sell me some?" he jokes, knowing Mick would never part with the hard won feed. "I'll give you five dollars a bale."

Monte and I push the older cows into a small holding pen. As they move forward I call them by name and tease Monte that I expect he will remember that Goldie needs her toes trimmed, and Red Eye will need extra attention to her large udder when she calves. Mick stands at the gate and sorts off twelve cows. Squeezing a dozen 1,000-pound animals into a twenty-one-foot trailer is not easy. As Monte pulls away, his diesel truck grinding up the long driveway in low gear, Mick and I stand arm-in-arm watching the departure, then head off to feed the bred heifers.

Later, three more trucks with trailers arrive to load out the other thirty-six cows. Mick stays to help the drivers, but I retreat to the house. I make a nice lunch, the only kindness I have to give. Mick raised each cow from a yearling heifer, and it took seven hard years to build up the herd. Now the cows are gone.

"Loaded up like a bunch of Holsteins," he reports when he comes in. Dog gentle, hand-raised cows that had never been off the ranch were stubborn to load. "The guys were patient and gentle," Mick says, reinforcing my belief that the cows are going to a good home. "Ole Red Eye balked," Mick says. "We got her front feet in, then she stalled. We pushed, pulled, prodded, coaxed. George even sweet-talked her, called her Grandma and Sugar-Booger. Finally, we manhandled her hind end in." The cattle will go south to lower, warmer country, where they will calve in a month's time. The money they've brought in will pay our taxes, insurance, and feed bills for another year. The seventeen first-calf heifers and twenty-six yearling heifer calves left on the ranch mean we are still in business.

Blue and Mick. Photo by Laurie Wagner Buyer.

Sunday, February 16th

Monte called to tell us the cows arrived safely near Buena Vista and that Miss Sally follows the tractor wheel just as she had followed the right mare's flank on our Percheron team while feeding with the hay wagon. He said he ear-tagged the cattle and put them on a liquid protein along with hay to give them a pre-calving nutrient boost.

Since we have no cow herd to feed, Mick turns the draft mares, Cookie and Candy, out on pasture with the saddle horses. I forget the strange change and go into the horse barn to harness up before I remember the new routine. With the remaining stock confined to the corrals, Mick and I feed with the four-wheeler. Our plan this morning is to bring the heavy two-year-old heifers in from the west pasture.

Holding firm at twenty-six degrees, the day beams balmy warm with welcome sun, a delicious break from the cold wind that hounded us the past two days. As we bounce across the home pasture riding double on the four-wheeler, Mick exclaims, "Damn!" I peek around his shoulder.

Mick hauling wood with the four-wheeler and ski-boose.
Photo by Laurie Wagner Buyer.

One of the heifers has calved. We stop long enough to order Blue, our Australian shepherd, onto the ATV to prevent his curious interference. The heifer stands to lick her shivering calf. Mick maintains a leave-well-enough-alone philosophy, so he opens the wire gate on the division fence to allow the rest of the heifers to come through, then shuts the gate so the horses won't pester the newcomer.

Used to following the feed wagon, the heifers trail toward home as Mick calls, "Here, girls . . . here, girls . . ." Once they are corralled, we feed them, then head back up-country to tend to the horses and bulls and give the lone heifer some hay. Later, Mick tows a snow machine ski-boose behind the four-wheeler and rescues the new calf. To prevent unnecessary struggling, Mick ties the legs, loads it, then drags the sled with reluctant passenger home at the end of a long lariat rope. Instinctively, the heifer moos, sniffs her moving calf, and follows. Mick beds them down in a shed before the sun sinks and the night chill arrives.

Monday, February 17th

After morning chores we make a hurried trip to Salida to buy calf feed, loose mineral, and groceries to stock up for another month. Now that calving has started, I won't leave the ranch except to go to town for mail, and Mick won't leave at all. He will have many chores and a great deal of careful watching day and night, with little or no sleep.

Tuesday appears with clear skies and twenty-three degrees. On Wednesday, however, the temperature dips down to six. Mick remarks on Thursday, "You can tell we're calving; it turned winter on us again." He puts three heavy heifers in the barn.

Friday, February 21st

Sleep never comes easy for me after a dose of cold air during my midnight barn check. I say my prayers. I count. I practice deep breathing. I stare out the window at the cloudy, but still bright, moonlit sky. Mick drifts off, breathing low and slow, his arm curled across my waist. I match my breathing to his and think of the new calf ensconced in the shed and hope it will get up and suck. Something warm in its belly will help carry it through the bitter night.

At 4:00 a.m. Mick says, "Stay in." I mumble in reply. I hear him go out and come back in. "Okay?" I ask. "Everything's fine," he answers. My ears catch the crumple of newspaper as Mick starts a fire in the potbellied stove, then the coffee perking, the wood fire crackling and popping, the rustle of paper in the gingersnap box as he gets a handful of cookies to dunk in his coffee. I doze off. When I wake again I listen as Mick gets a bowl from the cupboard, milk from the refrigerator. Cold cereal for breakfast doesn't sound that good. Though every one of my muscles curls tight and every joint aches from yesterday's work, I make myself rise.

Chores go well despite the six degrees. The high-altitude sun makes us feel warmer. I hike the upper part of the west pasture to the river. Walking through the untracked snow demands effort. Running ahead, Blue bounces along like a kangaroo, entertaining himself by burying his muzzle in snowdrifts to search out mysterious smells.

After noon dinner, Mick leaves to load hay for feeding the following day, and I head to town to pick up mail and visit the library. The scary ice-slick roads require a turtle's pace. On my return, getting out to open the ranch gate, I sense cold air sinking down from the high peaks. The steaming river exhales silver-blue mist. Mick has done the evening chores and put two more heavy heifers in the barn. He watches Bullnanza Rodeo while I write letters.

Saturday, February 22nd

The digital clock flips to 3:30 a.m. Mick sits up.

"What?" I ask, knowing that long years of calving have developed Mick's gut-instinct foresight.

"Something's wrong." He pulls on pants and shirt over his long johns.

I start a fire in the kitchen stove. When he comes through the porch door, he says, "Freckles had her calf in the corral. Damn! I turned her around three times today, but she didn't have any bag and I figured she'd go a day or two longer. Calf's still alive."

I pour him a cup of coffee and he gobbles down a handful of cookies. I creep into the living room to look at the thermometer. "It's fourteen below."

"Okay, let's get the little bugger inside," Mick says.

A brown plastic tarp serves as a makeshift sling, which we use to alternately drag and carry the calf to the house. He is a big lunker, chilled down but struggling. Freckles only had time to lick him partially clean before the frigid air turned the birth mucus to ice on his hide. We heave the calf into the bathtub, tarp and all. I crank up the furnace to seventy-five.

Thawing, the newborn turns wet and shivers. I administer an all-over body massage with an old flannel sheet and use the blow dryer to warm his legs. His ears, which had been as stiff as cardboard, droop, drip melted ice, and turn transparent, a sure sign that they will fall off. Crop-eared, but alive.

I dub him Icicle. The more I rub and massage, the more he quivers and shakes, and the more I sweat with exertion. I croon as I work and shush Blue, who whines outside the bathroom door. Finally, I let him in so he can investigate. He covers the calf's soggy face with sloppy dog kisses. When Icicle's circulation returns, he tries to stand. I turn down the furnace so he won't overheat, then head out to help Mick.

Light snow falls. My pack boots squeak on the trail calling out, cold, cold, cold. I chop ice off the stock tanks, and open the water holes on the river. While Mick puts the space heater on his old 1937 Chevy truck, I split several giant rounds of firewood. Blue follows me in and out of the house, insisting we check on the bathtub-bound calf. Icicle's eyes are bright and he responds to touch.

We feed the yearling heifers, then rumble up-country in the '37 to feed the bulls and horses. Blue and I brave the cold to hike and are rewarded by myriad elk tracks in the virgin snow.

Icicle is up, stumbling around, and trying to suck. We shuffle him back to the barn where Freckles goes into mothering mode.

In the afternoon, we trek across the county road on the four-wheeler with the rubber-wheeled cart behind to the timbered acreage bordering the national forest. Our woodpile is low. The forecast calls for another storm. The snow drifts over my knees in the spaces shadowed by trees. I walk the last half mile of trail so Mick can maneuver through the aspen and pine. Blue flushes a rabbit from the underbrush. Dog and cottontail turn into milky blurs against the snow-draped landscape. Tongue lolling, Blue returns. When I scold him, he takes my harsh words as a licking. When only a pup, he learned that chasing deer, elk, coyotes, birds, or any other game was forbidden, but I've been unable to break him of running rabbits. Since Blue will never catch one, Mick thinks there is no harm in allowing Blue the joy of pursuit. Still, I insist that Blue mind. Mick calls me a sour old schoolmarm.

While Mick trims lower limbs from a fifty-foot, dead-standing Douglas fir, I pull the branches away to create habitat for small animals. Mick rings the tree with one smooth, circling cut of the chain saw. An ominous crack sounds deep within the seasoned trunk. We freeze. The tree stands firm. Mick glides the saw in the open wound and cuts deeper into the heart-wood. The fir lists, rights itself, then falls, striking the ground along our back trail with a thunderous boom, and sends clouds of snow flying sky-ward. Watching an old-growth tree give up an honored spot in the land-scape excites and saddens me.

After cutting through the eighteen-inch trunk, Mick sets the saw to stop on the upper part of the tree. I duck in to pull the round out and carry it to the cart. Fifteen big rounds later, the cart sags under the burden. My

Blue. Photo by Laurie Wagner Buyer.

ears echo with the saw's reverberation. Covered with sawdust and snow from the waist down, Mick stores the saw in the box on the front of the ATV. The four-wheeler growls through the snow in low range, and I push the cart from behind on steep rises. Following wearily, Blue has forgotten his scolding, but not his dream of someday catching a rabbit.

Sunday, February 23rd

Snowing again. Eight degrees. The tiers of new wood wear lacy collars when I head out at midnight to check heifers. The snow sifts down in a fine iridescent curtain brightened by full moonlight. Calm, snuggled in hay beds, the heifers chew their cuds, grunting and moaning in patient contentment. Expectant and unconcerned, the heifers' bellies bulge up from their broad backs like whales sounding.

4:30. Still snowing. Mick checks the heifers again while I fix bacon, eggs, and toast. Half-awake and still tired we do not speak. Silence hangs between us. Dishes done, I shift into high gear to strip the sheets from the bed and put them into the washer, clean the bathroom, and vacuum the carpets. I stuff sheets into the dryer, toss towels in the washer, water the plants, dust the furniture, make the bed, then hurry to get into my outdoor clothes, and rush outside to help Mick by first light.

Completely sealed shut by fallen and falling snow, our world remains hushed. Mick has the heifer and her new calf fed and watered. The yearling heifers have had their pellets. Like cogs on a chain, we click into our daily routine. I fall through the river ice while trying to scoop away collected snow and suffer two wet feet and one soaked hand. Because it is above zero, I can survive without going in to change.

Kicking up clouds of fresh powder, the horses buck and run. They shake heartily, spilling snow from broad backs. Icicles that dangle from their manes, tails, and shaggy belly hair clink together like crystal wind chimes.

Back at the house I rebuild the fire. Mick and I stand, rumps-to-stove, to thaw out. After lunch I sit by the stove and stitch a piece of beadwork until my eyes droop and water. When Mick goes out to pump water into the stock tanks, I give in to an hour's nap on the couch.

When I wake, the sky hangs gray and low, but the snow has stopped. I bundle up and strap on skis for a short trek. Blue is not around to accompany me. I assume he is with Mick feeding the calves their evening hay ration. The swish-glide of skis and planting my poles in the new snow stretches dull muscles. I love moving across the winter landscape, not as an outsider, but as a part of the snow and sage, the seemingly touchable sky, the white-cloaked pines on the ridge. I ski past horses that glance up in prick-eared curiosity before returning to paw for bunch grass between clumps of rabbit brush. Alone time equals salvation and I return home renewed.

Blue is still absent. Mick and I make the rounds of the ranch buildings calling his name. We find him closed in the horse barn. Confused by his temporary confinement, he leaps and barks, then races circles in the snow.

Mick checks on the heifers at eight, then heads for bed. Watching a TV movie, I manage to stay awake until ten. Then I doze on the couch, buried under a half dozen blankets because I hate to burn too much wood. At midnight my silly alarm clock wakes me by playing "You Are My Sunshine" in a rinky-dink computer piano tune. Groggy, I trudge to the barn. Four of the late calvers sleep in a circle by the windbreak gate. They never budge from their beds as I wend my way through the obstacle course they create. Their backs are covered with a thick crust of snow. Another two inches have fallen during the dark hours.

The six heifers in the barn lie quiet. One red heifer rests awkwardly with her back legs sticking straight out. She stretches and her tail kinks up to reveal the red vaginal lining with a thin string of white mucus attached. The calf inside her moves and a huge ripple rolls across the ball of her belly. She glances back over her shoulder and sighs; then burps up her cud and chews, her eyes half-closed in a bliss only bovines understand.

Monday, February 24th

After so many springs of unsettled night hours, waking becomes instinctive. At 3:45 I struggle upright.

Mick asks, "What?"

"Nothing," I say. "I'm gonna go check the heifers."

"No," he says, "I'll go. You already went."

"I'll go. I'm already up and awake."

"No," he starts again, but I cut him off.

"Why in heaven's name are we arguing?" I pull the covers up over his shoulders and slide out of bed into the silver-snow glow of moonlight cast on the bedroom floor. I relish the sensation of walking on water as I make my way in semidarkness to the kitchen. I perform a mental checklist before leaving the house: boots, coat, gloves, scarf, and flashlight.

The premonition that woke me was right—the red heifer has calved. I peek through a crack in the barn boards. The calf shakes its head. A glassy shine of mucus covers the red slick hide and a thick gob of womb sack halfway covers the blinking eyes. If the pall had covered the calf's nose, he would not have been able to breathe. Struggling to stand, the calf breaks the umbilical cord. The heifer, too, tries to rise, but cannot. Her hind legs have no strength. I wait, giving her time to recuperate.

Entering the east side of the barn, I leave the gate open behind me to let the other heifers ease away from the new mother. The calf stumbles in a small circle as I gently boot-shove the heifer into rising. She wobbles and staggers, but finally gains her balance and turns toward her calf. Pandemonium breaks loose when the heifers spook, dashing and crashing every which-a-way, trying to move away from me. I hold my breath until they shift into the center section of the barn. The red heifer calls her calf, then butts it halfheartedly. The calf goes down and I back off. With time the heifer warms to the idea that this wet hunk of hide belongs to her, and she begins the mothering task of licking her calf clean. I slip out. Calf number four, another bull, is alive and vigorous. When I return to the house, the intense cold glistens from more falling snow. The temperature reads four degrees.

Wary and on edge, Mick and I snap at each other. We are only ten days into calving with another month to go, but already we are worn, tired, and crabby. I force myself to hold my tongue. I do some stretching exercises after breakfast to ease the tension in my shoulders and spine. I will be amenable. I will not bite back when Mick hollers. I vow not to have hurt feelings and indulge in stubborn silences. Instead, I'll serve leftovers for lunch. I won't cook. I won't make the cake I promised. Store-bought cookies will have to do for dessert. My silly little war, one fought many times before, is irony because no one wins. We end up two losers who snarl and growl until we tire, sign an uneasy truce with tentative smiles, and begin again.

This afternoon I write. Doing something I love gives me clean comfort. Creating rough scribbles on a yellow pad fulfills me. I keep to the kitchen. Mick holes up in the living room watching TV in between checking heifers, vaccinating and castrating the new calf, pumping water, and going for another load of wood alone. He asks me to go along but I tell him I'm too busy. He leaves, slamming the door. It's okay; we'll heal. Just this once, I need time to do something for myself, something apart from the calving and the ranch, the work and the worry. Writing feeds the beast that prowls the outer reaches of my heart, gnawing at my contentment. I write to be sweet-tempered again.

The phone rings several times after supper. Mick's son's wife Mary Ann checks in. A local reporter calls to do an interview with me because my new book of poetry, *Glass-eyed Paint in the Rain*, is a finalist for the Colorado Book Awards. My boss at Arrowhead Ranch, where I seasonally manage a fly-fishing resort, wants to start planning the 1997 season. In between calls, I watch TV with Mick as an attempt at a truce.

At 8:00 p.m. Mick checks the heifers again. I sack out on the couch fully clothed, pile on the afghans, and put the alarm clock within easy reach. I never mind getting up in the wee hours, but dressing and undressing irritates me. This way all I need to do is put on my coveralls, coat, and boots, then head out into the cold.

Tuesday, February 25th

In the frigid midnight air, my face stiffens in a yawn when I step through the porch door. Ringed with a purple-blue haze, the moon makes the night sparkle. Stars hang willy-nilly, like spilled crystal beads. Window-length icicles hang from the roof's edge looking like glass bars. The house fires have long since gone out. No whiff of wood smoke mars the sharp, pure air. My nostrils flare and stick, the telltale sign that the temperature rests below zero.

Half the corralled heifers curl against the windbreak. They rise and stretch, leaving craters on the ground where their bodies melted the snow crust. The others up on the hill pick through the remnants of the day's hay. Moonlight outlines their four-legged forms so I can see that all are eating; none have calved outside. The barned heifers blink rapidly, adjusting their eyes to the overhead light I switch on. In the quiet, their bellies rumble, sounding like they could use a big dose of Alka-Seltzer. In the relatively warmer barn, the scents of urine, still-steaming manure, hides, hair, and damp hay create a heavy, heady perfume.

Way before first light Mick goes out to check again. I sleep in until 5:30, relishing the lazy warmth of the bed. I stretch and squirm and wiggle my feet, reluctant to exchange cozy for six-below-zero cold. Mick smiles sleepily when I shuffle into the kitchen and opens his free arm for a one-sided hug. His other hand clutches a cup of coffee.

I chop wood. I chop ice. I shovel snow and fork out hay. One yearling heifer will not eat. She stands alone by the feed bunk with her head down. Froze up, she may be fighting off pneumonia. Mick eyes her as we feed three barren cows down by the riverbank. "Figures," he says. It irks him to see sickness sneak in. He's been around cattle all his life, helping calve out since he was fifteen, raising his own stock for over forty years. Still, he never becomes accustomed to the hard knocks.

"I don't know how I've stuck with it this long without killing myself," he says.

My ears sting. The memory of Mick's daughter's ex-husband's suicide slices my mind. Sy's history of depression and the rifle bullet that claimed his life seep dark and slow back onto the sharp edge of my consciousness. I'm on the bed of the '37 Chevy, pitchfork in hand. Mick walks away from me toward the river to break away the bank ice so the cows can drink. Even with the bulk of his heavy winter coat, he's lean as a whip. His legs, clad only in long johns and jeans in this terrible cold, are barely steady as he walks through the snow. He's sixty-five. His knees shot, he holds himself together with wrapped will, like a broken corral pole pieced back together with baling wire.

When he returns I ask, "Want to tell me what that's all about?"

"Shit!" He spits in the snow. "In South Dakota ranchers are killing themselves. Five feet of snow on the level. No way to feed. No one to help them. One guy lost six hundred head. As if there's one son-of-a-bitch in this country that cares!"

What can I say. The cattle market is pitiful. Political and economic decisions made by the government have great impact. Mick's family has been ranching since 1860. Each generation came up the hard way, and he is the last of his family ranching in this broad valley of native grass that is called South Park. "Quit" isn't in his vocabulary, yet every year he takes on more work. Someday he won't be able to lift a pitchfork or heave on a harness. Cows are all he knows. This scares me, but worse than fear is the helplessness of knowing neither of us can alter the charted course of age and change.

"Want me to get that black one in?" I ask.

"No, leave her. She's in the sun right now. She needs the light to thaw her out."

Midmorning my father calls me and I leave the ranch. For several years Dad has complained of an unidentifiable pain in his chest. He phoned to tell me he is scheduled for some new tests. He needs me to drive him and Mom to and from the hospital. In a matter of minutes I fix a hearty noon dinner of elk meatballs and gravy, mashed potatoes, steamed carrots, and salad, enough for Mick to have leftovers while I'm away. He is not a man who cooks and he has survived leaner alone times on fresh-caught trout, or milk and crackers. I worry about leaving Mick, but I cannot stop to think about him or the calving. I pack and clean the kitchen. As I drive away, I honk and wave at Mick who stands near the barn waiting as stock tanks in the corral fill. His wide-reaching wave in the rearview mirror calms me.

Before I can even begin the seventy-mile drive to Mom and Dad's home in Woodland Park, I have to go in the opposite direction to Fairplay to get gas, pick up the mail, and attend to errands that cannot wait. By the time I pull out of the bank parking lot, the storm predicted to strike tomorrow hits full force. Even on the fastest setting, my wipers cannot clean the windshield. I fear traveling through the storm over the mountain passes. I want to go home and sit by the fire. I'd rather argue with Mick and worry about heifers' calving than think about my father's health. Intellect spars with emotion, but when the road forks, I turn south into the heft of the storm.

Within five miles, my prayers for decent roads are answered. The storm fades and splits: to the north, a wall of low, black clouds and snow-obscured mountains, to the south, blue sky and puffy summer clouds that look like foreigners in February. Driving east, straddling storm and sky, I am blessed by the magic of safe passage on dry roads.

When I carry my suitcase up the walk to Mom and Dad's house, the snow returns and small starlike flakes drift down from the leaden sky. Tension and fear disappear, leaving a metallic, old-blood taste in my mouth. My shoulders slump empty and heavy. The dining room table set, Mom cooks supper. Pale and drawn, Dad remains jovial and relaxed. He says he is not afraid, but he hopes the doctors find out what is causing the pain in his chest. Even though he has survived three open-heart surgeries at ages forty-one, forty-six, and fifty-five, the doctors assure him that the pesky pain is not cardiac related. At sixty-six, Dad is looking hard for answers.

Thursday, February 27th

The storm leaves a couple of sloppy inches of snow in Woodland Park and none in Colorado Springs, where we take Dad to Penrose Hospital.

Mom and I sit in the waiting room at the GI Lab ward. I stitch beads to buckskin while Mom reads pamphlets like "Your Digestive System" and "Irritable Bowel Syndrome." We have no time to get restless because the nurse appears saying, "He's out. Waking up—asking for Scotch!"

In the recovery room Dad dozes, mouth open, snoring, looking alien with needles and tubes and a beeping heart monitor. His doctor arrives and explains Dad's complicated plumbing problems: inflammation of the esophagus, surface ulcers, no cancer. He needs to change his diet (no alcohol—there goes his Scotch—caffeine, chocolate, citrus, peppermint, fatty foods) and take medication. The doctor instructs us to call for biopsy results and reschedule more tests in two months. Dad wakes again and asks for the bartender, but the only thing the good-natured nurse will bring him is cranberry juice. In less than three hours, we are on our way home. Dad still feels woozy, but he insists on stopping for dinner at Gertrude's, a new natural-foods restaurant in Old Colorado City. Creamy tomato basil soup, green salads, fresh rolls, and apricot hazelnut cheesecake; food never tasted so good to me.

The three of us sit on the couch in the family room to watch a movie. Wrapped in a blanket, Dad drinks hot herb tea. Mom drinks a Coke and eats chocolate-covered raisins. I sit in the middle where I can reach out to hold hands or pat knees. Before going to bed I call Mick. He says he is worn out, but still going after being up all night. Two heifers calved within thirty minutes of each other; another is in labor. I'm anxious to go home.

I find Mick working in the corrals. He looks tired, but he smiles and kisses me. He tells me he has moved two cow-calf pairs up to the enclosure near the cabin where the calves will have freedom to run and buck and play, but still have access to a shed to get out of the cold weather. Two more pairs are in the corral shed. Another couple rest in the "executive suite," a large garage-type shed adjoining the cow barn. During my fifteen years with Mick, I have never come across him outside when he isn't working. He puts his boots on at dawn and leaves them on until he crawls into bed at night.

The phone rings while I fix supper. It's Dad.

"Hi," I say, "how was your day?"

"My day was fine," he replies, "up until about a half hour ago. The doctor's office called. They found some cancer."

"Shit!" I've never used such language in front of my father.

DM cow and calf. Photo by Laurie Wagner Buyer.

The biopsies came back positive. I hear Mom inserting comments into the conversation. Dad's voice is strong and calm. Mom's is tight, tinged with fear. Chest X ray. CAT scan. The doctor is getting in touch with cancer specialists. All our elation melts into a flat muddy puddle reflecting an uncertain future. I tell Dad I will come back down, but he insists they are fine. He will call if they need me. We hash over the pros and cons of calling my sisters, Karen, in Honolulu, and Eileen, in Chicago, and decide we should wait until Dad knows more.

"Hell," he says, "I don't think I'll die in a week." He laughs and I join in, my own voice small and hollow.

"I'm sorry," Mick says, when I tell him the news. "That's too bad."

He sounds sincere, but I cannot help thinking of all the times he has complained about my father, about my city family. Mick is a staunch individualist, a judgmental, critical man; not out of ignorance or meanness, but out of a rigid sense of self that cannot accept anyone or anything outside of his own rural code. He considers my parents city folks from the east (they are from Chicago, the Midwest really, but everything east of the plains states is East in capital letters to Mick, and therefore, an interfering and unwelcome element in the West). My dad spent his life as a career military man in the Air Force, and Mick is disparaging about both the military and the government since he spent an ungodly time span in Korea on the front lines. The list of inequities goes on, a tiresome record, which I coach myself not to replay. I want someone strong and wise and understanding to hold me and tell me everything will be all right.

Instead, I do the dishes. I find comfort in running hot water and a warm kitchen. I envision the ache inside me being scrubbed and rinsed and washed away, expelled from the end of the sink drain into the side yard where I often watch strutting magpies peck at remnant food in the dish water.

In my kitchen sanctuary, I write checks, pay bills, sort through the pile of mail and book orders. Mick wanders in several times to stand and watch me. He is concerned, but we are unable to reach past our awkwardness. We exchange pleasantries about the heifers, the neighbors, and the weather. He returns to the TV. When I'm finished at my desk, I join him in the living room and set up a card table with all the materials for the Arrowhead Ranch annual mailing: brochures, applications, return envelopes, ranch maps, cover letters. Silent, I stuff eighty envelopes. Mick asks, "Are you all right?" I smile yes and nod okay. The action of my hands reaching, stacking, evening, folding, stuffing, sealing, stamping, reassures my mind that I'm functional. My heart speaks a different story. It beats, but barely, the dull thud under my left breast somnolent, too tired to rouse true emotions.

Friday, February 28th

At midnight shift one of the new mothers bellers incessantly at her calf. I peek in to see if there is a problem and watch the heifer nudge her calf until he stands and begins to suck. Does she know it is below zero and the milk will keep her young one warmed from the inside out? How much do cattle think and how much is pure instinct?

Friday dawns snowy, windy, and below zero. Mick has completed the

4:00 a.m. check and is drinking coffee by a roaring fire. I join him bleary-eyed. I have a big day ahead of me. Scott, my boss at Arrowhead Ranch, is driving up from Colorado Springs for lunch to help me finalize plans for the mailing.

In between getting breakfast, making the bed, and straightening the house, I bake a cake and scrub the bathroom. Chores go well; the stock seems to be handling the weather all right. Mick seems to be handling the fact that we're having company. By 9:00 a.m. I'm back in the kitchen, reheating a pot of vegetable soup, making a salad, frosting the cake, and making dough and sauce for a homemade pizza. Mick wanders in and out doing more corral chores, watching the news and weather on TV, and teasing me about making enough food for an army.

My friends, Gary and Valerie, who are permit holders at Arrowhead Ranch, also come to lunch. Our conversation is eclectic. Scott and Gary trade fish stories. Mick is regarded as the expert cattleman and range-management consultant. Valerie and I put in our two bits regarding human nature and the needs of the resort clientele. As a clinical social worker, Valerie has helped me understand people and their problems. Gary is an avid outdoorsman, a keen observer of wildlife, and a dedicated pursuer of elusive trout. Scott, who has taken over the family ranch trust since his grandfather's death last fall, is an urban dweller who spent much of his growing-up years summering on the ranch. He is anxious to learn whatever he can about fish biology, habitat improvement, riparian protection, and the pros and cons of livestock grazing.

The conversation takes a swift plunge when cattle bashing begins. Mick is quick to respond, "What do these yuppie fish-lip rippers wear on their feet, frog hides?" We laugh. Gary points out to Scott that Mick is a conscientious manager: his cattle are healthy and well-cared for, his land is not overgrazed; the stretch of river flowing through the DM Ranch has never been stocked with fish, but it is full of small to medium brown trout with an occasional brook or cutthroat. I am so proud of Mick that my throat tightens and my eyes sting.

By the time the company leaves, I am exhausted, but Blue begs to go for his daily hike. The skies have cleared, but the ground ice is sharp edged, promising zero or below past dark. I strap on my skis. Blue and I make a fast foray up to the ranch gate on the county road. When I return thirty minutes later, my hands are frozen clubs incapable of bending, my face as tight as wallpaper.

His evening chores done, Mick relishes the supper plate served to him while he watches TV news. Two heifers are in the process of calving so he returns immediately to the barn. It is five degrees below zero. A big, red Saler heifer whose mother was a part-Simmental cow Mick was fond of has a huge bull calf. "That's one long-legged-look-like-a-colt calf," he says when he returns to warm up. "He was as slick as greased lightning, and the steam just rolled off of him when he hit the ground." Mick has placed the new pair in the corner jug to make room in the alleyway for the black brockle-face heifer to calve. Her calf's front feet show, but Mick wants to give this smaller heifer a little more time to get the calf's head through her hipbones. I never named this particular heifer, yet I remember her well. I attended her difficult birth two years ago on another cold night. Though her mother was a big heifer, the calf was good size and we needed the puller to get her born. The calf hip-locked, and we had a few pan-icked minutes when we thought we'd lose both the heifer and the calf. We managed to get the calf freed. With her lungs partly collapsed, she could not breathe well. We worked on her for an hour, alternately shaking out fluids, massaging her rubbery limbs, and compressing her lungs. I tried to tease Mick, telling him that it was the first time I'd ever done CPR and I feared the patient would die. Mick advised me to give up on the calf, that I was just wasting my time. She had a thready pulse, her eyes were glazed over, and she made no attempt to breathe or move. Mick was busy trying to maneuver the down heifer into a position where he could get her up. She had lost all her strength and showed no interest in her calf. On and on I worked until I felt the calf's heart rate speed up and she gave a stran-gled bleat. The heifer halfheartedly replied, and we left them alone, the still slimy calf covered over in hay to help maintain its body temperature. We had little hope that the calf would survive or that the heifer's natural instincts would kick in, but they did. Now, that calf was on the verge of being a mother herself.

MARCH

↩

Saturday, March 1st

Mick's internal clock goes off at the same moment my couch alarm rings at midnight. He is up and out to check the cattle: nothing but damn cold, a west breeze, the two new calves nestled down in the hay. We crawl into bed together and sleep. At 4:00 a.m., Mick's mental alarm goes off again. He is up and out the door before I can turn over. For an instant I feel a twinge of guilt that he has done both night checks, but I snuggle into the warm spot where he slept and drift back into brief dreams. In ten minutes I'm instantly awake and up, hurrying to build a fire in the stove and put on coffee. I know another heifer is calving.

"Which one?" I ask Mick when he comes stomping back in.

"The black. She needs more time. Why are you up?"

"Thought I'd make you bacon and eggs for breakfast."

"Well, you're a good woman," he says. "Call me in half an hour." He goes into the living room, coat, boots, and all, and collapses in his chair. I check the temperature. It has warmed up to zero. I turn out the light so Mick can sleep, then make myself a cup of tea. I sit at the kitchen table writing while the bacon sizzles.

Before I can wake Mick at 4:35, he is up again and out the door. He's back in five minutes. "Heifer calf. It's a good 'un." I set his coffee in front of him, but he shakes his head no. He needs another forty winks and returns to his chair. I sneak in and cover him with an afghan.

The sun rises fast and fiery in a clear sky. When my house chores are complete, I split wood and carry it in to fill the wood boxes. I watch Mick lugging five-gallon buckets of water to his three new pairs in the barn. Four other pairs are in the corral. Later he will trailer the two older pairs up to the calving enclosure where they will be on clean ground.

I'm in a rush today to get to town and mail the Arrowhead Ranch packets, which are stuffed, stamped, and lined up in a cardboard box. I change clothes, grab an apple, leave Mick a homemade TV dinner crafted with meatballs and gravy, mashed potatoes, and baked beans. "It's on the stove," I shout as I run out the door.

I stop at Arrowhead Ranch, which joins our ranch to the east, to plug in the office phone and answering machine. Once members receive their 1997 packets I will be besieged with calls for cabin reservations. Coated with melting ice and slush, the highway is nasty so I inch along at forty-five while the weekend ski traffic roars past, apparently oblivious to dangerous conditions.

At the busy post office the Division of Wildlife officer, Mark Lamb, stops to give me a wildlife calendar and a landowner's application for an elk license. The DOW remains intent on weeding out the overpopulated elk in South Park. Back at home Mick is finishing his heated dinner, so I make myself a bowl of soup. We sit together reading the week's mail until it's time for him to go load hay and plow snow. He leans over my chair and kisses me: sweet, soft, full of affection and tenderness. I sink into the warmth. Then we are on the floor making love, ignoring dog hair, rug burn, and cold

Laurie and Blue. Photo by Laurie Wagner Buyer.

air seeping in from the west wall where the wind buffets the logs. We laugh at the wonder of discovering how much we need each other.

Because it is bright and sunny and comparatively warm after all the below-zero nights, my energy seems boundless, so I decide to ski. Blue wags his stub tail when I say "walk?" He leaps and barks at my skis slicing through the snow. I stop by the barn to tell Mick I'm headed east.

I slog through a half mile of trackless ankle-deep snow along the ridge that parallels the river, then sluice down off a drifted-over hill to our ranch boundary fence. I wrestle unsuccessfully with the tight gate. Giving up, I remove my skis, coat, and pack, and squirm through the open space between the fence post and the gate stick, then wend my way through four hundred yards of willows and brush before I hit the neighboring road, which has been packed by truck tracks. Shifting into high gear, I swish along, Blue trotting at my side. We pass twenty bulls wintering on an open meadow near the river—an interesting mix of horns and hooves—Hereford,

Salers, Red Angus, Watusi, Longhorn. They lift their huge heads from the feed ground and glance our way, but not one moves a step in our direction. I'm grateful for some moments alone where I find peace. I set aside the worries about my dad, our calving season, our difficult ranching decisions, our roller-coaster marriage, the upcoming work at Arrowhead Ranch. I ski into bliss, a blessing that doesn't come often enough.

In the evening, after finishing his gopher (go-for-more) cake, Mick goes to bed though daylight still tints the windows. I ask him if he is okay, to which he replies, "Yes. Just tired." Once Mick has burrowed under the bedcovers like a mole in its tunnel, I go in and kiss him lightly on the forehead. He says, "Check at eight and midnight. I hope the damn wind doesn't blow."

But the wind kicks up its heels. When I head out to the barn, the moving air has caused the temperature to moderate at sixteen degrees, the warmest we've had since we started calving. At least wind is good for tugging the thermometer off zero. Stars are strewn against the dark sky like little gems of captured light, and a strange wisp of silver cloud hangs on the southern horizon. I cannot open the swinging gate to the corral. The bull's big butt blocks my entrance. He will not budge, but by squirming sideways I'm able to get inside then squish myself between his bulk and the windbreak fence to reach the barn door. "You big galoot," I say, "Move!" but he pays no attention.

Sunday, March 2nd

Groping, I manage to find the alarm with one hand, and throw off my assortment of covers with the other. I sit up and listen. I hear Mick breathing evenly in the bedroom. Blue yawns from his bed in the corner of the kitchen, stretches, whines, gets up to beg for a head pat, his stub tail wagging. Even in the middle of the night it makes me giggle to see his whole rear end wag, as if he can compensate for having no tail.

On the porch three cats sit sphinxlike on scraps of carpet atop the woodpile. They like being close together at night. They used to hole up in the barn, nesting down in the hay for warmth, but when they discovered they could come in a broken window to the porch they took up night residence. I like the comfort of having three feline guards at the back door.

Molly (top) and Patches. Photos by Laurie Wagner Buyer.

Molly, mother of Patches (whom Mick calls Tubby because he is so fat) and Midnight (a solid black tom named by my young niece), eyes me but never moves. Her sons flank her sides. Their tails curl around tucked-up front paws.

The night breeze wafts from the southeast and the stars shimmer as if they too are being moved ever so slightly by cosmic wind. The bull has given up his bed by the gate. All is calm as I breathe in the barn smells that tie me to the earth.

When I return Mick is standing in the hall looking vaguely confused and very vulnerable in his long johns and T-shirt. "Okay?" he asks. "Okay," I answer. We tumble into bed for four more hours of sleep.

The warmer air soothes, balmlike, when I carry the trash out to the burn barrel. Even the river reflects the warming trend—slush instead of ice.

Up-country the horses stand in an even line against the willows absorbing solar warmth into their thick-haired hides. My gelding, Brandy, is markedly more sway-backed and potbellied this year. At nineteen, he is still a pretty picture—his copper penny-colored coat in direct contrast with his snowy blaze face and stockings. I've owned him for fourteen years, and after all my childhood years of hoping and wishing and dreaming, I never tire of knowing I have my own horse. I seldom ride anymore. Not for lack of desire, but for lack of time and the fact that the four-wheeler has replaced horses as Mick's main means of moving and checking cattle.

The new cow-calf pairs at the enclosure fare well. The babies have learned to seek the relative warmth of the shed that is blocked in front with two-by-twelve boards to prevent the cows from entering. Mick forks hay for the cattle off the back of the '37 Chevy while I open up the water hole at the spring.

Past the small set of portable corrals, Mick bumps his way across slough hummocks to feed two older Hereford bulls while I remain resting, waiting, holding open the barbed wire gate. A sound stills me and I hold my breath to listen: the distant drone of a jet bound for Denver, the nearer roar of the river under winter ice, Mick's truck grinding in grandma gear, twin squeaks of magpies fussing in a spruce tree. I listen harder. There! The liquid trill of a blackbird. Our first, but often premature, sign of spring. The thrilling notes send shiver-ripples up my spine. Not even the notes of late-returning robins mean as much as the blackbird's cry.

I walk home along blown-in truck tracks, struggling for footing. Mick digs out his John Deere crawler tractor to plow snow. I split the day's wood. If I hit a round with a perfectly placed ax blow along a seasoned crack, the log will split neatly in two. Even the toughest heartwood gives way. Everything depends on the aim.

Dusting duty annoys me, but I tackle my weekly female penance with

Mick feeding the cows. Photo by Laurie Wagner Buyer.

a vengeance. Once done, I feel sanctified and set for another six days of real work. Mick hooks trailer to truck and hauls two more pair to the enclosure. Now there'll be room for the three calves born Friday night to be out in the corral shed in the sun. On a cold below-zero night the barn is a haven, but on a sunny, no-wind day it seems damp and chilly.

I settle in a chair by the window where there is good light to bead. An elk evolves out of the tiny stitched pattern. Beading is a time-consuming task, but it is an occupation that keeps my hands busy while my mind drifts and dreams. One of my infamous headaches seeps up my spine to settle under my right shoulder blade and at the base of my neck. Soon the pain will creep upward and crouch behind my eyes like a lion ready to leap.

I wake stiff-necked in the living room chair. Country Music Television is playing "Moonlight and Magnolias." Mick dozes opposite me. I move slightly, and my head feels like a moldy bale of hay balanced on my neck. With caution, I ease to the floor to do some stretching.

Blue has been lying on the floor beside me, his lowered head unmoving on his paws, but his eyes follow every leg lift, every sit up. When I whisper, "Walk?" he leaps up, crouches with his butt in the air and barks.

Blue bounces out of the house, and I shuffle after him with another sack of trash for the burn barrel. Icy-stiff, the west wind slaps at the warm backdrop of sun on snow. A blackbird flits past the haystack and lands on the top corral pole. It bobs and hops, but does not sing. I want to believe the harbinger has come especially with the message that we are on the edge of spring.

I follow a set of arrowhead-shaped rabbit tracks up the plowed road to the ranch gate. I lean against a post and swallow the sight in little tasting sips: to the north the dark timbered bulge of Black Mountain, to the east, blue skies with wispy clouds over the Tarryalls, to the south, interspersed aspen and pine on rolling ridges, and to the west, facing into the wind, the massive breast of the divide, snow covered, draped with a pewter phalanx of boiling clouds. The air tastes damp, foreshadowing snow. Far out across the pasture, I see a moving speck. Mick must have woken from his nap and is now returning on the four-wheeler from feeding his heifers an evening bale.

My evening is interrupted by phone calls from each of my sisters, Eileen and Karen. We talk for hours about Dad's illness. We are a close-knit family and I'm grateful for the weave that binds us into a warm, comfortable, aging, but serviceable sweater of love. I explain to them both that Dad seems positive and is following the doctor's orders. Even Mom, whom we all tend to worry about, seems strong and optimistic. On Wednesday they will meet with oncologists at the Rocky Mountain Cancer Center at Penrose Hospital in Colorado Springs.

By the time I hang up the phone the second time, Mick has gone to bed, his supper dishes placed considerately on the kitchen counter. I try writing letters but my eyes ache, a dull thud echoes back and forth between my ears, so I gather my blankets and curl on the couch, the alarm clock close.

Monday, March 3rd

Twenty degrees—a heat wave. As the sun struggles against an overcast and dreary sky on the eastern horizon, snow spits through the air. At midnight it had been clear, calm, moderately warm, the sky like a black velvet cape covered with rhinestones.

Bone-reaching dampness rides in on the west wind making chore time miserable, but the water holes are ice-free and the trail Mick plowed up-country is easy to travel. Forty head of elk string out along the hill. Mick, who has much better eyes than I, says the one in the lead is a decent size bull. To me they are tawny gray shapes that move magically against the screen of pearly snow. I watch them a quarter mile away while Mick feeds the bulls. Near at hand, a chickadee hops around a piece of exposed rabbit brush pecking at seeds. His tiny black-capped head looks religiously solemn, his peeping cheeps cheerful as the ringing of tiny bells.

The horses jostle for position as I kick flakes of hay off the bed of the truck. Despite warmer temperatures, the damp wind takes a toll. They are hungrier. The elk, spooked by the nearness of our work routine, mill with raised heads, then spill across the pasture to stand bunched by the county road fence. During the night they tap-danced all around the stack yard trying to maneuver a mouthful or two of hay from in between the eight-foot-high board panels protecting the pile. Mick fusses and worries that the snow cover has buried available feed. For seventeen years in Wyoming, he fed 650 head of elk on his ranch for the Department of Game and Fish. He developed such an affinity for the herd that they trusted him and grew unafraid of his team and sled that daily delivered hay to them all through the fall, winter, and spring. Even in summer, when they sought the high, undisturbed country above Sawmill Meadows, the elk recognized his voice and would come close when he called, the cows with their new calves, the spike-horned bulls. In later years, bound to them by some spiritual connection, Mick gave up hunting and abhorred the spectacle of the living wounded that showed up on the feed ground after the snow drove hunters back down to lower elevations. He never got used to the sight of elk with broken hips, missing legs and hooves, damaged backs, and gutshot skeletons that trailed in for the security and protection of his ranch. Despite the fact that it was illegal to dispose of wounded elk (firearms on the feed ground were strictly prohibited), more than once he administered relief from suffering with a blow from his ax. Now, five hundred miles south and ten years after he cared for the Green River elk, South Park elk are drawn to Mick's ranch because of the willow-bottom protection, plentiful forage, and limited hunting. Rather than use his landowner's elk permit, Mick will give the license to a reputable hunter who needs the meat.

Cookie and Candy hooked up to the sled. Photo by Laurie Wagner Buyer.

The day continues dreary and chill so I am content to mother up to the stove and rest.

Before dark I trudge up the road to breathe in a dose of damp air. A raven flies off a post and dive-bombs Blue calling "rock! rock!" When I return, Mick tells me that another black heifer has calved, and she was on the fight, head down, ready to charge when he closed the gate on her in the center part of the barn and retreated, figuring he was better off to leave her alone with her calf.

I'm making sandwiches for supper when Monte stops by to visit. No, he doesn't care for anything to eat or drink. He's tired. He pulled four calves today at the prison facility in Buena Vista where he runs the inmate agriculture program. The problem: small heifers, weak calves. We talk for several hours hashing over the cattle market, hay prices, the local real-estate boom, neighbor gossip, elk, the weather. Mick relaxes and enjoys the company. He seldom leaves the ranch and rarely has a chance to talk to folks. Monte is thirty-seven years Mick's junior, but they can talk like lifelong buddies. Both of them are ranch-raised, bust-your-butt workers.

Monte tells us about a cow who prolapsed her uterus and had to be shoved back together and stitched up. An onerous task: the internal organs had to be washed clean in soapy water, then rinsed with disinfectant iodine. The whole slimy, awkward mass needed to be pushed back through her vaginal canal. The cow was given an epidural to prevent her from straining. The modern method to deaden an area is to use an injection of Novocain, but Mick insists that the old timer's remedy of using 200-proof Everclear alcohol works even better. Monte laughs because his prison inmates, his incarcerated hands, were gape-mouthed over the whole routine. Most of them came from city environments and despite having seen or been part of gang violence, murder, rape, and drug deals, they had never seen anything as gory as a prolapsed cow. Up to his shoulder inside the cow, struggling to keep all her innards in place, Monte told his top hand, who was holding up the cow's tail, to stick his fist up the cow's rectum.

"What, boss?" the inmate asked.

"Stick your fist up her rectum to keep her from straining so I can stitch her closed," Monte repeated.

"No way, boss, not me!"

At the end of his weary rope, Monte shouted, "Jam your arm up her ass, NOW!"

The inmate complied, turning a sickly pea green. Quickly, Monte sutured the cow closed, cleaned off all the equipment and scrubbed up his arms. Drying his hands on an old feed sack, he said to his group of silent students, "Okay, let's go eat lunch."

Unable to handle the horrors of being home on the range, the green-horns said, "No thanks, boss, think we'll pass."

Tuesday, March 4th

Inside the barn, the black heifer that had calved at five is still nervous and ready to fight. Her calf lies right where I need to walk to reach the light switch so I can peek in at the heavies. I flatten myself against the wall and scoogie along. The heifer stands over her calf like a lioness protecting a cub, a fierce gleam in her eyes.

With the electricity on, I see all the heavies are standing but one. A bald-faced, red-necked heifer stretches flat out in the middle of a contraction. Through legs and tails I spot the expelled water bag. The glisten of the calf's foot shows through the sack.

"One's calving," I whisper to wake Mick.

"What? Huh?" he says.

"The red-necked one's calving," I repeat.

"Who?"

"The bald-faced, red-necked one."

"Oh," he says, struggling to toss off covers. "You mean Miss Marble Head."

"Who?" I laugh.

"Miss Marble Head. She's out of that dorky marble-headed polled bull I bought, remember?"

It may be lack of sleep or Mick's inventive name for the heifer, or the fact that he looks like a punk rock star with his hair sticking out in every direction, but I get the giggles. Gasping for air, I retreat to the kitchen to wait for him.

We parade out of the house. Mick with a flashlight, me, Blue, Miss Molly the cat. Mick cusses at the wind. "How cold is it?" he asks. "Twenty-two," I answer. I explain to him that the black heifer—Miss Excitability—was still on the fight. "Okay," he instructs, "stay outside. Keep the dog back."

Blue and I wait in the darkness where the first few flakes of a new storm tickle our faces. The barn light streams through the cracks and knotholes creating artistic patterns on the manure and snow muck. The light swirls like sacred auras, and snowflakes, drifting willy-nilly through the night, flash past like miniature moths dancing. I hear Mick latch a stall door, rearrange panels, and spread bedding hay on the wet areas of the dirt floor.

Sensing that he is ready for help, I go in and we maneuver the heavies around and sort off Marble Head. We put her alone in the midsection where we can reach light and equipment if she needs help. Mick splits the full water bag with his pocketknife, and the fluids gush onto the hay and dirt. The precaution prevents the calf from being hooded by the womb sack and suffocating. Only one calf foot is barely visible. The heifer needs more time.

We doze on couch and chair, fully clothed. I cannot sleep, but find myself listening to the wind whistling around the house, sighing down the cold stovepipe. At 2:30 Mick says, "Let's check," and we parade again out to the barn.

Miss Marble Head's down and straining, but still only one foot of the calf is in sight. Mick notes that she never has had much spring in her vaginal area, but she has a big enough frame for a first-calf heifer. As we stand, waiting, Mick puzzles over what to do first. He fingers the wrapped wire snare in his hand and says, "God, this thing is old. Dad bought it back in the '50s. All those years he pulled hundreds of calves with it . . . and now me . . . I can't believe I've been at it this long and still goin' at sixty-five, when Dad died at sixty-four. How in the hell have I done this all these years? And now everyone's gone."

I stay silent. The history of the Buyer family is a long one, reaching back to 1860 when Mick's great-great-uncle, David F. Miller, came to South Park by oxcart. He was a miner, and then a homesteader and rancher, first on Current Creek near Guffey, Colorado, then on the Middle Fork of the South Platte River outside of Fairplay. Following in his footsteps, came Mick's grandfather, John David Buyer, who was raised by D. F. Miller after his parents were killed in a train wreck, then his father, John Henry Buyer, then Mick, whose real name is John Robert Buyer. All those generations of cowmen tied inexplicably to this cold, high, tough, and unforgiving land. All have died, including Mick's sister, Arlene, and all his cousins. The only ones left in the Buyer family are Mick and his eighty-eight-year-old mother, Mary, who has lived in New Mexico for the past seventeen years. Mick sighs. I squeeze my eyes tight and clamp my mouth shut. Platitudes are not what he needs. He needs a resurrection of spirit, but I know that one is not forthcoming. Aging is slow death. Aging in a dying way of life is unbearable.

Mick turns the heifer into a corner, juggling the snare in his right hand. He loops the wire circle over the calf's protruding foot. I pass the nylon strap over the snare's handle and push it all the way up on the calf's leg making certain it is above the dew claws so when we begin to pull we won't damage the calf's soft, fleshy hooves. Mick reaches up forearm deep in the birth canal to find the calf's other foot and we repeat the procedure. The calf's mouth and tongue are visible. This is a good sign. It means the head has passed through the heifer's hipbones. For more leverage, Mick hooks a lead rope to the nylon straps and I wrap it around my hips and pull with the weight of my whole body each time the heifer heaves and Mick pushes down on the straps. Finally, the calf's head pops out, the tongue extended and bluish. Not good. Large strings of thick mucus pour from the mouth. The calf has been trapped in the birth canal too long, ingesting fluids. Eyes blink, showing life. Pull. Pull. Pull.

Marble Head goes down with a crash and Mick jerks the calf back and forth trying to pull the hips free. I reach down and clean mucus from the mouth. The calf gasps, barely breathing, limbs immobile. We work quickly, strap the hind legs and raise it dangling from the rafter above to drain fluids, then we rub and massage and coax the little one into breathing by compressing and releasing the rib cage. A puddle of blood collects beneath Marble Head. We may have waited too long to help.

We kick and slap Marble Head to make her rise. Otherwise, she'll ignore her calf and concentrate on her own misery. She's wobbly, but heaves to and stands, stumbles over to the gasping calf and begins tentatively to mother. We back off and hide behind a stall wall. "Fifty-fifty chance," Mick whispers.

We go back to bed at 3:00 a.m. The dregs of my headache plop behind my eyes like sour, week-old coffee grounds. My brain buzzes with frenetic thoughts, but Mick pulls me to his warm body, wraps me with his arms and legs, imprisons me in his ironlike hold. I breathe into the union, willing myself to relax, to sleep.

When I appear in the kitchen hours later, Mick smiles at my tousled appearance. "How's the calf?" I ask, afraid.

"Still alive, but flat out, weak. I put him and Marble Head in the jug and propped him up. The red heifer calved and her calf's a little slow too."

I count newborn calves. Twelve in seventeen days. "Boy! The bull sure worked, didn't he?" Five heifers left to calve.

A still, silent day; everything muffled by snow, surrounded by snow, two new inches on the ground, flakes in the air, the mountains obscured, the pines cloaked in white. When I stand unmoving, I hear the snow falling and the sound of my heart thudding in my ears. Walking is a major challenge. The warm days and cold nights have softened, then crusted, the snow into an obstacle course of hard spots, soft parts, hidden holes, buried brush. Walking is a misnomer; more like shuffle, trudge, stumble, trip, slide, twist ankles, wrench back, fall to the knees. Anyone watching would assume I was down-and-out drunk. The half mile home feels like a mini-Olympics.

After noon dinner, I cobble together a quick shopping list. Tomorrow I must go to Salida, an hour away, for groceries and a semiannual mammogram. Because of Dad's recent cancer diagnosis, I'm predictably skittish.

After dishes I make a fast trip to Fairplay for mail-bank-library-county clerk's office to catch up on errands. The small town where Mick was born and spent his first thirty-two years has changed drastically since the '30s, '40s, and '50s when he was growing up. Ranching and mining were booming then. Fairplay had a hospital, numerous bars, several churches, three car dealerships, a dentist, two barber shops, a bowling alley, a theater/roller rink (removal of the rows of seats left the wooden floors open for skating), drugstore, a trio of grocery-hardware stores, a bank, a youth center, a Legion Hut for community dances, a telephone office, two hotels, and a handful of restaurants. The train ran through until 1938. When we moved back to Fairplay in 1988 (twenty-four years after Mick had left to ranch in Wyoming) the town was dull and depressed, trashy around the edges, and weighted with years of poor economy. Since then, within the past five years, Fairplay has again experienced a boom time: tourists heading over the divide to the ski areas, out-of-state investors, front-range (Denver–Colorado Springs) deserters who are looking for a slower-paced, simpler life. Real estate prices have doubled. Rental homes are scarce. Old dilapidated buildings are being renovated and reopened as art galleries, antique shops, restaurants, and real estate offices. I hear rumors that Fairplay will soon have a beer garden, yogurt shop, RV park, snowboard factory, and a fly-fishing shop. The face of the town has been scrubbed and lifted—remodeling, painting, yards stripped of old junk. Equipment dealers, propane contractors, construction companies, lumberyards, sawmills, and firewood peddlers have all been banished to the highway commercial strip away from the center of town. An air of hopefulness drifts through Fairplay now, transitory at best since tourism and absentee landowners don't necessarily spell stability.

The past still holds some sway. History is a living, breathing entity in South Park, evidenced everywhere one looks by old homesteads, ranches, and mines. The outdoor museum, South Park City, has preserved an incredible number of historical buildings. In recent years the South Park Heritage Resource has been trying to find funding to purchase development rights to keep Park County's agricultural lands for open space. Personally, I teeter on the cusp of the old and new. I'm drawn backward in time by Mick's family history, his love of the old days, and the nostalgia of a better way of life when ranching was in its heyday. I am also pulled forward by my involvement in Arrowhead Ranch's fly-fishing resort, which caters to urban dwellers in search of solitude, stress relief, the miracles of fish and river, sun, and sky.

I spend my evening soaking up silence, disturbed only by the woofing of the wood stove and the bare whisper of the night wind, which, since dark, has softened in its dying. At two degrees above zero, we are back in Ma Nature's icebox with little hope of thawing out anytime soon.

Wednesday, March 5th

When I wake at midnight, the power is off. No refrigerator or freezer running or the little heater that warms the back room to keep pipes and pump from freezing. I stumble around trying to find my flashlight, which I thought I left on top of the refrigerator. Finally, feeling my way, I find it on the Hoosier cupboard shelf. I'm ticked, not because the power is off, but because I'm so ill prepared and have become spoiled by having electricity. For years I lived without power and modern conveniences. I recall too well how honed my senses were, how alert I was to everything around me even in the darkness of blackest night.

The wind roars out of the northwest, an arctic express heading hell-bent to the southeast. The spruce trees groan, and loose pieces of tin on the barn roof flap and squeal. The night spooks me. The flashlight beam seems little comfort.

I force myself to stand face to the wind and look up at the gray-blue-black sky. The stars are strangely still, like pinpricks of light seen through a velour stage curtain. I make myself stay awhile, ignoring the buffeting wind that beats my coat and hood against my body. I long to absorb the darkness, sink into the elements of the earth that once sustained me beyond the false security of house and home, the technology that has softened me, leaving me untough, untested, and unreliable. I will my booted feet deeper into the ground, reaching for unseen roots that I know are there, roots that stabilize and hold me firm, making me strong.

Our world at dawn undulates, a constant wave of movement created by wind and snow. We are surrounded by shimmering air the color of aluminum silver. In a second's time whole ridges, buildings, vehicles appear and disappear like mirages. Every chore is ten times more difficult. Mick's patience stretches thin and snaps as he backs the '37 into an obscured panel corral around the haystack. I'm hollering "whoa," but my words are whipped away faster than I can shout. I race toward him waving, but he cannot see and the panels slide and buckle. Finally, I reach the truck and pound on the door until he stops.

"Goddamn son-of-a-bitch," he spits out. "You work and work and work. All for nothing!"

Easily cowed, I back off, picking up the hand-forged horseshoe taillight protector he made the summer before to keep the cattle from knocking off the truck's lights. Miraculously, the taillights are intact, and there is no damage to the panels except for scrapes and dings. The only wreckage is Mick's sorely bruised ego.

He forks hay onto the truck bed with cussing vengeance. Blue and I retreat to the lee side of the shed, as out of the wind as we can be. With the truck loaded, Mick pulls up, and Blue and I climb into the cab. I keep my mouth shut. The '37 bucks and grinds up-country through blown-in, concrete-hard, snow-packed ruts. We finish the chores in silence. Ax in hand, Mick starts back to the truck after chopping open the horses' water hole. I turn to head for home when he touches my arm and says, "I'm all right now."

I force a smile, but am unable to say anything.

"It's too cold to walk," he says, "Ride back with me."

Though I'd rather walk and be alone, I accept his gesture of apology.

After lunch I am on the road again to Buena Vista. Despite slushy patches of wind-driven snow, the highway is mostly clear and dry, the sky's blue, and the sun shines with a piercing brilliance that forces me to squint even behind sunglasses. I mentally tick off the ranches I pass: Sy Rodgers, McQuaid's JP homestead, the Harrington, the 63, the Salt Works, all old names Mick has taught me with reminiscences of the people that built the country. Newcomers now own the ranches, but the old names hang on the places like badges of honor.

A huge, year-round RV park hunkers under the hill north of Pony Park. I can still hear Mick say, as he does every time we pass this place, "Jesus Christ, old McQuaid would roll over in his grave." A true pioneer, one of the first to run cattle in South Park, Tom McQuaid married into the Hall family, who homesteaded the Salt Works Ranch, the oldest working ranch in the state of Colorado. At one time Quaidy ran thousands of cattle on hundreds of thousands of deeded acres plus federal lease land. As the story goes, he never had children of his own, but he and his wife raised many orphaned boys from the State Reformatory in Buena Vista, calling them all "Button" in turn. When the government decided to put in Highway 285 bisecting McQuaid's ranch, the old boy, riding horseback, met the cat skinners with his buggy whip in hand. Cutting and slashing he drove them off their equipment. In the end he lost that battle, and eventually the war, surrendering the old ways and better times to death at the age of 105 when, it was rumored, he still drank a water glass of whiskey and smoked a big cigar before breakfast every day.

Bath Hill, Trout Creek Pass, Chubb Park, Trout Creek Canyon, Johnson Village—at one time a service station and a diner—now a haven for rafting companies, truck stops, motels, quick-rip convenience stores, and burger joints. The reformatory, now a full-fledged penitentiary, rises monolithic on meadows near the river not far from where the old stage road to Leadville used to run.

Buena Vista is still a sleepy town, quaint in its own way with some historic buildings, lovely old homes, and a duck crossing at the park on Cottonwood Creek. At the cemetery I cruise the freshly plowed narrow roads between the grave markers looking for Marilyn and Willie Johnson.

Mick's first cousin, Willie, died in 1986, and his wife, Marilyn, just died in February, after a long four-year battle with progressive cancer. Marilyn had been a schoolmate of Mick's and a wonderful friend to me. With bright red hair, she was Irish Catholic to the core, opinionated, a super-tough cookie with a soft heart. She was also quick to laugh, ready to help anyone anytime, and was a staunchly loyal schoolteacher who defended proper education for forty years in Park County.

I have almost given up my search when I spot what I am looking for: a small, gray twin stone with double interlocking hearts half-buried in the snow, surrounded by four posts and a sagging plastic chain. I stop, leave the engine on my Explorer running, and crunch through the ankle-deep snow to reach the stone. I place my hand over Marilyn's name. There are a few sad-looking faded flowers next to Willie's side of the stone, evidence that Marilyn had made her faithful visit to see him last Memorial Day.

In recent years, Mick, Marilyn, and I had made the rounds to the Como and Fairplay cemeteries near the end of May to clean up the graves and set out new silk flowers to remember Mick and Willie's grandparents, Mick's other grandparents, his father, sister, and great-uncle and great-aunt. Afterward we always took Marilyn out to lunch during which time Mick and Marilyn would rehash the past half century of history in the county. Now, belatedly, I wish I had had a tape recorder to preserve their comments and observations: who married whom, who lived where, the town drunks, the misfits, the pillars of society. I halfway crouch over Marilyn's resting place, disappointed that I did not attend her services because Mick did not want to go, or that even at this late date I did not bring any token to grace her grave. A small pine branch sticks partially out of the snow, so I dig with my hands, scooping away the hard crust to reveal an evergreen wreath decorated with frosted cones and plaid ribbon. Exposed, it will absorb the sun and melt away the surrounding snow and serve as a small reminder that I finally came to say good-bye.

The last weeks of Marilyn's life, both in the hospital and at home, were difficult ones as she slipped in and out of consciousness, often not even knowing who I was. Once though, she smiled and said my name clearly as I smoothed the salt-and-pepper chemo bristle of her hair. I kissed her scaly forehead where the South Park sun had burned and blistered her fair Irish skin and I told her I loved her. Her bright blue eyes flicked open, burning, and she said, "Love you too," words I'd never heard her say before. Then the light faded and she closed her eyes, sighing.

Here, weeks later, at her grave, I talk to her as I always did, telling her about Mick and calving and the weather, and the local gossip. Then I whisper the Lord's Prayer and walk back to my car, leaving her in the protective shadow of the Collegiate Peaks.

Salida seems busy even though it isn't livestock sale day. I circle the Main Street block hunting for a parking place. I dash several blocks to the

Farm Bureau office in hopes of catching our agent, Jill Long, to go out to lunch with me.

An hour later, after filling out paperwork at the admittance desk, I request a visit with the radiologist. For two hours the technician takes X ray after X ray, repeating some, using different equipment. In between series, I read *People* magazine. I'm astonished at what goes on in the real world, especially the fact that Kevin Costner's *Waterworld* went over budget by gross millions. That money could feed people, or save desperate ranchers, or find a mammography technology that didn't stretch, squeeze, compress, and punish a woman's breasts.

The kind technologist gains me entrance to the radiologist's secret office where light tables and X rays cover the walls. Distant at first, the doctor gradually eases into his explanation of why my breasts are so difficult to read. Head to head, we stare at multiple images of my small, midlife breasts: dark gray globs splashed with white bursts. No, not cancer. He takes time to reel the mammographer ahead in fast-forward: here is a woman with breast cancer. He circles the bright white outlined mass that has rays reaching out from it. It is so small, smaller than the tip of his pen. More breast X rays whiz by. Here is a woman with lots of fat tissue in her breasts, a uniform grayish appearance. If a cancer appeared in this woman's breast, they could identify it easily. But, in my case of very dense breast tissue with little fat, the X rays do not penetrate well. Therefore, there are lots of splashy white bursts that could cover or hide or disguise a potential cancer. "Nothing serious," he says, "but you bear observation."

Leaving the hospital I am wrung out, as thoroughly stretched as an old rubber band that cannot snap back into shape. Visions of film-captured breasts flip through my mind's eye. I wonder about the woman with the cancer. Did I know her? Could I help her? Marilyn's cancer was first identified in her breasts, and she had a mastectomy and radiation. Then the cancer crept into her lungs. Lung surgery. Then in her lymph system. Chemotherapy. Then the disease invaded her brain, leaving her incoherent and in pain until her death.

At Safeway I sort coupons and puzzle over prices. I run into our vet's assistant, Gail Denison, and we swap calving stories. Like us, she has five head left to calve. All of her cows calved out fine except for a breech that she couldn't get. She called Hutch (short for Wendall Hutchinson, DVM, age seventy-two), and he came and supervised while she did a cesarean. They saved the cow, but the calf was dead in the womb. While I tell the story of Marble Head's calf, several people listen intently. Are ranch women such an anomaly that we stop traffic in the grocery store?

Gail grins mischievously, showing off a fine row of perfectly white upper teeth. I slap her on the shoulder and shout "Hooray!" Last fall, while helping Hutch preg-check cattle, Gail was running the head catch on the chute when the fiftieth cow flung her massive head and hit Gail smack in the face. Teeth and hat went flying. Blood splashed over the front of her jacket. She told me she was so embarrassed she grabbed her hat, stuffed a couple of tissues in her mouth, and went back to work because there were still ten cows to go. Hutch never even knew she was hurt until they were packing up to go home. The blow fractured her upper jaw, broke off two teeth, and loosened two others so badly that they had to be removed.

The first time I met Gail she told me a joke. She and Hutch had come to our ranch to doctor a seriously ill first-calf heifer that staggered, was going blind, and was unable to swallow. Hutch and Gail gave her enemas, drew blood, injected antibiotics and vitamins, and discussed every possible disease and its symptoms. Gail pulled me over and whispered, "I know what this cow has—need-a-dick-itis!" It took me several seconds to figure out the strange sounding malady, then I laughed until I was sick, leaving Mick and Hutch to stare stupidly at me. No prompting on their part could make me share the joke.

When I pull in the driveway, Blue barks and leaps and tries to cover my face with doggy kisses. Subdued and shy, Mick finally asks, "Well, what did you find out?" I try to explain the complicated good news about my breasts as we carry in groceries and supplies.

"Your dad called," Mick says. "The CAT scan showed no spread. The cancer is localized."

Soggy with relief, I say, "I'll call as soon as I . . ."

Mick cuts me off. "He said not to call. He'll call you tomorrow after he's talked to his surgeon."

This irks me.

"Have you had supper?" I snap.

"Not yet," he answers.

"Well," I reply, "let me put these groceries away and I'll fix you some."

My brain switches into a Miss Bitch mode. I don't know why, except that I'm tired, all my worry spilling into a cautionary relief. I want to call my dad. I want someone else to put away the groceries. I want someone to fix me supper and bring me a cup of tea and rub my back. I want someone to hold me.

I stiffen my spine as Mick leaves the room. I yank open the refrigerator and pull out ham and butter and bread and pickles, then slam the door shut. I jerk open the cupboard doors to get a plate, glass, and knife. I slap together a sandwich and toss chips on the plate and march into the living room to Mick, who, beer in hand, mumbles thanks. I am an expert at playing the martyr.

By the time I stash the groceries and heat up a bowl of soup for myself, my unidentified anger has died. I attempt small talk with Mick.

"How was your day? Any more calves? Did the wind blow badly? I see you got more wood."

He replies with stony yes and no or grunts. I try to explain my cranky demeanor: I'm tired. My breasts hurt. I'm worried. I need someone to lean on. I want someone to talk to. He replies, grieved, "Well, I don't have anyone to talk to either."

We square off in our separate chairs and stare at the TV news.

At seven, Mick checks heifers and washes up for bed.

"Should I get up and check at midnight?" I ask.

"No, I'll do it," he says.

"Why?" I say. "Because you are mad at me?"

"No, because it's MY deal. I've done it alone before and I can do it alone now!"

"Fine," I say.

I curl on the couch in a misery of my own making. Why can't I keep my mouth shut? Now we are enmeshed in another no-win war. I try to read, but my eyes pool with tears and I cannot see. I pile on my covers and repeat my childhood prayers until I sleep.

Thursday, March 6th

I do not move at midnight when Mick comes into the living room for his boots, nor do I say a word when he returns from the barn. I do not stir at daybreak when he rises again, goes out to check, comes back in to make his own coffee and breakfast and build a fire. I need to get up and make an attempt at civility and kindness. My anger is gone, leaving a hole in my heart like a hollowed out, empty nest.

Peering from under the hood of blankets around my head, I watch Mick peeking around the corner to see if I'm awake.

"Hi, honey," I venture.

"Hi," he says. "How'd you sleep?"

"Good. I slept really good."

He comes over, tugs a fallen blanket up and lays it across my shoulder.

"Why don't you just stay in today? Don't come out at all."

"Okay." My throat tightens at his caring gesture.

My morning passes slow and golden-rich, like thick honey poured from a gallon jug into a small clay pot. I drink tea, read, write, do the dishes, and exercise. Occasionally I glance out the window to watch Mick's progress with chores. Sunny, but only zero, an arctic blue sky grows out of the pearl-colored dawn.

We strike a kind of careful truce. Mick cuts and hauls in firewood. I build a fire for him in the living room. He asks me about the calls I've gotten for Arrowhead Ranch accommodation reservations, and I fix him his favorite lunch: hamburger, fries, and a chocolate milkshake.

I hole up in the house all day: grinding wheat and oats into flour, whipping up a new salad dressing recipe, working on Arrowhead Ranch files, writing. Late in the afternoon I receive a phone call from a reporter for the *Rocky Mountain News* asking me questions about my first full-length book of poetry, which is a finalist for the Colorado Book Awards.

My dad calls: radiation and chemotherapy for two months, surgery to remove his esophagus after that. He'll lose his hair, maybe, and have sores and blisters in his mouth, or become ill from the treatments. Not a great diagnosis, he teases, but better than a doctor telling him he has only six months to live. We discuss his life insurance, the bills Mom would have, liquid assets, timetables on treatments. He feels okay, he says, some pain but bearable. Finally, we talk about the Colorado Book Awards. I have tickets for Mom and Dad. I hope they can make it to the banquet. I know Mick will not come.

The evening air is knife-sharp, and I soak up every fading ray of sun as I walk Blue up the plowed road to the ranch gate, then up the plowed trail to the horse pasture. The snow is scabrous, sculpted, carved out by hard wind. Every drifted lump leaves a blue-black shadow on its east face. Here and there, in places where Mick has dozed the snow away, the exposed earth leaves patches of mud where I purposely walk just to feel dirt underfoot, a new and different sensation to my booted feet.

Over fried-egg sandwiches we watch Country Music Television. A beautiful young woman sings out: "When Daddy's gone, what in the world do you do if you're Daddy's little girl?" Tears needle my eyes and I dash for the bathroom, closing myself in with my fear and grief. I try to coach myself back into a positive attitude, but my composure is gone. I let the tears come until I am cried out, then I lie a long time on the floor feeling like a wrung-out dishrag meant for the dirty clothes basket. I wish I had someone to hold and reassure me.

Mick leaves to check on a heifer that has been restless and anxious all day. He's been worried about her. The smallest heifer, she is slab-sided, with no extra weight or body fat. Even as a calf, she didn't grow as well as the others, wouldn't eat grain or pellets, hung back from the herd, shy and timid. When Mick doesn't return in fifteen minutes, I don coveralls and boots and go out to help. Both the calf's feet and the head are visible. Mick has the straps on and is pulling hard, trying to help the heifer as her contractions come. I grab onto the lead rope he attaches to the straps, and together we give it the old heave ho, but have minimal success. Mick gets the calf puller, and we fasten the leather britchin' to the heifer's butt and insert the metal rod in the holder. Mick cranks the handle in evenly timed movements and pulls down to try and get the calf's head free. The heifer stumbles and teeters. "Going down!" I say in warning. We lower the equipment with her. Now, more at ease, she strains and pushes. Two more pulls and the calf is free to the hips, the head lolled back at an awkward angle. The calf breathes well, shakes its head. The heifer's exhausted, yet bright in the eye. We get her up, but she seems stupefied. We hide around the corner to give her some privacy and space, but she continues to stare in our direction, ignoring her calf. We've hurt her by helping, and she's suspicious of our presence. It's up to her now, whether or not she accepts her calf, whether a mothering instinct will kick in or be absent.

The hardy calf struggles to stand. It has a fighting chance if the heifer will come around. Tiptoeing out the barn door, we leave their fate in the hands of the gods who grant new life.

Friday, March 7th

The illuminated dial reads 3:44 a.m. when I push the turn-off bar on the clock. The furnace clicks on. When I venture off the porch the air is still, soft, cool as silk, but not cold. Without the wind's pervasive bold voice, I hear the river running, a long-missed melody of rushing trills, crescendos, and decrescendos as water cascades over and under ice, around snow-drifted bends.

The new ma hovers over her black calf that lies in a heap, legs askew, evidence that he has tried to stand. He hasn't made much progress, since he is only about ten feet from where we left him when we pulled him from his mother. He has not been licked clean. Birth mucus has hardened on his hide like shellac. One piece of the womb sack, plastered along his back, gleams white and transparent as a wedding veil. When I approach, ma "mmhhhs" at the calf. At least she knows he's hers. Because he lies in a damp, squishy spot soaked with birth fluids, I drag him forward by a front leg onto drier ground where there is old hay and good footing. With a concentrated heave on my part, I get the heavy bugger to stand, splay-legged and quivering, alert and anxious. I steady him while he takes a few wobbly steps; then I back off. Ma comes over, curious: "mmhhh." To calm her, I throw a jag of hay at her feet and she grabs a mouthful, chewing voraciously. Slowly, I reach for the iodine on a high shelf and crouch, aiming carefully, to spray the calf's damp, dangling umbilical. He flinches at the caustic sting of the disinfectant and staggers under his mother's neck, then turns toward her flank. If he will suck while the heifer stands and eats, he will have a grand start on the first day of his life.

Many ranchers disapprove the notion of leaving the heifer and her calf alone to work out the complicated details of their bonding. Some would wash and dry the calf, get it up, confine the heifer, and make the calf suck, fiddling and fooling around, anxious and worried that the calf would die. Mick, raised in an outdated but still commonsense-oriented school of thought, believes that nature is the best teacher. He learned his skills from years of following his grandfather and his father, and I have learned from following him through fifteen calving seasons. Human interference creates an unnatural circumstance. We, with dominion over the animals, have unprecedented power in our hands. Power, wisely used, means interference only when death is imminent, as in pulling the calf when it was obvious the heifer could not birth him on her own.

As I stand hidden behind the stall wall, watching the new calf suck, I think of the process of natural selection. How, in the wild, a young animal ignored is certain to die. The weak and stupid fail. The strong and smart survive. Here on the ranch there must also be a line that demarcates which cattle are kept, which culled. If this heifer had refused her calf, Mick and I would have worked with her to get her to accept motherhood. If her mothering instinct never kicked in, we might even grant her a stay through the summer, to fatten up on grass, but come fall, she would be on the truck headed for the sale barn and hamburger row.

Many elements are involved in raising cattle. Genetics play a huge part in the livelihood and well-being of a cow herd—traits such as mothering ability, milking ability, udder size and shape, overall frame and weight, and coloration, are passed down from one generation to the next. Large, pendulous white udders are prone to sunburn and blistering, which requires doctoring to prevent cows whose bags get sore from kicking off their calves. White faces or pale pigment around the eyes make cows more prone to pink eye, which requires treatment to prevent blindness, or cancer eye, which means they must be sold. A tendency toward poor feet can lead to hoof rot. Damaged hearts or lung problems can lead to brisket, a disease that is fatal at this high altitude. Sometimes pelvic sizes are too small, or birth weights are too high. Uncountable things can cause illness, injury, or death.

On top of all that, mother nature plays her pervasive role: cold, snow, wind, too wet, too dry, long winters, short summers, no grass, toxic weeds, lice, ticks, worms, innumerable diseases, predators such as coyotes, cougars, bears, and natural hazards like badger holes, bog holes, swift rivers, and lightning.

Finally, the rancher remains the central character in the whole scheme. Do his cattle have enough space, enough grass, access to clean water, shade, shelter, salt, mineral, cake, hay, vaccinations? Is the rancher sharp enough to cull smartly, breed wisely, watch the market trends, buy low, sell high, and have enough income to keep his outfit together another year?

In the fifteen years that I've known Mick, first as his hired hand and now as his wife, I have seen the lows of this business outweigh the highs. An optimistic eye may count one out of every five or six years as real successes. He is a man born to the land, bonded to earth by his birthright and by his stubborn, even zealous, dedication to a way of life. He is not a businessman, and though he eyes the money situation, the majority of his decisions are based on gut instinct, and everything begins and ends with the cows. He is a cowman. He lives, breathes, eats, drinks, and sleeps on their timetable, not his own. He doesn't take vacations or go visiting. He never wants a night out on the town. An evening in front of the TV, watching rodeo or the Nashville Network, is the extent of his social life, unless a neighbor drops by to visit. When he does have a day away from the ranch, it is usually because of a bull sale, a draft horse sale, a calf sale, or because he needs to go to the feedstore or pick up parts. Once in town, he may stop by the Chevy dealership to chitchat with the salesmen, and going out to lunch means grabbing a burger and fries at McDonald's.

While at times I'm definitely irritated by Mick's narrow worldview and his unwillingness to broaden his horizon, to go places and to do things, I realize that his whole identity is centered on the ranch. His single-mindedness is the reason he is still in business after fifty years of calving out cows. It is also why the Buyer family has a long-standing reputation of being fine cowmen, good, strong, serious stewards of the land. Mick's bottom line has never been a dollar bill. As a matter of fact, he has probably lost several fortunes by refusing to sell agricultural land to developers. His bottom line is the land. Love of the land. It doesn't pay much, but the fringe benefits are invaluable. I have seen Mick stand at the kitchen window and soak up a sunrise wearing a look of pure bliss. I have seen him sit a horse and count cattle through a gate, as a king would survey his realm.

Nowhere have I ever met a man more grounded, more intact, a man in close touch with who he is and what his purpose on this earth should be. While I deeply respect his perseverance, dedication, and stubborn determination, these are the very traits that make him a hard man to live with.

He gives me grave reason to worry. What will become of him when his age finally tips the scales and he no longer has the physical strength to pitch hay, buck bales, chop ice, shovel out an irrigation ditch, saddle a horse, pull a calf, carry a bucket of water, or even just walk out to the barn?

No one remains to carry on. No one to follow the trail he has marked out with boot prints and hoof tracks. Each year I watch, holding my breath, as he rides less and walks more slowly. Long life is a wondrous thing if you can grow old gracefully, allowing the world of mental and emotional pursuits to take over the pleasure and necessity of physical activity. But already plagued by arthritis, shot knees, stiff joints, crippled fingers, aching back, and constant fatigue, growing older isn't going to be a carnival ride for Mick. Acceptance, grace, resilience, and peace of mind will never be his strong suits. In my mind's eye, I see him ranting and raging against his increasing age, strung together with anger and sadness. I see him with a grubby, but hard hold on the handle of his life, refusing to slow down, to let go, or accept change. In the end, like a monarch bull elk, massive antlers weighting a weary head, he'll go down with dignity. In the silence of the barn, I pray that God will be kind to Mick. I pray that his health will last for a few more years, and that his dying, when it comes, will not be long, drawn-out, or cruel.

Returning to the house to light the morning fires, I see a bright bold cluster of streaming stars, a comet, on the northeast horizon. Old timers felt that comets were an omen, a foretelling of things to come. I stand and study the stars, searching for answers, any answers, but there is only an eternal stillness that leaves me feeling alone, without guidance or direction.

In the darkness surrounding the house, I sense movement, then see Mick's darker shadowy shape in the porch doorway, waiting for me. I shake my head, knowing he hasn't slept in, knowing he's chomping at the bit to get started on the day. I take a step toward him. Then another. It isn't much of a map to follow, but for today, anyway, I know where I am going. There's breakfast to cook and cows to feed. There's a man, with a heart as big as all the heavens, who needs my helping hand.

Checking the thermometer I'm surprised to find it is only six degrees. Without wind, the air feels balmy. Today I take time to clean ashes from the wood stoves and cart them outside to a barrel reserved for their collection. A few more winks of sleep have cheered Mick considerably. A warmth like wine flows between us, the sweetness heady and contagious. We hold hands over breakfast; he hugs me from behind while I do dishes.

We have our first springlike day. The calves at the enclosure buck and play, butt heads in exuberance as their fuzzy hides absorb the sunshine like dark sponges. Blue and I walk home the long way via the county road, which, having been plowed, gives me solid footing. A chickadee sounds notes from the dead limbs of a tall old spruce guarding the roadside. In the stillness, the tiny bird has the heart and volume of an opera singer.

Mick crawls into bed at 8:00 p.m., and I settle down to watch a movie video, but I'm interrupted repeatedly by the telephone, or as Mick calls it, "that goddamned thing!" There were years when I lived so far from people and settled places that I never had the luxury of a phone and relied exclusively on written communication to keep in touch with family and friends. Even though I often feel beleaguered by the phone's demanding ringing, I still appreciate the convenience and never take the privilege for granted. Mick considers the telephone an annoying, obnoxious play toy. I consider it a necessary tool that allows me to run the Arrowhead Ranch business from home and gives me the ease of contacting other writers and friends. And now, with Dad's recent cancer diagnosis, it provides me with a lifeline to him and Mom. On this evening, for once, I'm pleased that Mick's partial deafness (from being under army tanks during the Korean conflict) prevents him from hearing the phone's insistent jangle.

Saturday, March 8th

I check the lone heavy heifer in the barn at midnight. Mick checks her at 4:00 a.m. At 7:00 he returns to the house dripping sweat, panting.

"I got it," he says, then chugs a drink from the water pitcher. "Hip-locked . . . had to get a rope onto the straps and tie off to a post, but got it."

I tell Mick he had a call from Franklin Nash: There's a bull sale, the fifteenth, in La Junta. "Tell Mick he can buy a dang good Hereford bull for pretty cheap down there." Mick laughs. He bought many Hereford bulls from Franklin Nash in the old days, the late '50s and early '60s, before leaving South Park and moving to Wyoming. Mick says he doesn't think he needs another bull. He is tickled with the Limousin bull he bought last spring from Nate Patton. The bull, naturally named Nate, is only the third non-Hereford bull Mick has ever purchased. He tried a Saler and a Red Angus on his heifers the two previous years and only had fair to good results. Mick thinks Nate is some kind of bull. We count the days on the calendar. In twenty-one days, fifteen heifers have calved, which means that Nate has a "good set of pants" and knows how to get to work.

Chore time is pleasant. I hear another blackbird. It tells me we are one step closer to spring. The earthy landscape has turned lunar overnight. Snow and exposed ground create fantastic shapes, bulges, and craters. I spot round-headed gray-green clumps of sage and the tiny star burst dried flowers of rabbit brush that rise like miniature treasures. Surrounded by slopes of snow, pyramid casts of elk droppings shine like black pearls.

Blue and I tromp the dirt road, pausing to gather flint chips where the Indians camped long before the word "road" existed. I stop for a moment at a grove of aspens where the fence strings through the trees in a straight line and recall the day Mick and I had set the posts along this south boundary during the first summer we called the ranch home. We lived in a twelve-foot-by-fourteen-foot wall tent while we built fence. One Sunday, the sun growing hot, the air sultry, and thunderheads blossoming in the western sky, a familiar brown car had slowed on the road. Mom and Dad shouted out the window: "We brought hot dogs and beer!"

Scanning the gravel roadbed, I spot a bent and rusted eight-inch spike. I pick it up, flip the large nail over and over in my hand. The spike could have been part of a bridge timber or a homestead log. It could have fallen out of a wagon or a Model T. Whatever, it turned up here, probably buried when the road was built and then rediscovered by a grader's blade and a scouring wind. I pack the spike home knowing Mick will take time to pound out the kink and use the nail again.

At the tall dead spruce, no chickadee sings. The day holds so quiet that I hear only Blue's crunchy carousing in the snow and the sound of my own steps. I wait and listen. A soughing breath of wind, the snow warming under the morning sun and settling with a muffled sigh. Far off, barely audible, the dip-and-sway chirping of snow buntings. I stare across the pastures, but cannot see the flock. Way to the east, the Trophy Lakes at Arrowhead Ranch glisten like twin mirrors, the ice cover tossing light back up into the sky, signaling the sheer brightness of the day.

Late in the afternoon I water houseplants, remembering the origin of each as a gift from a friend. I must content myself with these plants until wild flowers rise phoenixlike from the dust and spring melt: lavender and white pasqueflowers coming up through the snow, a scattering of butter-gold dandelions pushing up through new grass, silver and purple loco, the shocking orange brilliance of Rocky Mountain lilies hidden in the spruce bogs, the royal rich purple of fringed gentian in the hay meadows.

The first summer and fall we lived in this place I immersed myself in studying the plants and wild flowers. Even now their names enchant me: bird cage evening primrose, cancer root, mariposa tulip, fairy candelabra, elegant camas, and, of course, the columbine. When the fragile blooms arrive again out of their long sleeping, I love calling them each by name as I touch their ephemeral petals.

The afternoon flies by while I do mundane chores. By the time Mick comes in from evening chores, I'm polishing the bathroom mirror. He clicks on the TV remote control and gets nothing but a roar of snow.

"What'd you do to the TV?" he hollers.

"Nothing."

"Well, it's broken."

I enter the living room feeling timid.

"All I did was dust," I say.

"Did you dust these?" he asks, holding up the remote controls.

"Yes, I always do," I say feeling sheepish and defensive.

"Well, don't dust them. They don't need dusting. You pushed something wrong."

On the verge of being angry, I defuse the situation as best I can. Arguing amiably, we both alternately push buttons with no success. Our conversation sounds like something out of a Perry Mason movie:

"Did you move the TV?"

"No, I did not."

"Not even a little?"

"I did not touch the TV except to dust it."

"Did you touch the satellite receiver?"

"No, all I did was dust it."

"Well, you must have pushed something. There's no reception."

I dig around my file cabinet until I find the manuals. I call the Echo Star man and leave a message "Help! Trouble with the satellite!"

Disgusted, Mick hangs on the edge of anger. I opt for a walk with the dog, fuming the whole time because my day is now shadowed by argument and accusation.

Returning home, I worry: how will we survive an evening, a day, two days without Mick's TV. I get the giggles. Surely he isn't so mothered up to the damn thing that he'll die from lack of Weather Channel nourishment. I scold myself and encourage a kinder perspective: he works hard, he's tired in the evening, TV is his relaxation. At least he isn't out in the bars, drinking, or picking up women. I plaster on a smile and take the whole deal lightheartedly, but I pray the satellite man will call quickly.

The ocean sound of TV snow fills the living room. I volunteer to put on a video so Mick will have something to watch.

"No, thank you," he says.

"Well, can you turn down the snow, it bugs me."

He punches the volume button and the snow recedes into a foggy whisper. Determined to get in a siege of sit-ups and leg lifts before I shower, I unearth my exercise mat from under the couch. Attempting to be funny, Mick counts for me: 7, 3, 26, 14, 58. I grin, then set my jaw, concentrating, thinking of how and what I touched when I cleaned. I jump up and check the plugs on the TV and the VCR. The TV flashes on.

"What'd you do?" Mick asks.

"Pushed in a loose plug," I say.

I slip into the kitchen and call the satellite man, leaving a message on his machine: "Warren, this is Laurie. No need to call or come over. I found the trouble . . . guess I just saved my marriage!"

Sunday, March 9th

I thought being able to sleep a whole night through would be welcome. Instead, Mick is restless and awake. I keep looking at the clock, longing for my quiet couch. Finally, in the wee hours we both drop off, then force ourselves to stay in bed until 5:00 a.m. We rise looking and acting like we'd been up all night partying. Readjusting our routine is hard work.

In an effort to erase the remnants of last evening's animosity, I fix Mick a batch of pancakes, which he calls flapjacks or saddle blankets. "Blond or brunette?" I tease, aping the story he has told me of the ranch cook they had when he was a kid who asked every hired hand the same question while flipping cakes on the wood cookstove griddle.

I love the smell and feel of pancakes under the spatula, how the tiny heat bubbles rise and pop, telling me when it's time to turn them over. Saliva gathers in my mouth as I watch Mick spread butter, then pour on maple syrup, but I close my eyes against the tempting sight and content myself with my ordinary oatmeal and herb tea.

Blue skies. Twenty degrees. A slight breeze sighs. Chores click by like clockwork. The cull cows, Coonie, Broken Toe, and Blackie, wait by the riverbank for their portion of hay. Fifteen heifers with new calves are parceled out in different places, all in the early sun, calves frolicking, the older ones nibbling their first tastes of hay, mimicking their mothers. I train my eyes to search each baby butt for signs of scours, each head for dull eyes or droopy ears that would signal the onset of pneumonia.

I shiver. The first year I worked for Mick in Wyoming, he had eighty heifers to calve out. The season stayed cold, wet, and miserable, the snow piled as deep as the fences were high. With no shelter from the bad weather, the calves sickened and scoured. Their weak bodies littered the feed grounds. Mick had had knee surgery and was stumbling around on crutches while his son and I, both greenhorns, tried to rope calves and poke pills down their cold, raw throats. That feeling of death on my fingers never left me. Neither has Mick's story of his first spring in Wyoming when he was feeding 600 cows alone because his hired man had fallen off a haystack and broken his leg. Calving out in the snow and muck and slush and goo, Mick dragged 120 calves to the dead pile. "The season of death and destruction," Mick calls springtime in the high country.

I forego my walk to hurry home. I want to bake a cake. Mixing, beating, kneading, pouring—the motions of kitchen work calm me, make me feel as if this, in the end, is the most important work of all: to feed and nurture, to give of myself by preparing food.

Mom and Dad arrive and greet me by oohing and ahhing over how lovely everything smells. Fighting pain all morning, Dad has been swigging on a bottle of Maalox, which leaves his mouth chalk-white and ghostly. We eat and discuss cancer treatments and when Dad is scheduled to go to the hospital. Not a pleasant topic of conversation, but I am glad we don't shy away from the issues.

After soup, salad, and a tiny piece of cake, Dad chooses a chair in the living room to rest. He has gone gray, his face the color of washed-out gravel. The pain has returned, kicking double time. He tells me even his arms ache. I build up the fire and put a blanket over him, then sit by his side, rub his arms, and talk of insignificant things. Mom comes in to check on him, bringing a damp cloth from the bathroom for his forehead.

"How is he?" Mick asks while I clear the table.

"Not too good."

"Guess I'll go out and fill the stock tanks," he says.

Mom and I sit on the couch. I read the little blue book on cancer and all the information sheets from Dad's oncologists. Mom reads about esophagectomy in my medical journal. As Dad rests, color creeps back into his face. Soon he is strong enough to talk again. His biggest fear, he confesses, is that the pain will worsen when he starts the chemotherapy, since nausea, vomiting, and esophagitis are common side effects of the cancer-killing drugs. The thought of throwing up terrifies him.

As soon as Dad feels well enough to drive, they head for home, leaving me waving from the doorway. I have a counter full of dirty dishes to deal with and a dull empty feeling in my chest.

Monday, March 10th

My blackbird returns. How I hear his clucks and trills over the sound of an incessant breeze is a mystery. During the night the wind whipped into a flurry and now spits dirt and dust and crusted old snow onto everything. Mick and I are both quiet. He heads out to do chores. I split kindling and wood and haul it into the house. When I've finished, Mick has headed up-country alone, so I strike out with the dog for a walk along the county road. Blue scares up a rabbit, and again the race is on, the dog yipping and pouring on the steam, the rabbit easily outdistancing him over the patchy snow. I haven't any energy to scold him. Far up the road he waits dejectedly by an emerging sagebrush. The gray-green crown of the bush obscures his ducked head until I am abreast of his hiding place. He looks up ashamed, waiting for his punishment. I sigh. He is so euphoric when chasing something that he can't seem to help himself. I stay silent, and Blue falls in beside me as if I've given him a command to heel. This

Mick and the woodpile. Photo by Laurie Wagner Buyer.

is his apology. Side by side, we pace the long mile up the road, breathing dust coughed up by the northwest blow.

My face is gritty and my lips plastered with grime when I finally reach the house. Mick is peeling a banana when I come in. I change clothes, then slice an apple to eat. He goes back outdoors, starts up his JD crawler, and hooks on the hand-built rubber-tired wagon he made one summer in Wyoming. I watch from the window as he trundles up the driveway.

All afternoon the wind whistles a mournful song around the windows, but the sun is bright. I watch a batch of chickadees flitting in a willow bush as the wind rocks the branches back and forth in a rhythmic dance.

I go out to unload the wagonful of wood that Mick has brought home. The biggest rounds weigh well over fifty pounds and are difficult to wrap my arms around. Blue and I head east. The wind and sun has softened the snow so my boots slice through the ankle-deep slush like knives through freshly made goat's butter. My old hard-packed ski tracks stick out of the landscape like miniature railroad tracks heading across the dull-colored pastures. Here and there patches of river ice have collapsed and left open water the color of slate-blue skies. I think about the fishing season coming up and of my Arrowhead clientele who will return to cast again and again into the rushing South Platte waters in hopes of catching a rainbow or a brown. For myself, I only hope that my awkwardness eases enough so I can make a decent cast. So far my limited experience has me endlessly tangled in tippet, line, and leader, snagged by a nameless fly.

Mick never talks much, but today he has not offered more than six words to me. The longer Mick and I live together, the more alienated we become. Marriage abides with constant struggle. Like milking the family cow, the relationship demands that I tend to needs every day to maintain health. Still, my marriage often seems neglected and uncared for until problems erupt like a mastitis infection in a cow's udder, then things become inflamed, sore, hard as a rock, untouchable because of intense pain. What can I do then except doctor the disease as best I know how and hope for healing? Unfortunately, it seems that one part of the whole stays sour and unproductive, a constant reminder that, though function-ing fairly well, overall good health is unattainable.

Hemingway's transcendent female character in *The Sun Also Rises* says, "It makes one feel rather good deciding not to be a bitch. It's sort of what we have instead of God." For my part, I try to meld not being a bitch with God's mercy and hope for the best.

Mom calls in the middle of the evening. Dad was put under a general anesthesia and had a Groshon catheter inserted in the left side of his chest this afternoon. Mom, garnering her courage, drove home from the city. Now she sounds weary. Dad, whistling in the background, is telling her what to say. Exasperated, she says, "Will you please go sit down? You're sup-posed to be resting!" Returning to her conversation with me, she says, "I guess I'm going to have to tie him in a chair." Though Dad is the one who must suffer the discomfort and pain of his cancer, Mom is the one who must suffer and deal with Dad. With forty-eight years of practice, she'll rise to the occasion with her usual grace under fire. I only hope the barrage of rapid shots coming her way will not leave her shell-shocked and unable to cope. If I could, I would gladly take her place on the front lines.

Fourteen years ago, when I first went to work for Mick and his wife,

Margie, on their O Bar Y ranch in Wyoming, it startled me to find Margie sleeping alone on the couch in the living room. She and Mick had been separated for several years, with Margie going south to Arizona to escape the long, dismal winters and Mick staying ensconced on the ranch to feed the cattle and plow the endless snow. In the summer, though, with clement weather and singing birds, Margie returned to the ranch to keep house and help with the haying. During the early days that I worked for them, I slept in their son John's room while he was away at college. I often woke early to make coffee and start breakfast and found Margie on the couch, rumpled and tousled, wound round with sheets and blankets, struggling to sit up. "Stay there," I'd offer. "I'll bring you your coffee." Then we would talk in women whispers, sharing our stories. When I asked her why she slept on the couch, she said, "It feels like someone's holding me here."

Her words cross my mind on this night as I unfold blankets and place my pillow just so on the couch, the same couch Margie slept on years ago. I squirm, nestling into the soft, butt-worn cushions, seeking a warm spot for my toes, pulling an afghan up to cover my chilled shoulders. Before I drift off into troubled sleep, I realize Margie was right, it does feel like someone is holding me here.

Tuesday, March 11th

Sleeping alone brings many rewards. The biggest and best is the fact that my vision has cleared, and I am able to focus my eyes on what matters most to me. My solitary night on the couch has refreshed me more than a week's vacation. Mick appears out of the bedroom with a totally changed demeanor. I venture a cheery "good morning."

"I'll be fine," he offers.

"Good," I smile.

"Didn't you want to come to bed?" he asks.

"Well, I just thought I'd give you some space and time to work things out."

"I was cold without you," he confesses.

So, with a few kind words exchanged, we slide back on track. My fear of a serious derailment and a dangerous wreck is set aside, but it is not forgotten.

In a celebratory mood, I fix bacon and eggs and toast for Mick, the old standard ranch breakfast that cannot be matched by granola, yogurt, oat bran, or fat-free muffins. Protein, fat, and carbohydrates, though they say the stuff will kill you, are what give an outdoor worker enough bottom to weather the cold and wind and long hours. The timeless phrase, "make sure you put a biscuit in your pocket" pops into my mind and means I ought to build a batch of biscuits soon.

The round of finished chores is given a grand finale when a pack of coyotes erupt in a clamor of yips and howls. Mick has driven on, headed home. Blue races east, hackles raised. "Nah!" I command and he stops, then sits, curious, listening, watching for shapes moving in the thick red willows along the slough edge. The coyotes raise their voices like a raucous choir. Are they rejoicing because the sun feels so good, the snow's melting, mating time is at hand, or because they found the bloody remnants of a cottontail discarded by an owl? No matter. Whatever causes them to cry out, they are lovely to hear now that the calves are growing old enough to be wary and their spindly legs are strong enough to carry them quickly back to the safety of the herd if coyotes threaten them.

Today, March 11th, marks twenty-nine years since Mick's dad died. It is a day we always remember even though Mick isn't one for making much about loss, grief, or loneliness. He misses his father and the old days of ranching. His sister, Arlene, died in 1990, just two years after we returned to South Park, and the original Buyer family homestead ranch outside of Fairplay was sold in 1994. There isn't much left for Mick except a few photographs and his own memories.

Mick's mother, Mary, at eighty-eight, has outlived her husband by almost thirty years. I think about Mick and me and our twenty-three-year age difference. Where will the future find me when he is gone? I have to achieve an identity apart from his and the fact that the ranch is his entire world.

Town today is slushy wet. Water runs in singing rivers everywhere. Puddles. Retreating snowbanks. Mud. Discarded litter and forgotten autumn stuff appears in yards and alleyways.

Once I'm back home, Blue and I strike out, splashing and slipping, sliding in remnant snow and increasing mud. The evening smells earthy: cow manure, horse urine, cat piss, wet hay, sodden dirt, a whiff of wood smoke, a smidgen of pine sap from the fresh-cut rounds of wood, and a wash of something dead that the dog has rolled in.

The soft ground gives underfoot. The drip and plip of water drops off the barn roof and the squish-mish of my rubber boots are pleasant. Even the river's tone is different, its voice deeper, faster, full of snow melt, mud rich. Sweatshirt, sweat pants, and a thin jacket make up my outside ensemble. I don't even need a scarf or gloves, so I tuck them into the pocket that isn't stuffed with baler twine. Without all my layers of heavy winter clothes, I drift light as dried dandelion seeds. The wind, whispery warm, caresses my face and legs and fingers and uncovered hair. I sing "spring!" with each step.

At my turn-around point on the hill overlooking the river I sit on a wide, flat rock and look south to the bulky shape of Buffalo Peaks. Snow patterns at 13,800 feet look like decorative icing on the massive chocolate-colored mountain. Clouds shift, and shade patterns the mountain's timbered sides, letting light and dark, occult expressions change the face of the landscape. I long to hold this peaceful beatitude forever.

Wednesday, March 12th

I wake at 4:00 a.m. While washing up, bleary-eyed, at the bathroom sink, I shiver as the electric heater's buzz of warm air brushes against my naked breasts and arms. Hot water from a tap, a real sink, real soap, a clean towel, carpet underfoot are things I never take for granted, and I bless Mick daily for giving me small comforts. Many mornings I've broken ice on buckets to get water to wash in a tiny basin with coarse homemade soap, no heat, the same thin, worn-out towel that never came clean no matter how often I hand-scrubbed it on the washboard. Whenever I bathe or do dishes or launder clothes in the washing machine, I think of all the buckets of water I hauled by hand from rivers, streams, or springs, and I am grateful for the physical ease I have in my life now.

I am out of bed at this early hour to give myself a chance to scribble for a couple of hours. The furnace never came on during the night so I check the temperature: twenty-two degrees, the warmest we've had for months and thirty degrees warmer than this day a week ago. Still, the fire feels good, the tea tastes sweet and hot, and I love the way my mind races when it is rested and fresh. Page after page of rushed words appear on recycled, gray pads stacked up on the kitchen table.

Mick says, "Honey, look at the sunrise." I turn and every view out the windows and porch doors is ablaze with orange and rose light where the sun squeezes between the eastern horizon and thick cloud cover. The sky is fiery hot, looking as if it could melt all the river ice in moments, but, in five minutes, the glow dies, leaving us a gray, angry-looking sky in the east, patches of blue and white in the west. Even indoors I hear my black-bird call and others of his kind join in.

I head outside to find Mick engaged in an all-out battle with a third of the yearling calves that crossed the river ice yesterday to a little island. Warmer temperatures melted the ice bridge and the cattle refuse to cross back over. Mick and Blue are both overheated and panting hard. A time out is called while Mick forks hay off the old Chevy flatbed into the feeders. The good calves, the ones who crossed over, begin to eat, hungry after their night marooned on the island. The remaining nine, the bad calves, beller plaintively, hanging by their hooves on the edge of the river ice. The over-cast sky darkens the river water so the depth is impossible to judge. The bad calves cannot tell if it is six inches or six feet deep. To make matters worse, when the good calves crossed back, a huge ice shelf broke off under their weight spooking the bad calves back to the safety of the island.

The river is really not bad to wade. We find several riffles where it is only inches deep. Mick patiently carries forkfuls of hay to easy looking spots. Blue and I make a wide circle, cross upstream on ice, and approach the calves from behind. Fifteen minutes later my coaxing and cajoling of the recalcitrant calves turns into an all-out cussing and hollering at ram-bunctious Blue. Mick joins us, pitchfork in hand. I pick up a willow stick as a weapon. It's a dangerous battle: ice, mud, frozen hummocks, slick banks, willow bushes, and stubborn, frightened, very fast calves. Looped ties on my coat catch on some brush and I go down. Blue dives in for a nip. A calf's hoof slashes open his cheek. In desperation, Mick tells us to quit, and we retreat, leaving the calves to their small, now thoroughly tromped and shit-covered kingdom.

Catching our breath, we struggle to regain our good-weather humor. I put snow on Blue's bleeding cheek. He whines, but does not pull away. Wounded in action, he knows we are proud of his efforts.

Up-country calves burst out of the sleeping shed and scatter like quail when we drive up. Some of them race in circles, bucking and kicking, others butt heads, then whirl and run, tails straight up like little flags on short poles. An all-out circus, the heifers mill, calling, trying to keep track of their calves. Things settle back down as Mick forks off their hay. He's feeding the heifers twice a day now and says he can't keep up with their voracious appetites. Keeping on their own weight, plus milking heavy to feed their growing-like-weeds calves takes a lot of feed.

When we head home, a bird flies from the pole fence in front of the cabin to a bare-branched aspen tree. Blue races forward, flushing it. As the bird flits to land on a rabbit-brush stalk I spot the telltale red breast. A robin. I hold my breath. Another joins the first. Silent, the pair wing from bush to bush, then they disappear. An advance guard? Early comers? Or just passing through? It doesn't matter. The startling surprise was like receiving an unexpected gift. Farther on, the chickadee perches in the dead spruce tree on the county road, chirping for all he is worth.

I spend my day doing little things to save my energy and acuity for tomorrow when I must drive to Denver for the Colorado Book Awards. I anticipate the crush of traffic and too many people with apprehension. To take my mind off the trip, I go see my neighbor, Mary, who trims my hair for me. She also massages my scalp, and brushes my hair, which provides the most wanton kind of ecstasy. We laugh and agree that hair brushing should be a prerequisite to marriage. If a man is willing to brush a woman's hair and rub her back, then he is a perfect candidate for a good husband. Mary twists my hair up in a French roll so I feel like a movie star as I scrub the clubhouse floor at Arrowhead Ranch, whisk dead flies out of the windowsills, and wash away five months of blown-in dust and grime from the counters, tables, and furniture.

When I pull into the ranch yard, Mick and Blue are back at war with the ornery calves. Mick whacks at their rough rumps with a large willow stick. Blue operates as his second-in-command with feints and rushes.

I study the front-line action from the kitchen window as I make chocolate-chip cookies. When Mick finally hobbles in, looking the worse for wear, I have oven-warm cookies and milk to reward his active duty. "Got all but one," he groans. "She went through the fence and is out with the cull cows. Wouldn't you know it, she's Broken Toe's calf! Walked right over to her mother and started sucking, not that she'd have any milk after losing her new calf. Weaned for five months, but the heifer still knows who ma is. They never forget."

I start a fire in the living room as Mick oozes into his recliner.

"Guess I've got a good heart," he confides. "I put it to the test, and I ain't dead!"

I peek in a few minutes later to find him sleeping soundly.

Thursday, March 13th

The air has a sharp edge, but the sun warms and gains strength as I lean uphill, walking the steep driveway to the county road. At the gate I stop, huffing, and study the small piece of wood wired onto the steel crossbars, a sign our neighbor and friend, David Neukirch, carved for us:

DM RANCH
MICK AND LAURIE BUYER

How often I've opened the gate with a sense of pride that I'm Mick's wife. Then I recall the times I've stopped at the gate, crying, so full of anger and resentment that I wanted to take my pocketknife and dig out my name to obliterate it from the sign, and then walk on, either way, choosing east or west, and just keep on walking, never looking back. Today, though, I feel calm and happy about the ranch. I walk with long strides, head up, arms swinging because I haven't much time. I must breathe in as much clear air and confidence as I can. Sensing my no-nonsense mood, Blue marches at my side.

A blip of blue makes me gasp. "Oh, hello!" I call out with joy. The blue bird returns, bouncing from fence post to fence post. A male, his color smears bright as a crayon mark against the sky. I wonder where his mate is and why he's early. He darts away, flying fifty feet to perch on the spire of a small spruce where he looks like a brilliant blue angel on top of the evergreen tree. I blink and he is gone.

The hoarse aerial call of a raven turns me south in time to see a pair of black-winged bullets shoot over the top of the aspen trees. "Crock . . . crock!" They roll and dive. Twist and spin. Blasting upward, one follows

Front gate sign made for us by our neighbor David Neukirch.
Photo by Laurie Wagner Buyer.

the other in an athletic Simon Says routine. "Rawck . . . rawck," I call, using my best raven imitation. "Come back . . . come back!" But the entertaining duo is also gone, lost against the dark, pine-timbered sides of Black Mountain.

Heading home I meet Mick on his four-wheeler going up to feed the pairs, the horses, and the bulls. He slows and stops, shuts off the puttering motor. We talk the small talk of spouses who worry about being separated. "I checked the tires and oil. Okay, thank you. Thirty-two pounds is good. All right. You be careful alone here; no Olympics, no heroics, call Rudy if you need help. I'll be fine. There's soup and salad and TV dinners and cookies. I know, I know. Well good-bye then. I love you. Bye, good luck; I hope you win." His last words surprise me. I kiss Mick's cold, leathery cheek, command Blue up onto the four-wheeler, tell him to stay, and walk away.

Mick struggles because I am a writer. He doesn't like the fact that I am an open book kind of person. Because he is an intensely private, closed, isolated man, the idea of people knowing about him and his life irritates him. He finds such openness unacceptable. We've had battles about my writing, in which there are no winners or losers, only scarred, stalemate practitioners, who shy away from each skirmish like horses spooking back from the fetid scent of a winter kill.

It is the tiresome merry-go-round of acceptance-rejection: I love you, but I don't like you. Yes, I want you to be happy, but not at my expense. I would like to take Mick's last words and frame them to hang over my desk.

As I pull the Explorer past the ranch gate, four cow elk cross the county road. I say good-bye again as their pale butts disappear into the shadowy timber.

I fight South Park wind the entire length of Highway 285 heading north to Denver. My wrists ache from holding the wheel hard, keeping the tires as steady as possible along the centerline. Plenty of times I've seen cars, trucks, trailers, even heavy semis, tossed off in the ditch like tinker toys. The roads are dry, though, and the sun shines. It helps me focus on the road ahead instead of the fear that sits behind me in the back seat. Paralyzing fear. The same fear my mother fights. Like the fear I once had of being alone. Or the fear I had of the dark. Or the fear I had of water. The fear of driving is my last fear to face.

After Fairplay, other towns and landmarks flash past: Como, Jefferson, Kenosha Pass, Grant, Shawnee, Glen Isle, Bailey, Conifer, Aspen Park. The traffic, which was nearly nonexistent, multiplies like batches of rabbits. Above the Jefferson county open space, I zing through a wall of heavy fog. Red taillights blink a warning and I brake. Glancing in my rearview mirror I see nothing but thick mist. I steer steadily along the curving white line that marks the edge of the highway. Pine trees loom and disappear. The car that was in front of me vanishes.

I slow to a crawl, pulling on my lights, occasionally braking on the tight turns and downslope runs where the Explorer gulps the asphalt, wanting to go faster. An eerie prickle flickers on the back of my neck, and my mouth goes dry. My hands squeeze the wheel. There is no place here to safely pull off. I must concentrate and stay calm. Coaching myself, I give instructions: turn off the tape player, open the window a crack, breathe, relax. Focus on the right fender, watch the white line, breathe.

Past Indian Hills, through the tight, winding stretch of Turkey Creek Canyon, the fog thickens with blowing snow. The highway darkens to a wet-slick, glossy-sheer ribbon. I search the roadside for signs so I won't miss my turnoff.

The gray ceiling lifts until the sky is dull silver, the day tarnished by the threat of snow. Wet and chilly, it is twenty degrees colder than it was in the high country. When I pull into Mick's son's driveway, daughter-in-law Mary Ann and Dottie, the boxer, appear on the front porch to greet me. Though my heart thuds, knees shake, and my legs feel as weak and wobbly as a new calf trying to stand, the last remnant of my fear retreats, slumps in the rear seat, and is forgotten.

With Mary Ann as chauffeur, we go out on the town to do things I never get to do in South Park, beginning with lunch at the Denver Salad Company, a quick shopping trip to Foley's, and a rush to find a place to park at the Mann Theaters. Parked next to us, a VW beetle is decorated a-la-'60s, complete with scrawled, spray-painted slogans: JANIS! PINK FLOYD! BOOTS ARE FOR FAIRIES! HONK IF YOU'RE HORNY! Mary Ann and I laugh and search the line of moviegoers wondering who owns the ostentatious rig.

A dark theater is one of my favorite places. I settle into my seat, ease into a state of relaxation I seldom find at home. My bones melt, my mind clears, erasing everything so I can totally absorb the story to be played out before my eyes.

Leaving the realm of movie land unleashes the real world once again. The day is darker, and the increased wind chill sends us shivering to the car. Back at Mary Ann's, John has returned from work at the United Airlines Training Facility where he teaches pilots the high-tech skills that all of us appreciate when we step aboard a jet. I give the kid my best step-mother hug and head upstairs to make a serious attempt at creating a sophisticated, aspiring writer out of a worn-down ranch wife.

The evening is wicked. Spraying slush covers the Explorer with waves of gray water. I envy the way Mary Ann sweeps along the freeways and maneuvers through the rush-hour traffic like a graceful lady matador.

In downtown Denver the loom of high rises and uncountable lights make me stare like a tourist. I read directions to Mary Ann who studies street names and one-way signs. It's all a foreign-land puzzle to me. I don't think I speak the language or even understand the obscure hand gestures of passing pedestrians making their way along the sloppy sidewalks. I try to remember my late teenage years in suburban Chicago, but the vague recollection is not enough to ease my sense of dislocation and of feeling seriously out of place. What I do remember are my acting classes, so I subtly shift from real person into actress on the stage.

Valet parking at the Holtze Executive Place requires a tip. I listen to Mary Ann's advice and hand over the proper amount of money. As we enter the gold-lit lobby, Mom and Dad climb up the stairs from the hors d'oeuvre bar and early evening drinks. Dad's hand is secure on Mom's elbow. Mom's head, turned back to listen to what he is saying, is a study in graceful repose. The rush of recognition and love washes over me.

Dad looks handsome in his dark blue slacks, sports coat, and carefully knotted tie. Mom looks like a breath of cool beauty with her short-cropped auburn hair, cream-colored suit, and fall-colored print silk blouse. Catch-up chitchat races past: not well early today; didn't think we could come; ranks of radiologists took up the morning; no, the drive was fine; yes, the room is nice; oh, here's the shuttle. We clamber into the minivan for the two-block drive to the Anaconda Towers, 38th floor, Petroleum Club, for the Sixth Annual Colorado Book Awards.

Hours drift and stir around me, a pale, fizzy-sounding dream in which I watch myself walk, talk, smile, and stand. The carpeted rooms are close, the air too warm and tight. I breathe in tiny shallow sips trying not to swallow too much of the strange atmosphere. The city stretches out in every direction from floor-to-ceiling windows. What I see is an ocean of fluorescent colors rising and falling on the waves of a winter night. If I were alone I would stand by the cool glass and stare for hours, soaking in the sights and sounds of the city. As it is, one presence in the midst of several hundred people, I am pushed and pulled by the tides of talking and listening, the overall roar of humanity that sounds like the voice of the ocean caught up in the curved conch I won in a sixth-grade writing contest. As a child, I often held that large smooth shell to my tiny ear to hear the seascape captured within, yet I never did understand what the voice was saying.

During the evening's introductions I try to paint myself as a study of elegant nonchalance. It is hard work not to show too much emotion, to have a pleasant smile in place, to have my hands rest unshaking on my

With Mom and Dad at the Colorado Book Awards.
Photo by Laurie Wagner Buyer.

lap, my legs crossed to keep them from jiggling. When the finalists for the poetry category are read, my name among four others, I feel a surge of certainty that I will win despite my prior certainty that I would not. A coiled tightness twists in my gut.

When Stephen Beal's name is called to honor his book, *The Very Stuff,* I uncurl like ribbons on a forgotten gift stashed under a bed. As Stephen goes by to accept his award, I grab his hand in a quick grip saying, "Thank you for winning!"

Dad leans past Mom to hold my shoulder and whisper, "You're still a winner to us!" I feel an unbelievable sense of relief. Not winning means my life will not change. A voice inside my head says, "It will be so much easier to tell Mick you lost."

While guest speaker Annie Proulx reads, my mind drifts and yawns. I am exhausted by the mechanics of trying to find firm footing, of imagining and believing in a future for myself. My eyes are tired from having seen too much. I want someone to shut my eyes with tenderness and put the copper weight of new pennies on my lids to keep them closed.

We leave Mom and Dad at the motel. Mary Ann circles the inner core of the city looking for signs and landmarks, then turns us true west toward the mountains and home. The roads are slowed by snow and ice. The elements are something I know intimately, and since I'm not driving I am not afraid. Tightly wound, I talk incessantly, sounding as silly and innocuous as a Chatty Cathy doll.

Mary Ann forgot her house keys. Shivering, sorry to wake up John, she rings the doorbell and sets Dottie on a barking frenzy. John answers the door in a pair of print skivvies. I start giggling and can't stop, teetering on the edge of fatigue drunkenness.

Setting an alarm for me in the guest bedroom, Mary Ann thinks I'm daffy to want to get up at 5:30 a.m. when it is nearly midnight. I want to call Mick before he leaves on his rounds of morning chores. In this pretty room that glows with the white-gold light of a bedside lamp there is a card on a paisley pillow in the middle of the bed. I take the colored paper in hand and read John's message to me. Among confetti, streamers, and star bursts it reads: "Congratulations, Laurie! You have a lot to be proud of. You should be very proud of yourself and all you've accomplished. We sure are proud of how far you have come. You're someone who deserves the good things to happen and I have a feeling that there are a lot more good things in store for you! Keep writing those great books! We Love You, John, Mary Ann, and Dottie."

In the darkness I stand at the window peeking through the lowered blinds at blocks and blocks of houses sleeping in the snow, the streetlights casting a warm luminescence against the stark white night. There is so much light here. No one ever walks in external darkness like I do at home, under the stars and moon, with the wind walking with me. Internal darkness terrifies the city, those places that remain lightless and untravelable. I have family and friends who are candles and mirrors. My inner horizon blossoms with sunrise, starlight, or moon glow. I crawl into a cushy big bed, blanketed by down duvets, cradled by overstuffed pillows. But on this night of comfort and peace, I cannot sleep. The hours slip by as I watch them pass on the digital clock, awake and anxious.

Friday, March 14th

Dawn grays from pewter to silver to near white with no traces of blue. In front of the bathroom mirror, I wrestle a brush through my shellacked hair and there, bright as a beacon broadcasting my age, is a single shiny albino strand amid the red-blond waves. Surprised and amused, I pluck the gray hair from my scalp and twist it into a tiny curl to tuck into my eye shadow case. I intend to give it to Mick, saying, "another milestone."

Mick answers on the second ring and I whisper an overall account of my big night out on the town. No snow at home. Just wind. He may take the cull cows to the sale today.

In a flurried rush of leggings, T-shirts, sweatbands, and walking shoes, Mary Ann and I head off to her aerobics class at a local health club. This is a world I haven't seen since my college days: loud music, lights, mirrors, women in skintight outfits who jump and sway, step and reach, working themselves into sweaty oblivion. In ten minutes I'm pooped and forego trying to keep up with the difficult dance routines. Instead, I bounce in place like a marionette on loose strings. The last fifteen minutes of the hour-long session are reserved for slow stretches and ab-work, the new catch-phrase exercise for abolishing potbellies.

Weight machines take up the next hour. Mary Ann knows which buttons to push and how many reps to do. I'm like a kid in a video arcade trying out everything that beeps, blips, or buzzes. All around us scantily clad people are walking, running, pumping, pedaling, lifting, stretching, swimming, sweating: all that precious energy going to waste. What we couldn't do with it on the ranch: pull calves, fix fence, feed cows, shovel manure, split wood, irrigate hay meadows, buck bales, wrestle calves, break horses.

At home John makes himself lunch. We talk about their application to adopt a child. After three miscarriages and the loss of a son in the fifth month of pregnancy, then facing the specter of infertility, John and Mary Ann have opted for adoption. They are nervous and excited, even apprehensive, but certain about their desire to raise a son or daughter. A more difficult subject, which I broach cautiously, is Mick's age, his concerns and worries over hanging onto the ranch, his inability to envision any other lifestyle than that which is intimately entwined with cattle and hay, water and grass and sky, weather and weariness. He has worked constantly with cows for over fifty years. I would like to see him slow down, but pulling the reins in on Mick only makes him balk. I relate the recent story of trying to help Mick fork hay on the truck after he'd had a strenuous workout chasing the yearlings. When I attempted to take the pitchfork from his hand, he said, "Just try it! The day I put down this fork is the day I'm dead!" I'm about two-thirds Mick's age, and John is half his age, but we both agree he is tougher than a boot and can easily work us both into the ground. Still, we worry and discuss, look at options, hash over things like income taxes, estate taxes, and the dismal future of agriculture. In the end we agree on only one thing: Mick's life isn't something we can control. He alone must decide his uncertain future.

As I drive home in the dull half-light of an after-the-storm day, my sleepless night accosts me and I struggle to stay awake. At the ranch gate I'm greeted by cheek-slapping gusts of wind that I gulp down, breathing in deep, erasing the odors and fumes of city life and traffic from my lungs. Mick and Blue wait for me on the porch.

Saturday, March 15th

I can barely walk when I rise to write in the predawn quiet. Every muscle screams in distress, especially my calves, which have iron vises squeezing them into knots. Funny and pathetic, I crab around like a sand critter out of its protective shell. Helping with chores, I stretch and bend and lift and pull and push until every city ache eases.

A sight worthy of being painted appears in the upper pasture: five horses—three blacks, a buckskin, and a copper-colored sorrel—back-dropped by winter-browned grass and leafless brush while a pair of electric-blue bluebirds flit around them as they line up along a spill of bright green hay. Back at the house, standing in the front yard, I hear the honking cry of geese. A mated pair angles with athletic grace across the azure sky far to the south. Piece by piece, spring fits herself together like a five-thousand-piece puzzle.

All afternoon I write. While Mick loads hay and rewires a broken ignition switch on the backhoe, I sit at the kitchen table and scribble, my pen racing along the blue-green lines of a legal pad, forming patterns like lines of ants on a sidewalk.

Yesterday, while I was gone, Mick loaded up Broken Toe, Coonie, Blackie, and Lefty. He hauled them to the sale yard in Salida only to find that the yards were closed and not expected to reopen. Now he will have to trailer his cattle another eighty miles to Monte Vista, or 125 miles to La Junta, or more than that to Fort Collins. An agricultural landmark disappears, marking a time when ranching was the lifeblood of the Arkansas valley. Most of the water rights in South Park have long since been sold off for millions of dollars to thirsty, wasteful front-range cities for green lawns, multiple daily showers, and car washes. With the water gone, the hay has vanished. Ten thousand haystacks used to line the river bottoms on the eighteen-mile stretch between Fairplay and Hartsel. Now, there are none. Hay is trucked in and sold at exorbitant prices. The ranchers are selling out, moving away. We can count on the fingers of one hand the people in South Park who make their living solely off the land. The closing of the sale barn is another death knell.

"What about the girls?" I ask Mick.

"Leonard was at the yards. He said they would send a truck in from Monte Vista to haul 'em to the sale there."

"What about the Salida yards?"

"Rumor is they will doze 'em down to make way for a trailer park."

We're on top of the mountain looking down at the wreckage of the times—age, inability, financial impossibilities, an anti-ag attitude in the community where city dwellers and out-of-state environmentalists encroach thoughtlessly. I change the subject to avoid the sadness.

In the evening Mom calls and relays the terrible side effects Dad suffers.

"Can you believe it cost $102.00 for pills for three days? I hope insurance will cover it," she says.

"Mom," I break in, "are you holding up okay?"

"Oh, I'm fine now. I kind of lost it this morning. I couldn't stop crying. Told Dad I couldn't do this. Was going to call you to rescue me, but I felt better after I had a shower. It's hard to see your father so sick. I rub his back. That helps."

Everything says, "Pack a bag and go." I hang up the phone and stay near the kitchen door looking out at the night, holding onto Mom's last words: "It could be worse. We may need you more later on."

When to go? When to stay? What to do besides worry and think and pray? What I see is a horror that harbors the end of my father, and the vulnerability of my own life. All right. Fine. If that's it, that's it! But I won't back down without a good fight. Snarl, death, you son-of-a-bitch. Show your teeth. I've got a club of love here to beat out your stupid brains. The ugly anger that grabs me from behind is ridiculous, but it keeps me from me crying.

Sunday, March 16th

My brain says, get your butt out of bed. My body says, stay awhile, sleep. My heart says, Mick, hold me. Hearing my silent plea, he turns, a warm wave of flesh and breath wraps around me, kissing, stroking into an unspoken symphony of love that reaffirms the living.

When he slips from bed, I roll over to where he has lain and bury my face in his pillow, allowing the body heat and the scent he has left behind to soak into my bare skin. What would it be like to wear Mick's hide? Would life be any easier if I were six foot one and 180 pounds? With his absence, the bed grows chill and damp.

Looking at the thermometer cheers me: I write twenty-seven degrees on the calendar with a smile. Soon I'll be writing thirty and thirty-two degrees; then, when we break above the freezing mark again after months of cold, I too will thaw out, loosen my perspective, and re-embrace another beginning.

The morning air is fine, as feathery and light as May when it is still March. It feels funny to walk on solid ground again. Despite eight inches of wet snow that recently melted into the earth, the road is powder-dry. Dust puffs up from each footfall.

In a crack in the roadbed I spy a glimmer of red glass. I pry it sparkling like a gem from the earthen den. On a spring day sixteen years ago, Mom and Dad came to visit me in a remote cabin on Dickson Creek in the Bitterroot Mountains of Montana. Dad had had trouble with his van during the trip, so he drove back down the mountain to an auto body shop. He had to leave the van there, so he hitched a ride part way back, then walked the highway's edge before climbing the last mile up the dirt road. On his trek he collected bits of roadside glass: Seven-Up-bottle green, beer-bottle brown, taillight red, Coke-bottle white. When he returned, tired and sweaty, he handed me his grubby treasures. "Here," he said like a little boy, "I brought you presents . . . diamonds, rubies, emeralds, topaz."

I follow his footsteps on a different road in a different state, scanning the red-brown dirt for jewels. I find two small diamonds to match my ruby, no emeralds or topaz, but just at the cabin gate I spot a carat-and-a-half diamond. Now I have treasures to take to Dad.

Monte stops by at noon, and I invite him to share our steak and potatoes dinner. He says no thanks, he has had a big breakfast, but I see him eyeing the homemade rolls that have just come from the oven, so I set a plate in front of him anyway. I love to watch working men eat. Monte has just come from cutting, hauling, splitting, and stacking a pickup load of firewood. Mick is just in from hand-pitching an 800-pound bale of alfalfa into the feed crib for Pauncho, the last heifer due to calve, and Nate, the Limousin bull.

The men talk, as always, about cattle and the weather. Monte has had a tough week with his inmate crew at the prison. The heifers they are calving out are small, not grown out, and barely able to have a calf. He has had two cesareans and three prolapses this week alone; they lost fifteen calves from that bunch. It angers him that the cattle were not well fed and were bred too young. In his own home herd of cattle in Cañon City, where his dad is calving out over a hundred head of heifers, they have only lost two calves. At the prison he also had to have the vet come out to remove the eye from a bull who had a three-inch willow stob stuck in behind the eye socket. The vet is a young woman who specializes in large animals. While she and Monte work together in the blood and gunk to remove the eye, the inmates turn green and move away. "Hey," she teases, "I thought you guys were supposed to be badasses!"

Monte fills us in on the cows he bought from Mick. Goldy and Society Red had their feet trimmed. Lindy had twins and is over her lameness. Miss Sally is close to calving. He has ten calves out of nine cows, so he's happy.

The pan of dinner rolls disappears and I replace it with a plate of cookies. The guys make a decent dent in those before moving outdoors. For the rest of the afternoon they lean against the tractor in the yard, shooting the breeze, discussing the portable shed Mick bought, eyeballing Mick's yearling heifers who curiously hang along the yard fence, analyzing the pros and cons of Monte wanting to purchase a 300-cow outfit in the San Luis valley: Will it pencil out? What about the debt load? How much hay? What kind of water rights? How tough are the winters? What about finding decent hired help? An afternoon in the sunshine trading guy-talk proves to be a tonic for Mick. He leaves to tackle his afternoon chores whistling, his step lighter and freer.

Tired of typing another manuscript, I call Blue to join me for a walk before dark. A piercing screech pulls our eyes upward to search the sky. A killdeer swooping west is one more sign that winter's hold on us is easing. A flock of blackbirds peck and scratch in the yard where Molly waits in a half crouch, tail twitching, behind a log stump. Everything about the evening says "Ah!"

Monday, March 17th

Wind in the willows. Dim sun. I split wood until I work up a sweat. For the first time in five months, I leave my heavy down coat on a peg on the porch wall. Instead, I don a vest against the chill breeze. Chores flow by. Mick croons to his mares, chatters at the calves, and roughhouses with the bulls. Spring's soft hand tempers his disposition, and consequently, mine. There is tenderness today, a cautious watching and waiting anticipation. I search the dull, yellowed grass for sprigs of green. Way too early, but I plant the idea anyway. More snow, some rain, lots of sun, and our world will dance a greening jig.

When I call Mom she tells me they're going to try to get Dad into the shower without getting water on the chemo pump box attached to his side. A friend will drive them down for the first dose of radiation. The slow-crawling poisons needed to beat the cancer will become Dad's reason for waking each day for the next six weeks.

On the spur of the moment, I decide to run over to Buena Vista to buy groceries. When Mick offers to drive me, his gesture pleases me like an unexpected present. We are only gone for a few hours, but the time away from the ranch is like a date. Mick waits in the truck with Blue while I shop. Going home, I sleep in the truck like an infant, the road hum and country music radio serving as a lullaby. Mick teases me about being such an exciting date. I respond that if he were more talkative, I wouldn't nod off!

The river purls a new tune, singing, "Ice free—ice free—ice free, free, free."

The river at flood stage near the barns and corrals.
Photo by Laurie Wagner Buyer.

Tuesday, March 18th

A meadowlark's warbling splits the morning like a spontaneous smile. "Listen," Mick says. We wait, ears cocked to hear the luscious notes ring out again. From every corner of the ranch then we hear ravens cawing, squabbling. My big chore jacket buffers the breeze, but in an hour I strip down, tying the coat around my waist like an apron. One of the new calves, a wanderer, has strayed away from the bunch to check out the bulls waiting by the gate. The cartoon caption of a 75-pound calf sniffing noses with a 1,800-pound bull could read, "Are you my dad?" The herd sire looks back with an expression that Mick calls "bull with a bastard calf." The little rascal figures out that he's alone. He turns toward us, looks puzzled, bawls once, then heads straight at us, tail up, running like a buck deer. He skids to a stop, breathing hard, the look on his face a study in comic disbelief, then he spots the cows in the willows and spins away.

At the spring I wait for Mick to close the pen gate and examine a willow branch going gold with new buds. One has opened a minuscule amount to reveal a pinhead's worth of white fluff. Another week of warmth, and the pussy willows will appear.

I walk the county-road loop, stopping long enough to study a tiny bunch of aspen Mick planted on the hill above the cabin the first summer we were here. Too many dry years have taken a toll: the grove looks like a mini Mt. Saint Helens with dead trunks and cracked off branches littering the ground. I gather the debris into a huge armload and carry it cross-country to stash it in the sagebrush. A few small saplings still have a green tinge and are springy to the touch. Maybe, with rain, they will revive and reestablish. On the way home I find a shiny topaz on the road.

In today's mail a package comes from Marcia and Bruce Plankington, the new owners of the old Buyer family ranch that Mick's brother-in-law, Walt Coil, sold in 1993. The box contains Mick's sister, Arlene's, high school scrapbook with a note from Marcia saying: "Mickey, I rescued this from the ranch after the Coils had taken what they wanted. I hope you will enjoy having it." We take turns leafing through the dry, brittle, yellowed pages of the dilapidated book. There are birthday cards, Christmas and other holiday cards, news clippings, dance cards penciled in with the names of boys Mick remembers, letters from friends, school news, report cards, dried flowers, the account of Arlene's fiancé being killed in a plane crash during WWII. A girl's treasure trove of memories gathering dust, Arlene's ashes now scattered over the ranch where she was born and raised.

Wednesday, March 19th

A post-perched raven croaks out an alarm-clock call. A female bluebird sits on the TV antenna looking dull and drab against the brighter blue of the sky. Mick mentions that it must have been a colder night since the stock tanks were covered with a half inch of ice. Our chores go round like a carousel, smooth and easy, the music of a light breeze in the trees, the faraway song of the river punctuated by bird call and calf beller. The bulls lumber in. Beginning to shed off, their hides hang in reddish buffalo-like patches where they've rubbed off hair on willow sticks. On my walk I find an old rusted washer, but no jewels. A car passes Blue and me going ninety-to-nothing, leaving huge plumes of dust in its wake. This first intruder in our world means I need to find a different hiking route. Spring means more traffic, more people, more litter, and more gates left open. Back at the house, Mick saws up weenie-edged slabs for kindling. When he finishes, I swing the double-bitted ax for an hour, splitting each chuck into finer faggots for starting fires. Hot on my face, the sun feels like a thousand kisses.

The road to Woodland Park unravels like a long black ribbon on this unseasonably warm day. The dichotomy of birth and death wrestles in my brain. Years ago in Montana, I learned about death and dying in a hands-on way: if we wanted meat to eat, we killed a moose, elk, deer, goat, rabbit, or chicken. Winterkills were common. Hawks, owls, bears, coyotes, wolves brought down the young or sick. I accepted how nature rebuilds through death and rebirth. Now, my father's life is in question. Can I continue to look at life with a "that's-the-way-it-is" detached attitude?

Five minutes after I pull into Mom and Dad's driveway, they return from the hospital in Colorado Springs. Dad driving is a good omen. His voice hoarse and croaky, he walks slowly to hug me. He teases me about Mom. "She's done so well with her driving," he says, tears in his eyes.

Mom replies, "Yeah, he gave me an A-plus, but then dropped me down to an A-minus because I blew a yield sign!"

At supper Dad rasps out grace, which makes Mom smile. I'm supposed to have my eyes closed during this thankful moment like a good girl, but I peek as I have always done to see who is not paying attention, who is sneaking tidbits from their plate. When we were young, my two sisters and I had to exercise extreme control not to giggle out loud while we watched each other disobeying the rules of mealtime.

I'm shocked at how little Dad manages to eat, but Mom is pleased. "That's the most he's eaten," she mouths to me.

We call my older sister, Karen, and Dad gets on the phone long enough to thank four-year-old Charlie for the drawing he sent because Grandpa is sick.

"I love my picture," my father says.

"It's about Bambi, actually," Charlie replies in a voice much older than his age.

"Oh, I see. Well, it is very good. Send me another one sometime, okay?"

Mom and Dad and I stand at the refrigerator to study the scribbles on an 8½ x 11-inch piece of paper with comments written on the side by Karen, who was instructed by Charlie, "Mom, you write what I tell you": orange and yellow=fire; black=smoke; green dots=Bambi's footprints; blue=sky; gray=clouds; pencil=clouds of smoke; purple= the ground; brown spots=guns; black lines=trees that burned; V shapes=geese.

The colors swirl and blend; the geese flee; Bambi is nowhere to be seen, but his fear and confusion are evident in his running hoof prints. Men are not visible, but the brown spots of their guns are ominous. The fire and smoke obscure the thin lines of earth and sky, and the black sticks of burnt trees remind us of the aftermath of human carelessness and insensitivity. A child who lives on the eighth floor of a high-rise in downtown Honolulu has managed to capture the primitive aspect of war in the West.

I curl in a jumble of blankets and pillows for the childlike delight of hugs and good-night kisses from my parents. With lights off, door closed, I squirm around to warm the sheets, then wait and listen to the sounds of retiring: faucets, the refrigerator, the furnace, and the humidifier all turn on and off, each one humming differently; the loud ticking of the kitchen clock; the faraway sounds of sirens and dogs and cars cruising dark streets. Straining my ears I wait and listen, then finally hear the whisper of voices from Mom and Dad's bedroom: "Our Father, who art in heaven, hallowed be thy name . . ." They are in bed, holding hands, Dad propped up by a slide of pillows to minimize his pain, Mom in her sateen nightgown lined in soft flannel. When they fall silent, I sigh and turn over to sleep.

Thursday, March 20th

At 5:30 my built-in ranch-time alarm wakes me. I dress, have a cup of tea, call Mick to make certain everything is all right at the ranch, and head out for a walk. It is thirty-five degrees, so I only need a sweatshirt and some gloves. The morning bursts with birdsong and dog bark. In two blocks I hear the symphony of eight dogs: the falsetto of a Pomeranian, twin bass of two German shepherds, oboe wailing of a hound, and the indistinguishable howls of other backyard inmates. Traffic is heavy, and exhaust hangs in the dawn air like a pall, tightening my throat, making my nose itch and twitch and pinch with each swallowed inhalation. The asphalt feels hard and ungiving underfoot, and I concentrate on taking long, light strides. In the roadside ditch along Rampart Range Road, there are bottles and cans, papers and boxes and plastic bags, fast-food wrappers, a Pantene hair spray bottle, cigarette packages and enough butts to pave a parking lot, a dead tabby cat on its back with paws reaching up as if to bat a suspended ball, uncountable diamonds and rubies and an old tire. Signs read: No Trespassing, Keep Out, Do Not Enter, No Outlet, Beware of the Dog. Other hikers, joggers, and dog walkers are aliens to me. I look down when they say "hello." I feel so exposed in town, as if my vulnerable emotional nakedness shows in front of so many eyes whizzing by in cars, trucks, and buses. I realize with grumpy dissatisfaction that there is no secluded spot within miles to squat and pee. When I return to the house, my ankles ache, shins sting, hips hurt, back throbs, and bladder burns. My ears ring from traffic noise.

We head down Ute Pass for Dad's daily appointment at Penrose Cancer Center. Dad opts to ride in the back seat, something I've never seen him do before. The cancer treatments have limited him, drawing his life into a tiny microcosm of self-aware neediness. Always before Dad has had an effusive personality, on the go, talkative, restless, opinionated, vitally aware and interested in the world around him. He read every page of the paper each morning and watched the news every night. Now his energy, what little there is of it, is drawn inward, concentrating on the smallest survival skills: try to eat and drink, try to sleep, try to go to the bathroom.

The Cancer Center is filled with sunshiny windows and daffodils on all the tables and counters. People recognize Dad and say hello, calling him by name.

I'm given a tour of the chemo lounge where comfortable chairs and fish tanks fill a large room. The scene, though outwardly pacific and calm, gives me a cold chill. People rest and relax, watch TV, visit, play cards, eat snacks, all hooked up to ubiquitous IVs that drip chemicals into their arms. A sign says: There are seven million cancer survivors living in the United States.

I want to ask how many have died. I close my eyes and see the image of the car-struck tabby cat in the ditch.

Dad needs blood work today, so I sit along a wall, the only young person in several rows of chairs, and smile at every person who catches my eye. Dad jokes with the nurses. Their musical laughter uplifts me. Always the charmer, Dad is a social expert at making others feel at ease, an action that puts aside his own insecurities and awkwardness.

Back downstairs, through a maze of hallways and look-alike doors, Dad slides a coded card through a scanner that allows him access to the lab. Technicians take us into a room where doors are plastered with warning labels: DANGER HIGH RADIATION AREA. The women are pretty and pleasant, looking oddly out of place in a room that is something out of a Star Wars scene. Dad teases: "I had to bring my daughter so she can see that I am getting my money's worth!"

Shirtless, Dad lies on a covered gurney, arms behind his head to expose his chest to the overhead eye of the machine. Laserlike lights key in on three tattoos marked on his sides and his breastbone. The lights go off, then on. We trail out leaving Dad alone in the impending darkness. It panics me to leave him there, but a technician shows me the video monitor where I can watch him and the intercom where they can talk to him and ask if he needs anything.

Standing on the street curb, waiting for the valet parking attendant to bring our car, we find the air is sharp with the smell of burning leaves. A breeze ruffles Mom's red hair. Dad nonchalantly drapes his arms over Mom's and my shoulders so we lean into each other forming a connected trio.

"What do you think about when you are under that horrible machine? Do you think about those rays zapping the cancer?" I ask.

Dad doesn't answer. I worry I have asked an inappropriate question.

"Actually," he says, "I was thinking what I could eat at Yakatori— Japanese noodles?"

"Rice and steamed veggies?" I reply.

"Shrimp tempura," Mom chimes in.

"Sukiyaki," Dad says shepherding us back to the car.

Mom and I sit out on the deck in the waning but still warm sun. A cranberry juice for me. A vodka for Mom. She and Dad have been together since they were nineteen and eighteen. Theirs has never been an easy road to travel, but somehow they have always managed to stay in the correct lane. Fender benders, flat tires, breakdowns, but no major irreparable wrecks. I admire their tenacity, resilience, their ability to accept and forgive, their willingness to go on loving despite human frailties.

"I love to watch the birds and the squirrels," Mom says. "This is my favorite thing to do."

We munch on cashews and pretzels and watch the breeze blow the spinning blades on Dad's miniature windmill.

My sister Eileen calls from Chicago. We chatter about her job, Mick, the ranch, her daughter Ashley's basketball games, the fact that Jimmy Buffett tickets go on sale Saturday and that she and her husband, Chuck, plan on going again to the concert in June. Eileen and Karen have it harder than I do because they live so far away and cannot come to help Mom and Dad.

Before bedtime Dad teases Mom, "Shape up, Joan, or I'll give you a smack."

"Oh, give it to me, give it to me," she chants. He slaps her lightly on the cheek, then kisses her.

"Me too, me too," I beg. "I want a smack too."

Friday, March 21st

Before the traffic's mass movement, before the dogs tune up, robins murmur morning mission notes. On my walk around the neighborhood, I study the trees and sky and the visage of Pikes Peak, ignoring the littered ground.

When I return Dad is up, trailing a sheet and blanket into the living room. He did not sleep well. He's grumpy, his hair rumpled and askew. The Groshon catheter on his chest no longer appears alien. He settles in his chair, and I help him arrange the covers, tucking corners around his bony shoulders. I rub his arms and kiss his forehead. He groans a muffled, gracious sigh in reply.

Wrens and chickadees peck in the brown backyard grass. Magpies strut their stuff around the pines. A black devil squirrel, his long ears looking like horns, bounds over and drinks from the birdbath. He glances my way, runs up to the door and scratches, his small, long-nailed paws pressed to the glass. I giggle at his beggar's plea. He backs off a couple of steps when I slide open the door and place five peanuts on the welcome mat for him. In ten minutes he has come and gone five times, each time rotating an in-the-shell peanut around and around in his paws before placing it in his mouth and dashing away. When all the nuts are gone—eaten or stashed—he scratches on the door again. "Okay, Piggy," I smile, "one more round, then I'm cutting you off." With his second helping gone, he insistently turns circles on the deck, climbs up on the firewood box, and hangs comically from the screen. When he leaves, a red-and-gray squirrel comes up to the door. Word must have gotten around that the Wagners have handouts.

Again, the hospital. A dietitian explains to Dad that he can eat anything. The more calories the better. He has lost ten pounds in a week and she doesn't want him to lose more. Years of brain-changing low-fat, low-cholesterol, healthy-heart diet go out the window for Dad. He must now reeducate himself to eat well and often, so his body can rebuild the cells the chemo and radiation are killing off. We joke and laugh, teasing him about French fries, milk shakes, biscuits and gravy, broccoli and cheese sauce, bacon and sausage and eggs. Pleased, the dietician says, "How wonderful that you haven't lost your sense of humor."

In the evening, I sit at the dining room table and write letters to each of my sisters with information about Dad's cancer. I include explanatory pamphlets from the center. Then I write six times over the same basic letter to close friends of my parents who I know would like to be notified of Dad's condition. The words seem sad and inadequate. To brighten the dark cast of each note I add, "The weather has warmed up nicely, and the birds have returned."

Saturday, March 22nd

When Dad wakes I bring him his morning paper, make him tea and cream of wheat, then pack my bags. We say good-bye at the front door. Mom in her nightgown, Dad in his T-shirt and running shorts, both look worn and aging. One of the hardest things I've ever done is turn away and drive off. They will be fine. They will call if they need me. Still, I feel like a deserter.

My trip back to the ranch is a mental kaleidoscope of changing scenery and childhood images. The places we lived (Scotland, Texas, Arkansas, the Philippines, North Dakota, Hawaii, Illinois), the moves we made (fourteen schools in twelve years for me), the relatives, friends, strangers that entered our lives every time we changed stages and rearranged the sets. Snippets of dialogue echo in my ears. Dad wasn't always this mellow. Mom wasn't always this strong. Anger, fear, and insecurity intermix with tenderness and love.

The only compensation for a troubled mind is busy hands. When I get home, I fix Mick a nice lunch, clean up dishes, tackle the house cleaning, laundry, the sundry odd chores that have escaped notice this week. Mick has been dragging meadows the past few days using his '37 Chevy and the English harrow. Dust and manure dirt fill the air, then settle in a fine powder on everything. Generator trouble shuts Mick down, and he changes hats from field hand to mechanic. The '37 part is shot and cannot be easily replaced, so he scrounges a generator off an old buck rake with a '39 Chevy engine. The wreck probably hasn't been moved in forty years, but the used generator works fine. In the family we joke that when something breaks down or needs to be fixed, it gets "Mickey-Buyered" or "we'll just Mickey-Buyer it." Mick reaches legendary status for his uncanny ability to repair things with handmade, cobbled together parts.

A chilly wind ruffles the otherwise mild evening, and we walk together. Mick, Blue, and I head over the ridge to a patch of timber Mick calls Jack's Camp because of an old log he found carved with the message: Jack's Camp, July 18th, 1911. The log is mostly rotten and covered with the thin lace of orange lichen and green moss. A few weathered boards, nails, and marks on surrounding trees are all that is left of a sheltered place someone called home. We have no idea who Jack was: a prospector, a sheepherder, a cowboy, or a freighter who camped in the spot when he made his trips over Weston Pass to Leadville. The wagon ruts of the old stage road are still visible where they cut through the ranch.

Sunday, March 23rd

Leaving me behind to dress for our trip to Denver to see John and Mary Ann, Mick rises early to take care of the cattle. He feeds an extra four bales of hay since he won't be home in time to do evening chores. When he comes in he says, "The calves are as slick and shiny as peeled onions." He warns me to stay out of Nate's corral. Close quarters and spring fever have put the bull on the prod, and Mick had to beat him back with a sorting stick to fill the water tank. He's not mean, just playful, but a ton of playful can get anyone in trouble.

John and Mary Ann live on the edge of what was once prime ranch land. Now C-470 cuts through the heart of the old meadows, between their home in Belleview Farms and Hogback Ridge to the west. A day's visit means Mary Ann and I sit in the sun while the dogs chase each other around the yard, and Mick watches John wash ranch grime off his truck. Mick bemoans the wasted water running down the concrete driveway to the storm sewer in the street. "All that water would water my cattle for a week."

In the afternoon Mary Ann and I hike a concrete trail that parallels the interstate. The roar of wheels on pavement at sixty-five miles per hour hammers at my ears, but I also hear the melodious call of a meadowlark that settles on a fence post in a patch of farm field with a trickle of irrigation water. The grass, what little exists between the roads and subdivisions, is emerald green and growing. Back at the house, Mick and John hang out in the four-car garage discussing snow machines, trucks, lawnmowers, chain saws. Any subject related to motors and power is open, but it is a conversation closed to women, a place where men speak a language incomprehensible to us.

John and his dad look at old photo albums and compare snow machine trips into Yellowstone Park. Mick was there in 1965. John and Mary Ann were just there. Thirty years span the gap. When Mick traveled through in a snow plane with Harley Mocroft, they never saw another soul. In places where the earth's thermal heat had melted the snow down to bare ground, they placed small lodge pole pine to act as rollers to push the snow plane across. "Harley," Mick tells us, "used to roll out his sleeping bag right on the bare dry road and would sleep warm as toast even on below-zero nights." Today, traffic through Yellowstone is closely monitored since as many as two thousand snow-machines zoom through every day.

The night sky is dark enough for us to stand out in John and Mary Ann's yard and gawk at the comet in the northwestern sky. A pair of binoculars brings the exploding star cluster into close range. Bright silver, it shimmers, so far away that what looks like a four-inch blast of brilliance is actually a gigantic ball of molten matter trailing a tail more than a million miles long.

When we are nearly home, I let Mick drive on to the house while I walk the ranch road in from the gate. Here the stars are so close I can almost reach up and snag one on my fingertip. I stroll in darkness softened only by a third of a moon and star glow. The comet flies like a luminous horsetail above the shadow of the divide.

Without fires all day, the house is cold. Without fanfare we crawl between the frigid sheets. Nestled spoonlike, our bodies create a catalytic warmth that begins in Mick's chest and my back and spreads with spectral radiance to our fingers and toes. The constancy of our personal orbits remains a mystery to me.

Monday, March 24th

The storm front catches us as we do chores. It is eerie to watch a roily mass of clouds spill over the mountains and collide with the blue sky. Colder air rides the clouds' flanks. The eighteen-degree warmth in the east gets slammed. Everything shifts and changes. The wind direction alters. The breeze becomes a blast. Our faces and fingers stiffen. In a matter of seconds, winter returns, riding hard to rout spring and send it flying backward in full retreat. Milling in circles, the cattle tromp the hay we feed.

As I cross the half-frozen pond of spring water collected near the willow bottom, I flush a snipe out of hiding. The shrill cry startles me. A long-billed, shy, and revered forecaster of real spring, the first snipe of the season appears during an obvious return to winter. In the evening, at dawn, even in the middle of the night, snipes' mating and feeding flights produce a strange ululating sound when wind rushes through their wings. For years Mick and his family have called them *who-who* birds because of their odd *whoing* sound. A favorite of mine, I memorize the perfect image of the marsh lover's stiff-winged flight.

Mick and I spread out survey maps of the ranch to study. Would it be possible to sell eighty acres in order to keep the rest? Selling land is anathema to him. Land is family to Mick. Deciding which piece to chop off and offer for sale would be like choosing which child to give away. Meadow and river, high, dry sagebrush pasture, a thick clump of timber, whatever choice was made would be sure to leave a hole in our hearts as big as a clenched fist.

For the first time in fourteen years we hesitantly discuss the tough issues of selling out, of leaving, of breaking up, even the possibility of divorce. No matter which way we turn, we hopelessly tangle in pain. Mick wants to stay with the ranch and preserve the entire acreage for his children. Yet, he is increasingly aware that he can no longer keep up with the daily grind of physical work and the financial stress and worry of keeping things together. I want Mick to keep the ranch even if our livelihood is failing, but can I afford to invest all my love and energy in a place that holds no future for me?

By midafternoon the snow returns. The wood fires warm our bodies, but our hearts are hardened by cold-blooded, unpalatable thoughts and questions with no answers.

My father answers the phone when I call to check in with him. His voice is strong. No weakness, no hoarseness. His mouth sores have healed. Drinking a root beer float his latest accomplishment. After I hang up I escape to the outdoors.

The sharp slap of snow against my face refreshes me. Awakenings are not always pleasant. If I lose my father, I still have this to hold close: the earth underfoot, the snow-wet air, the obscure sky, the challenging brunt of the storm.

Tuesday, March 25th

A pair of keening killdeer bursts out of the snow-covered sage. Eight below zero shocks every sensibility. False spring. The sun bakes the new snow. We must be grateful for the moisture. Mick eyeballs the calves with care, spotting only one telltale wet back, a sign of sleeping out in the weather. The rest were wise enough to seek the shelter of the sheds. Every animal greedily rushes for the hay we feed. The calves wrap tiny tongues around green wisps. Though still hooked to life by a warm udder, they are growing up and copycatting ma's need for hay and salt and water.

For some stupid reason Mick and I argue despite the fact that sniping words are a waste of time and energy. The essence of an argument is a desire for control. I despise arguing, but I am drawn into the vortex of fault and blame. A good arguer, a great debater, I line ducks up in a careful row and drop them one by one. That issue is dead. Next complaint? I'm loud. Strident. Hardheaded. Stubborn. Convinced I'm right, Mick's wrong. That is my father coming out in me—"I may not always be right but I'm never wrong." My point of view remains crystal clear and infallible. How can Mick be so nearsighted and narrow-minded that he cannot comprehend the obvious, commonsense, plain-as-the-nose-on-your-face logic of what I'm saying? I'm the one, though, who walks away, angry and frustrated, but determined not to let argument escalate into an all-out fight. I've been whacked across the face with a heartless hand years before I met Mick. I learned to watch the limit of someone's patience. But walking away leaves me feeling weak and defeated.

The anger, resentment, and bitterness ooze out of my feet, leaving my legs feeling rubbery. The earth balances and heals me, gives me courage to go home, fix supper, take Mick his plate with an apologetic smile, harboring a dim hope that maybe somehow we can muddle our way through the morass of our separate needs and continue to find a path of common ground to stand firm on. That is my mother coming out in me—the peacemaker, the calm presence, the elemental female need to fix, mend, heal, comfort, hold firm.

Evening comes quietly, a settling shadow that soothes the ache inside. No matter how often I bring up the subject that Mick must to find a way to provide a secure future for me if something happens to him, he remains implacable. Following some sort of old-fashioned family tradition, he insists on leaving the DM ranch, the cattle and horses, the vehicles and equipment, and his life insurance to his children, John and Melody. There are no cash assets or investments. When I say "What about me?" Mick likes to reply, "Oh, stop worrying. There will be a hoard of hairy-legged admirers waiting at the gate to take care of you when I'm gone." That grates against my heart like heavy-gauge sandpaper on polished wood. It irritates and frustrates me that because I am not a blood relation, I do not count.

For some secret deep-seated reason, Mick is unable to meet my need for a reliable future, either financially or emotionally. Why do I continue to expect things from him that he cannot give? For years I've counted on the notion that one day he would love me enough and trust me enough to consider me a true member of the family, a woman worthy of being taken care of. I've waited with patience and understanding. Now, however, I begin to feel that I only have one option: to sail alone. Uncharted waters require personal insight and courage. I envision myself untying my frayed rope from his aging, but still sturdy dock. There is no room in my small boat for anyone but me. The only thing I know about sailing is that the wind is everything. My responsibility is to learn which way the wind blows and tack appropriately to get where I want to go. First, I must choose a direction and decide on a course, but I am becalmed. No breath of wind stirs me. I stay in dead water, afloat and waiting.

Wednesday, March 26th

Snipe song ripples through the sky. Spring comes again fresh-faced and welcoming. When I walk the county road after chores, a pickup slows and stops. Our retired water commissioner, Mark Curry, has been put back into service to check well locations. There has been a panic to register and properly file on existing wells in this water district since the City of Aurora announced plans to tap a large underground aquifer in northern South Park. Water is gold, the valley's lifeblood. Every year more water disappears, going to quench the endless demands of front-range cities. Without water the high country returns to the desert it was before the advent of irrigation. Luckier than most, we have several miles of the South Fork of the South Platte, a quarter mile of Twelve Mile Creek, numerous springs, and wetlands. As the value of the ranch goes up, our ability to make a living goes down.

Warmth. The word slips sensually off my tongue like a kiss. The afternoon sun brushes my back when I hike the muddy trail up Copper Ridge. Elk tracks and droppings mark the earth, making a tapestry of moon shapes filled with black pearls. Reawakened smells of sage, pine, and dirt tease my nose. I pick up a pinecone with my ungloved hands to feel the prick of spurred bract ends. Ridgetop gained, I settle on an old stump to catch my breath and stare at the faraway snowed-over flanks of Buffalo Peaks.

I decide to trek the long way home cross-country through aspen stands carpeted with evergreen kinnikinnick and steep north-slope black timber where my footing is challenged by thick duff and slick downfall.

I study the game trails and spot a paw print in the mud that is much larger than Blue's. Another dog wandering alone? A big coyote? I know it cannot be a wolf because they were exterminated from this area decades ago. Except for the occasional caw of a distant raven, the woods are so silent I can hear the deepening roar of Twelve Mile Creek.

Trying to keep my feet dry, I tiptoe from hummock to hummock in a spongy slough bottom studded with dwarf willow. When I reach the eight-foot-wide span of rushing water, I skirt the banks looking for a beaver dam or ice bridge. I climb over and through an old wire fence that hasn't been repaired in a dozen years. An ouzel darts out of an ice-edged pool and sends Blue into a frenzied chase. In the sheltered protection of an overhanging willow, I find a bridge that holds up well under my weight so I leap onto the gravel bar on the opposite bank. Gone gray and silver, alternating colors where the water splashed over a riffle, the bar offers a secluded spot to stand and fish the upper pool. I have no rod, but I plant my feet and practice an imaginary cast. "Plip!" I place a phantom fly right near the grassy overhanging bank where I'm certain a brookie or a brown lies in wait.

Mick's north fence on the cabin meadow has been wiped out. For a quarter mile the stretched wires sag to the ground. The bulls pastured here might wander and cross the river and be gone. I lift the upper strand and string it here and there atop the posts creating a bluff that looks like a widow-woman's poorly patched together clothesline. A large herd of elk running en masse from hunters caused the damage. In a couple of months the cow elk will return to this solitary stretch of river to have their calves in the hidden sanctuary of the fifteen-foot-high willows. Then we will have cow-bark-and-calf-squeal music every day.

The lower stretch of meadow is littered with the debris of the 1995 flood: old fence posts, pieces of beaver-gnawed aspen trees, willow branches, sticks, worn boards off ruined head gates, anything and everything the high water left behind when it retreated back within the river's banks. I need to come back and stack the natural trash to make small game shelters. In the summer, wild iris and fringed gentians color the landscape purple, lavender, and bluish-crimson. An echo haunts my ears: the sound of snowmelt, the swelling river, and spring.

One by one, strung by fives or sixes or sevens, colored beads become a pattern I stitch to smoked buckskin. Cheyenne pink, surrounded by an earthy red, on a background of chalk white, encircled with deep blues. With a needle so thin I can hardly see the angles of self-directed design, I make the soft hide of a deer come alive in my hands.

Thursday, March 27th

Caught in lamplight before dawn, *The Very Stuff* beckons me. Stephen Beal's poetry is about "color, thread, the habits of women." I crave some tacit understanding of the nurturing I need, the cradling and hand feeding of my infant creativity. I hope Stephen can tell me about the habits of women from a male perspective. Maybe he can grant me access to the locked door of my own psyche.

A cresting blast from the west. A smaller, sharper blow from the south. Tall trees whip and recoil in the warm fury of this thirty-degree day. Chore time is tough and tense. Neither Mick nor I have much to say. It is hard enough to keep our feet and stand up against the wicked pressure of the wind without having to try and talk.

Mick announces he is going to Buena Vista. He asks me if I want to go. I hesitate. I know if I go, I'll be silent and grumpy. If I stay home, I'll worry and stew. Such a tradeoff. I opt to stay home to type manuscripts. The disappointment on Mick's face hurts. His blue eyes, like arctic ice, turn cold and distant. He leaves Blue home, which surprises me.

"Will you be home for lunch?" I ask.

"No," he says.

"Okay, I won't fix anything. Do you know where you're going so I'll know where to look if you don't come home?"

"No," he says and walks out the door.

Blue whines at the window. Is Mick upset enough and desperate enough to do anything foolish? His earlier despondent remark about killing himself returns. Suicide specters float in the room. Like pieces of raw meat crammed down my throat, ghosts choke my life. Shoulds, coulds, woulds, what ifs, and maybes gnaw at me. Could I have done anything to save Sy? What can I do to help Mick cope with his own darkness?

While the world goes crazy with relentless wind and a hurt husband roams the highways, I spoon hot soup into my mouth to ease the ache.

When Mick pulls in late, Blue leaps and barks like a wild dog. We manage to get through a semicordial supper together before our uneasiness and anger erupts again. We cannot seem to talk without verbal poking and stabbing. In between our outbursts, CNN exposes the mass suicide of Heaven's Gate people in California. We cannot imagine such alien craziness. By comparison, our inability to cope seems ridiculous.

Slouched in his recliner, Mick opens his arms to me. Craving closeness, I drop to my knees, place my head in his lap. Blue nestles alongside. We stay embraced until our arms ache. Making a wary peace, we take each other to bed.

Friday, March 28th

Maybe comet Hale-Bopp caused this unease. Perhaps we are caught in different orbits that insist on pulling us apart instead of bringing us together. Mick and I huddle by the stove and finally talk like friends. Easy for me since I'm an open book. Difficult for Mick, who harbors a closed, shy personality. We broach the subjects of disappointments, ruined expectations, our continuing struggle to make our marriage work. Many loving things and many not nice things become clear to us. I assume that marriage means mutual financial and emotional involvement. I learn that Mick never wanted to remarry after the trauma of his first, failed marriage, that he felt coerced into marrying me. He is lost in his aging and his growing inability to continue ranching. I'm lost in my middle-aged struggle to figure out how to support myself and build a future. We hash out the pros and cons of selling the ranch, divorce, going our own ways. It is an exhausting exhumation of all the bones beneath the earth of our marriage. How can we stay together; how can we survive apart? The only thing that shines in this gloomy conversation is that we love each other.

Dad calls and asks me to come on Easter Sunday for church and dinner out in Cripple Creek. I think of the long drive, of leaving Mick alone again with chores and worries and an unsettled personal state of affairs, but what can I say to my father, who seldom asks me for anything, except, "I'll come."

Saturday, March 29th

A skif of snow sugars the ground. A bunch of robins bustle at the hay pile. In the biting wind Mick waits for me at the ranch gate, an incredible effort on his part to walk the hill considering how his knees ache. We hold hands, smiling to walk the three-tenths of a mile down to the house.

"Go on," Mick says, "I'm holding you back."

"No," I reply, "I'm fine."

I color five hard-boiled eggs rose pink and write our names on them with magic marker: Mom, Dad, Mickle-Nickle, Miss Laur, and Blue. Then I hike to the cabin where I have a couple of Easter baskets stashed on the upper kitchen shelf.

The big, black, dusty draft horse mares block my path like trolls demanding payment. I croon to them: Cookie and Candy, Cookie and Candy, Mrs. and Mrs. McGoo, which are Mick's affectionate names for them. I scratch ears and necks and pat chests. They tower over me like avenging angels, but they are as sweet as pie, as gentle as gumdrops.

At the cabin, tears spring into my eyes when I see the collection of dead flies, cobwebs, and dust. In 1988 we scrambled to get the roof on before November first so we could move in. It had been a rough summer, living tough and grubby in a wall tent, trying to fence 250 acres so we could bring the horses down from Wyoming. All the cattle on the Wyoming ranch had been sold. Mick's old part-Dingo dog, Sam (Samuel Samson Kigilicutty Buyer), worked with us.

Mick's new land in Colorado had given us hope after the loss of the O Bar Y ranch on the Upper Green River. Mick's divorce had severed his connection to a place he had worked and loved for over a quarter of a century. His ability then, at fifty-five, to continue trying to ranch over 11,000 acres, to put up 900 tons of hay, and to run a small herd of 150 cows was diminished. Those twenty-five years in deep snow country had ground him down to a nub. A new start meant everything to us then.

Mick had been like a teenager that summer we spent in the tent: up early, way before dawn, working like a demon, climbing every ridge within miles to see what was on the other side, exploring the river, creek, springs, scouting for arrowheads and artifacts. Then in August, while driving treated wood posts on the rocky flank of Copper Ridge, Mick smashed off his thumb in the hydraulic post pounder. His horrified grunt and bloody

The cabin on the upper end of the ranch.
Photo by Laurie Wagner Buyer.

glove made me rush to start the tractor. The long drive to the nearest clinic thirty-four miles away, the even longer drive to Colorado Springs to see a hand surgeon, turned into a nightmare. Mick's thumb could not be saved. For weeks, as he wrestled pain and the healing process, we did not know just how much use he would have of his left hand. That one fateful blow, man against machinery, ended Mick's idyllic summer, the only one he would ever have.

We hired a crew to build the cabin that Mick had dreamed of putting up himself. The log walls went up slowly as we froze in our sleeping bags each September night. By October first, Mick refused to wake with frost on his face again. He moved our cots, sleeping bags, and a little gear into the partly complete cabin, and there, surrounded by sawdust, insulation debris, and work dirt, we settled in. The small propane furnace warmed us, and we began the task of making a cabin shell into a home. I had no inkling then that in six years we would move yet again when the half section of land to the east of us came up for sale. Mick mortgaged everything to buy the adjoining property that had an old homestead ranch house, barns, and corrals. It took Mick a couple of years to convince me to bring our household things a half mile downriver to a home where we had electricity and running water. I moved, reluctantly, and we left the cabin we had built to weather away.

Easter Sunday, March 30th

I give Mick his tiny Easter basket and card, and I hurry through breakfast so I can squeeze in a hike. The bounty of spring pulses in the cool air. The sun bursts open like a broken egg-yolk above the Tarryall mountains. I turn my face to the first rays and pray: for my dad to deal well with his cancer, for our family to have strength, for Mick to find a peaceful decision about his future, for me to have the endurance to go on loving him despite our differences. When I open my eyes, Blue sits facing east, ears perked, nose twitching. He looks at me as if to say, "Church over?" "Yes," I say, and he leaps and dances like a confined child set free.

On the long drive to Woodland Park I spot a pair of geese along the river preening on the bank in the sun, gray and black beauties, perfectly matched like bookends. Then, in the South Platte above Lake George, a lone gander paddles upstream, making no headway. When did he lose his mate? How will he weather the seasons to come without her?

A childlike celebration comes when I enter Mom and Dad's house: Easter baskets, colored eggs, candies, and cards. Dad looks much thinner, but his face blooms peachy radiance under the gray shadows.

The twisting mountain road to Cripple Creek is packed with travelers. Dad drives with his old aplomb, and seeing him behind the wheel again gives me secret satisfaction.

We talk of being children, of growing up, of wanting things early in life that most of us never get. My mother says, "For me it was horses." She robbed her piggy bank for enough coins to ride a pony round and round the block. The milkman's horse enchanted her. In later years she worked all day exercising trotters at Maywood Park to have a half-hour ride in the afternoons. A tomboy, she yearned to be a physical education teacher. Instead, she married Dad, became an Air Force sergeant's wife, and birthed girls. Her childhood desires were set on a back burner, then forgotten.

Dad loves to gamble. At the Gold Rush Casino, lights flash, bells ring, and the computerized one-armed bandits go clanging wild. The noise surrounds me like monstrous mosquitoes, a hard and steady obnoxious hum. This is the craziest kind of entertainment, but Dad soaks up the atmosphere like a country kid come to the big city. Dad plays eighty dollars, wins $176, and quits.

I grin at my parents' constant squabbling. My father remains a child at heart and very much a boy: he wants to play his game his way and be a winner. My mother still plays the little girl's role of perfect peacemaker: happy home, contented husband. She wants the world to be a nice place and continues to stretch her own equanimity to smooth out the rough places in life. The lucky middle child, I relish the safety, security, and well-being of having parents who really care about me.

Roaming the backyard in the mild evening air, I sense the atmosphere hanging on life's balanced scale, ready to tip into full spring with the weight of one more robin, one more blooming pasqueflower.

Monday, March 31st

I bring home the joy of colored eggs, marshmallow rabbits, jelly beans, chocolates wrapped in foil paper, but Mick, quiet and distant, will not talk. He reads the papers I've brought in with the mail.

"It's hard for me when you're gone," he says. "I get used to being alone. Then, when you come back, I don't know how to act."

He plans on cutting wood and goes to his shop to work on the chain saw. I'd like to curl up on the couch with a good book, but I need to make the effort to bridge the gap that yawns between us. I think of my mother and the years she patched the planks and repaired the approaches and examined the stringers on the bridge between her and Dad. She never quit trying.

I change my go-to-town clothes for boots and coveralls.

We look like a modernized wagon train heading across the sage flats. Mick on the four-wheeler pulling his homemade rubber-tired wagon loaded with toolbox, chain saw, ax, gas and oil, lariat rope. Complacent,

Blue and I walk behind, serene with the succor of sweat and work, the reward of wood to warm our house.

Mick picks a thirty-foot-long dead spruce, prickly with branches. Assaying the angle and lean of the tree's old life, he predicts the way it will fall. He saws with authority in his pose, placing his feet carefully in the wet, muddy pine duff and slush of spring. A timid crack splits the silence, then the resounding thud as the matriarch of this patch of timber goes down, her fall cradled by young aspen and the dead rotting trunks of her contemporaries. A solid tree with heartwood as pale amber as honey, no rot, no sign of bug kill, she lived her lengthy season, then died. Now she gives the last of herself to us.

As Mick saws with a rhythmic racing roar, I stack the rounds like puzzle pieces in the wagon. Blue lies on an old snowdrift, panting. In an hour's time, we retrace our trail. I use care to pat down the ground where the wagon wheels have cut the earth's crust.

Stacking the wood outside the porch door gives me solid satisfaction, but the fact remains that Mick and I have little or nothing to say to each other. This means something profound, but I'm not savvy enough to figure it out.

Ignoring the silence that lies between us like another woman, I say my prayers and believe tomorrow will be better.

APRIL

❧

Tuesday, April 1st

March vanished. Where was I? Fighting the beginning of a cold and wanting to do nothing but wallow in laziness. A simple line from Stephen Beal's poem "640" provides the life jacket I need to keep my marriage afloat. "Nothing," he says, "will die, or not come back, or not endure forever, if you love it enough." I imprint this in my mind, believing that repetition makes things come true.

A strange wind gallops in from the southeast, kicking up clouds of dust. On its heels, the roar of winter: sleet, tiny hail balls, and the nip of icy wind. As much as I hate to leave the house, I have to go meet my neighbor, Carol, at the Arrowhead Clubhouse to clean for the official opening date of the fly-fishing resort.

Brash, chatty, and funny, Carol tells tales of her job at a local restaurant and stories about her husband, David, and his cattle. We scrub and sweep and wipe, clean and polish and mop, and talk. The work of women is like belonging to a club. Mastering certain skills automatically makes you a member. It's ridiculous how we strive to make the world a better place by cleaning toilets and washing windows. How we believe that by providing a clean, well-lighted place in which to live, we hold the horrors of the world at bay. We live on ranches and help our husbands. We work outside the home to bring in enough money to help pay the bills and have a little left over to give ourselves an occasional self-purchased present. We are never wined and dined or given flowers or expensive gifts. We settle for hugs, thank-yous, a birthday card, and a Christmas gift, knowing that the tradeoff is the privilege of living on the land. Like me, Carol has no children. Like me, she wants to save their ranch even though it means scrimping and going without, struggling to pay bills, working all day, every day, without vacations, health insurance, or retirement benefits. If David dies before Carol, she says she will leave the ranch to the Division of Wildlife for elk habitat. She says she will never let anyone cut the land into small helpings and serve it to the public with a house on every square piece.

Wednesday, April 2nd

During the night, snow piles up on every surface in its northbound path. I hear the hard flakes hitting the windows, hear the quiet that muffles the house and yard. Eighteen degrees and ten inches of snow mean a return to winter. Worried about his calves and the weather, Mick has not slept well. This morning we sniff and cough, clear our throats, blow our noses. I probably carted the bugs home like little beggar lice to cling to the cilia of our lungs.

I swallow my guilt and stay indoors. I hope the calves have been smart enough to seek the shelter of the sheds. Tenacious pneumonia germs lie in wait for them. Shelter and feed is all we have as preventative medicine.

When he returns an hour and a half later, Mick says, "A foot or more up at the cabin. I couldn't see a shittin' thing. Going up-country I was all over the pasture." Whiteout means the ground and sky harbor the same color. When the brush is covered, landmarks buried and fence lines obscured, the ranch becomes a world untravelable by eye. It becomes a landscape to be traversed only by instinct and gut reaction.

All day it snows. Occasionally, the white essay being written outside is punctuated by bird flight. Mick comes in from plowing snow with the John Deere crawler: he's cold, wet, and achy from being jounced and bounced and jarred. "Fifteen inches," he reports. "A heavy fall, so full of water the snow is blue. It piled up in front of the crawler blade in huge snowball hunks." The temperature warms to twenty-five degrees, and the roof drips sonorously.

The storm is predicted to stick around a day or so. It reminds Mick of 1957, the year his father told him to save the cows and forget the calves. And of 1964, the year his daughter Melody was born, when they got twenty-two inches on the eighth of April. He was out plowing feed trails for the cows and new calves when he got word of Melody's birth. He had three hundred head of cattle to feed alone. When the blast of the pickup horn at the house alerted him, he had to leave everything in the hands of fate and head to Denver, ninety miles away, to see his daughter. Two days later it snowed again.

When the skies clear at dusk, new snow covers everything like a wet blanket. In the last light, Blue and I walk up the road where Mick has plowed off most of the snow. The ground has thawed, and we shuffle along in the slush and mud. I hear the earth drinking; her voice sounds like a sigh, a very tired, but grateful, loving sigh. The moisture means grass, and also predicts the possibility of ranching one more year.

Thursday, April 3rd

As I scour and scrub and dust, I watch out the windows catching glimpses of Mick making trails through the knee-deep snow. He looks old and frail, dwarfed by a landscape that has tried to take him down many times. Physically he is the toughest person I know, but it is his heart that has handled the winter battles. Without his magnificent heart he never would have made it through the first winter in Wyoming: 550 cows, his hired man out with a broken leg, twenty-six miles from town, snowed in with five and a half feet on the level, a wife, a toddler son, an infant daughter, 125 dead calves, and no help. He fed cattle from dawn until dark. Some days he never took a break to eat at noon. He and his folks had purchased the eleven-thousand-acre ranch the previous fall and he was $300,000 in debt. If Mick was going to make it, he had to buckle down and work. He worked until his arms were so worn out at night from pitching hay that their tingling numbness and constant ache kept him from sleeping.

Unaccustomed to the isolation and loneliness of the Wyoming ranch, Margie was frayed to a thin thread. With Mick gone all day outdoors, she had no one except two attention-demanding children, a radio, and a fifteen-party telephone line. To stay sane, she cooked and baked, baked and cooked. Come spring, Margie swore if she ever had to bake another loaf of bread she would go crazy. She confessed that she fought the notion of hanging herself in the barn. In the warmer days of May, her son, playing in the settling snow by an open shed, saw the alien brown color of earth. He brought a handful of the wet mud to his mother, saying, "Look, Mommy, dirt!"

For a long time, they stuck it out, Mick, Margie, Johnny, Melody, surviving twenty-five tough years before the family and the ranch fell apart. I wonder why I never considered the hardships before I married Mick. Did I believe I could endure where others could not?

I think a great deal about the history of the family I married into. I take the rough-cut pieces of their stories and try to fit them together to form a comprehensive and understandable picture. Huge hunks are missing from my view. Some pieces, if smoothed and sanded, would fit together better. I often want to rewrite their history to make the Buyer story end in a unified, instead of divided, way. I want their story to end the way I want my story to end: happy, settled, content. Instead, Mick and Margie's ending remains set in the concrete of the past, the hard, stiff, sharp-sided reality of divorce, the sale of the Wyoming ranch, enough resentment and bitterness to make friendship difficult.

Will history repeat itself? What if the mortar I use to chink the spaces in our walls is insubstantial? Will it hold for a while but eventually weather away? Will it fall out, brittle and useless, crumbling to the ground? When the winds of change blow, howling through the open cracks of lost confidence, they will wear my love away, making the walls that protect me thinner and thinner. Then the snow and rain of indifference will come in, chilling even my warm heart.

The west window wears icy armor because the roof leaks. Puddled snowmelt coated the glass and sill, and the night temperature froze the pane into a glistening mass. I scrape at the ice and mop the sill with ragged towels. Tired, Mick sighs when he puts on his chore coat, gloves, and cap and goes back outside to lug a ladder out of the shed. I hear him plop it against the house, then, for hours, I hear bang and clang, scrape and scratch, the muffled thuds of footsteps on the roof, as he shovels off snow and chips away at the ice. He replaces fascia boards and remounts the old galvanized gutter. After all his work, the ceiling still drips, the crack where the water seeps in hidden under the tangle of overlapping shingles and a century of patch jobs.

By late afternoon, I'm weary, but I need to go to town to run errands. I need company so I ask Mick if he will ride with me. "No," he says.

After cleaning the kitchen, I read Pablo Neruda's *Twenty Love Poems and a Song of Despair*: "Tonight I can write the saddest lines . . . We, of that time, are no longer the same . . ." My reflection in the bathroom mirror looks like a blond baby doll with sad, dark eyes. I hear Neruda again: "How could one not have loved her great still eyes . . . Her infinite eyes!" A shiver runs up my back and settles at the base of my naked neck. "Love is so short, forgetting is so long."

I do not sleep. I lie for hours and watch the eye-level stars on the other side of the window twist and turn, slowly wheeling in their constant spheres.

Friday, April 4th

I'm off again, this time for the Spanish Peaks Cowboy Poetry and Art Gathering in La Veta, Colorado. Driving away alone is not an adventure. It constitutes a night terror, an eerie, spooky, muddled dream where I am lost, running, but can't find my way, and home has disappeared.

Under an ultra-gray sky, Mick checks the oil and tires on my Explorer. "It looks like the heavens are ready to open up," he says. He heads off armed with a pocketful of scour pills to make his morning rounds. One of his calves has a touch of a bug: ears knocked down, a shitty butt, dull eyes. The warm days and cold nights, the wet and slush and muck and snow take a toll on the young.

As I pull away from the ranch house yard, Mick stands near the haystack, pitchfork in hand. The first flock of ducks, dark spots against an ash-gray sky, wing over, heading west. Mick and I wave and blow kisses.

The snow-and-mud road begins to thaw, but I make the highway without four-wheel drive. Within five miles, heading south, I hit slushy roads and falling snow, the large whirling flakes like white moths flying blindly into the light of my windshield. I take a deep breath and look in the mirror. Fear sits in the back seat. He is not leaning forward, malicious grin in place; he is sitting back looking out the window with consummate nonchalance. The storm is a show, an entertainment. I order my hands to relax on the wheel, instruct my heart to look forward instead of back.

In Salida I meet Jill and we drive out to her ranch to collect her bags. The warning clang of a railroad crossing stops me at the tracks and wooden arms come down in front of my Explorer. I watch as black engines and countless cars cascade down the line. I have not been stopped by a train in twenty years. The earth's shuddering beneath the vehicle, the roar and wash of pushed wind, the chattering clatter of wheels on iron, strike me as otherworldly. No wonder the Indians in the 1800s found a locomotive frightening.

Jill and I take a shortcut route down the Arkansas River to Cotopaxi, then across the wide, open Wet Mountain Valley, through Westcliffe and Gardner. Cattle country with huge expanses of grass and the distant miragelike vision of peaks. For hours we talk the talk of women, returning again and again to the mystery of men, how they puzzle us, confound and frustrate us. We decide if we had a dollar for every minute we have spent in our lives trying to figure out men, we would be wealthy women indeed.

Quiet and quaint, La Veta shoulders a solemn air of oldness. Here is one of the places where stories of the West were made. This is a town disintegrating in economic doldrums. Michael Martin Murphey and some local businesspeople schemed and dreamed until they created the gathering, an event designed to boost incomes and find funding to preserve the heritage and historic demeanor of the area.

After checking into the old-fashioned adobe La Veta Inn, Jill and I sprawl on double beds surrounded by brochures and menus, and plan our itinerary. An hour later, we are on the verge of leaving to investigate the area when my parents surprise us on the stairs.

The four of us take a drive in the day's last gold-edged light, traveling up the valley to the south, going past a new golf course and mini-ranches that dot the river's banks. Abundant deer graze on new-green meadows, and old snowbanks speak of the deep winter just gone. The storm that had harassed our day has disappeared, but a remember-winter wind cartwheels off the peaks with chilled intent, promising a cold night.

At a bar on Main Street the four of us find adjoining stools and order drinks. An older cowboy and his wife stop by our table to say hello. He is from the Lander-Riverton area in Wyoming and used to announce rodeos in Pinedale. As we chat we find out that he knows Jill's fiancé, Jerry, and has heard of Mick. The Wyoming ranchers' names he reels off are ones I recognize, a reminder that the world of the West is small, a place where someone you know always knows someone they know.

Weariness hangs in Dad's eyes. With little fanfare we say our good nights so Mom and Dad can retire to their motel. Jill and I go upstairs to the room to collapse on the beds again. We'd like nothing more than to put on our nightgowns, crawl in bed, and gossip, but we have tickets to a Michael Martin Murphey concert.

Positively Main Street is a warm haven after walking two blocks in a wind that rolled off the snow-drifted Spanish Peaks. An oak-wood fire burns in the large room's corner fireplace. Jill and I stand, rumps to the coals, and let the heat ooze through our jeans.

The warmth of packed bodies takes the ice off the night. Three guitars and a hammered dulcimer are tuned. Lights lower. The first strummed chords transform a mountain town cafe into a concert hall. Michael Martin Murphey shares the makeshift stage with Gary Roller and Paul Sadler. With music of the new West interspersed with songs of the old West and poet Colen Sweeten's ranch stories and homespun wit, the evening becomes a gathering of friends in someone's living room.

When the first wind-song notes of "Wildfire" whisper free of Michael's guitar, the room shifts and quiets. A collective sigh of pleasure spills against the instrumental opening, but this gift seems meant for me. While I mouth the familiar lyrics, memories canter past: I am a thirteen-year-old in Ewa Beach, Hawaii, passing the window of a five-and-dime store every day after school and coveting a plastic statue of a rearing bay stallion whom I name "Wildfire." I save every penny of my allowance for weeks. Finally, after forking over $14.95, I bring the stallion home to add to my collection of horses. Seven years later I've gone from girl to woman, from college in Illinois to the far reaches of Montana. On a static-filled, battery-powered radio, I hear "Wildfire" for the first time and believe in some cosmic, supernatural way that the man who sings the mystical song looked into my heart and wrote my story: "She comes down a yellow mountain, on a dark flatland she rides, on a pony she calls Wildfire, with a whirlwind by her side."

Saturday, April 5th

The magic remains when I meet Michael (whom his friends call Murph) at the high school gymnasium where many have gathered to watch Native American dancers from Fort Garland. While we chat, his love for and respect of the history and culture of the West are apparent. The heavy beat of a large rawhide drum struck by many mallets echoes off the tall walls. Though we sit on bleachers in modern-day clothes, the drums transport us back in time. The room whirls with buckskin, feathers, shells, beads, the flash of dancing feet, the otherworldly sound of a language at once foreign but also understood. Elders and toddlers, teachers and learners, we are graced by the mysteries of landscape and culture.

Poetry and music sessions are scheduled all over town. La Veta begins to buzz. Inside Positively Main Street it is warm, wild with the rush of talk and people. Outside it is cold, crazy with blasts of hard, tough wind.

I read new poems in between fiddle, guitar, mandolin, and harp melodies played by Cowboy Celtic from Alberta, Canada. In my second session, complemented by the ballads and blues of Los Dos (Paul and Pam Sadler), I read story poems from *Glass-eyed Paint in the Rain*. I choose "Loose Horse" for the old cowboys, "Madge" for the ranch wives, "Mud Creek Beaver" for the animal lovers, and "Mick and the O Bar Y" to honor the husband who has stayed home to care for the cattle.

After lunch at an art gallery, I find a bit of peace, an opportunity to just breathe, a chance to let go of the tension and breakneck pace I get caught up in when I read for an audience. I'm drawn to Gary Roller's sketch of an elderly woman who has the soul of ages captured in her eyes. She could be Mexican,

Native American, Eskimo, Tibetan, Andalusian, Polish, Celtic. The universe centers in her face. I wish I could ask Gary how he came to create her.

Before heading out for the evening, Jill and I call Jerry and Mick, checking to see if they are holding down the ranch forts while we are doing up the town. Like here, the wind screams like a bear-cat. The snow, reduced by half, rebuilt with two new inches. One more day, I tell Mick, and I'll be home.

Jill and I dash off to the Fort Francisco theater to watch a zany western review called "Back in the Saddle." Characters whiz across the stage in fantastic costumes: Calamity Jane, Annie Oakley, Mae West, Mark Twain, Elvis, Frankie and Johnny, cowboys, Indians, dance hall girls. The Galactic Amazon players are hilarious. I laugh until my side aches and my smiling face hurts.

Circle the Wagons hosts a dance and Michael plays again at Positively Main Street, but Jill and I, in our middle-aged way, head for the hotel and for bed. But instead of obeying our bodies' demand for sleep, we curl in our sweat pants and talk until midnight.

Sunday, April 6th

The morning hosts sunshine and no wind, well, maybe just a hint of breeze with a few errant flakes of snow. Trying to pack up and say goodbyes at the same time constitutes a whirlwind. At the last moment I hold Mary Murphey's hand, thank her, and ask her to pass on my appreciation to Michael. I hug Pam and Paul and tell them I'll write. I share a few words with Gary Roller while he's setting up to play another concert. He gives me a signed print of the elderly lady that I so admired, so I gift one of my books. In two day's time I have made a half dozen new friends. Jill and I pull out of town with a long three-and-a-half-hour drive ahead. The sun's glow softens the day.

The miles slip past as we roll along highways that cut through the heart of ranch country. As much as we've talked the past three days, Jill and I talk some more. We find common ground in our love of country life, our love of the West, and our love for our men.

I leave Jill at her Salida ranch house where Jerry has already been to let out her dogs and build a fire to warm the chilly rooms. During my last hour on the road, I'm alone with my thoughts. The odometer tells me the Explorer has driven four hundred miles. My heart tells me I have been over a million.

I crest the last hill, and the ranch spreads before me in gray-gold light. Unexpected tears slip onto my cheeks. In the cold wind Mick has walked the hill to open the ranch gate for me. The weathered wood sign and iron arms spread wide to welcome me back.

Monday, April 7th

My exhaustion shows in the shadows under my eyes, in the dull yellow tangle of my uncurled hair. Mick and I are as hesitant as strangers attracted to each other. We speak softly. Touch shoulders. I know he has had nothing but cold cereal for three days so I make him bacon and French toast with syrup. He knows how tired I am so he volunteers to do chores alone again.

When Mick returns we light a fire in the living room and sit together in his big chair nestled together like two huge puppies in the bright mid-morning sun. I say, "I'm too heavy." He says, "Stay." Our reserve melts, dries out, then kindles and steams into lovemaking. Somewhere in the tumble of shed clothing and nakedness, we find our old laughter and bring it rumbling into the light. Why did we have it hidden away?

Mick tells me that his friend, Dick, stopped by on Sunday afternoon and visited for hours. With the recent deaths of Mary Kay Snell and Edith Moran (both in their nineties, both schoolteachers from the early days), the old guard of Fairplay is mostly gone. For Mick and Dick, in their mid-sixties, the world has changed beyond belief.

Both of them shy and timid around people, especially women, Mick and Dick attended grade school together in Fairplay. Their backwoods beginnings give them a commonality they cannot find with others. When they are together they talk old times, old folks, and the way it used to be. They have no use for, or understanding of, today's modern world. Dick worked on ranches and in logging jobs all his life and today runs a one-man sawmill on the outskirts of Fairplay. He is a strong, handsome man who has never married, and he carries his shyness like a magic shield. Living alone in a trailer on the edge of town, he has no family nearby though he goes to Denver on holidays to see one of his sisters and goes to Arizona during the winter to visit another sister. His parents, both schoolteachers and hardworking folk of the earth, have long since passed away.

Mick tells me they talked of aloneness and loneliness, the bond they share. Even though Dick is a bachelor and Mick has been married, first to Margie, now to me, for a total of nearly forty years, they are both loners. They know lonely from the inside out. It is something they eat, drink, sleep, and wear. Lonely is like second skin to them.

"What did Dick tell you?" I ask.

"That it's something you never get used to," Mick replies.

Before bed, calm and complacent, I search the star-filled sky outside the darkened window. Where is Hale-Bopp? Her sparkling, iridescent streak does not shine within view.

Tuesday, April 8th

I muster enough energy to help Mick feed. The calves have sprouted like gangly weeds, all legs and ears and eyes.

"Nate tried to nail me again," Mick says. "I had to beat him off with my glove to feed him. Now I crawl over the chute to fork his hay. You stay out of that corral."

I nod and assess the shrinking hay pile and mentally count the days until June when we can hope for the first green grass. Surrounded by a sea of concrete—six inches of semimelted, settled, wind-packed snow—everywhere I look is white. Nothing could paw through this crust to find even a bite of old grass.

"Can we make it?" I ask.

"Stretchin' it . . . fed the last sack of pellets to the yearlings yesterday."

I nod again, then reach out to hold Mick's gloved hand. He's uncomfortable with my kindness and shrugs away, quickly picking up the cut strings of twine off the fed bales and wrapping them into an untidy ball to stash in his coat pocket.

"Gonna hike?" he asks.

"Yep," I say and start off with Blue trotting dutifully at my side.

I hear a snipe calling insistently: "pip . . . pip . . . pip—pip . . . pip . . . pip."
I try to imagine Mick in any other environment. Without the pastures,

meadows, timbered ridges, the high divide, and endless sky behind him, he simply disappears. I can see myself going on, working or cooking on another ranch, or living in town in a little house, helping out at the library or the Seniors' Center. I can envision some sort of future for myself separate from the ranch, but for Mick I envision nothing at all. Across the valley, a raven's imperious call echoes rock . . . rock! I walk toward the sound because it is someplace to go besides home.

Desperate to stop the skin-crawling itch that he has battled for a year, Mick puts straight seven-percent stock iodine on a large red patch on his arm. He wants to get rid of the annoying urge to scratch so he can sleep. When he asks me if he should do it, I reply, "No comment," knowing if I say not to do it, he will anyway, knowing, like he does, that it is going to burn him like a scalded hog. After his shower he walks past with his arm painted shoulder-to-elbow in orange-red. I say nothing. Within minutes he is howling from the pain. Pissed off at his stupidity, I cuss him into the bathroom, and start applying ice-cold cloths to his arm.

"Goddamn it. It burns like hell!" he spits out, his teeth clenched.

"Well, you stupid idiot," I want to say, but don't.

I slap his hand away when he tries to rub the burn.

"Leave it alone."

"Why didn't you try to stop me?" he groans.

"Because you would have done it anyway!" I snap back.

I smear aloe vera gel in a thick paste on his arm. He promptly wipes it off with a tissue.

"Why won't you let me help you?" I ask.

"Because I don't need any help."

"Take some Tylenol for the pain," I say.

"No!"

"Let's put some ice on it for a while, then."

"No!"

"Okay, Mr. Stubborn. Suffer!"

I suspect Mick's skin condition is the erupted fire of old stress, building and building until it manifests itself like lava in his pores. We have done everything we could think of to combat allergic reactions: changed soaps, changed his diet, changed his clothing. He went to the doctor twice only to be told he would have to learn to live with it or go see an allergist, which Mick refused to do. We have plastered him with cornstarch, bathed him with baking soda, slavered him with creams and lotions and gels, gone through tubes of cortisone, tried herbal concoctions like Emu Oil and parasite eliminators. We investigated eczema, psoriasis, shingles, Lyme disease. We never suspected kidney disease.

Wednesday, April 9th

The last holdout heifer, Pauncho, has been put in the barn every night for a week to get her used to being confined. Beginning to spring, she makes a little bag. If she has a live calf, that will bring our total to sixteen heifers and sixteen calves, a good enough number to start over with. Another herd in the making, if somehow, some way, we can figure out how to keep the ranch.

We eat breakfast while the snow piles up with a rising shush. We talk about the letter Mick received from his old ranch hand in Wyoming. For the past eight years, John Fandek has tried to run Mick's O Bar Y ranch for new owners. It has been trials and tribulations for him all the way, a battle of old commonsense ways against a modern we-have-the-money-we-can-do-anything mindset. John loves the ranch and has stayed loyal in part because of the legacy Mick left when he sold out. It isn't something newcomers understand or appreciate, but it is something we cherish: the thought of the ranch we loved being cared for by a man with good hands, a strong back, and an old-time mind. Now it looks like the keeper of the flame must lower the torch and another light in the western horizon will blink out.

John writes, "Am sending my farewell to the O Bar Y (a copy of his resignation letter) . . . I've never known a place where I felt I belonged more than the O Bar Y . . . I have job offers from Black Butte, the Quarter Circle Five, and Frank Natarus, or I may just say to hell with it all and go to Alaska for the summer." John's letter to the owners of the O Bar Y ends with these words: "I suppose I will always feel some sense of belonging and obligation to the O Bar Y. But, as wise old Jack Schwabacher once told me, 'It is foolish to love something that cannot love you back.'"

Mick picks up John's letter and reads it again and again, as if John's quitting is as hurtful to him as it is to John. For the new owners the solution is simple. They run an ad in the local paper: Ranch Hand Wanted.

Near dusk, tired and stiff from sitting and typing freelance articles, I pile on double sweatshirts and pack boots and head out to hike. I go east, away from the wind. Mick's plowing has exposed patches of earth that run water over softened, grainy, rich-smelling mud. Everywhere else the ground is hidden under snow, a white mantle settled on spring's shoulders like a furry stole. The sun has melted the six inches of new snow into watery slush. Mine are the only tracks across the land, and with each step I sink into the ground and leave behind a hollow impression that immediately pools with water. The squishy sound sings a hopeful song, the lyrics repeating green grass . . . green grass. Blue bounds down the ridge to the riverbank, and a great blue heron lifts up out of the royal-colored water into a paler sky like a puff of pine smoke. Wings flapping in lazy waves, legs dangling, the bird makes a wide, graceful circle over the pasture, then flies downriver to look for another fishing hole. If we lose the ranch, we lose not only our identities and way of life, but we lose the daily connection to wildness where something as simple as a snow bunting can release my earthbound feet and gives me reason to believe that I too can fly.

Today is Mick's daughter's thirty-third birthday. We call Melody in Arizona. She is resting after noon dinner while her baby daughter, Savanah, naps. Soon she will prepare a chuck-wagon supper for guests on their Arizona Trail Tours in Patagonia. Her husband, Dan, is out on a ride showing the guests the grandeur of the San Rafael valley. In some intimate way, Melody and Dan's struggle to keep their small outfitting business going is akin to our own struggle to keep the ranch. I want little Savanah to grow up knowing about horses and cattle, about grass and sky.

The night sky is misty with clouds left over from the storm, but I search the blackened window screen for Hale-Bopp to the northwest. Thinking I see a milky smear, I feel around the dark room to Mick's dresser where I hunt for the binoculars. Mick stirs in bed and asks, "What's wrong?"

"Nothing," I answer, "I'm looking for Hale-Bopp." I adjust the glasses carefully.

"For who?"

"For the comet—ohh, ohh, look."

Focused in, the comet becomes a bright ball trailing a wild pony's tail made of a trillion stars. I stare and stare until my eyes water. I scan the sky. The dipper sparkles like a cup lined with diamonds. The slivered moon, half hidden in a veil of wispy cloud, is haloed with a gold-blue aura. This is a feminine panorama—all dark mystery and compelling light, as far away as dreams, as untouchable as a cloistered virgin. When the cold air seeps through my nightgown and chills my skin, I give up my voyeur's watch and crawl into bed.

Thursday, April 10th

Mick and I snuggle together like kittens curled in sleep. The return of winter reverts us to a hibernation state of mind, and we hate to leave our warm bed. We mumble to each other, trying to decide whose turn it is to get up first. Finally, we agree that since I'm younger, Mick has statistically faced more cold mornings and built more fires than I have, so I roll out, flip on lights, open the damper, crumple newspaper, place kindling and a small split of spruce log just so, and strike one carefully held match. The fire catches and roars. On his bed next to the stove, Blue yawns and stretches, pads over for an ear scratch, then waits at the door, his stub tail twitching, anxious to get outside to Molly.

Molly winds her way around Blue's legs begging for attention. I brush her arched back and fuzzed-out tail and recognize my own animalistic craving to be touched and petted, to feel cherished and cared for.

One of the things I like best about Blue and Molly is their ongo-ing affair. Blue is Molly's second love. Her first love was Sam, Mick's Australian shepherd–dingo cross, who was nine years old when Molly was born here on the ranch. She grew up under Sam's watchful eye. She adored him. She followed him on walks. She slept with him in the sun. When he was old and ill, crying in pain, she paced the porch, crying too, telling us to help him. We put Sam down and buried him in the side of the ranch yard with his bed and bowl, brush and collar, with a marker that Mick hand-carved and I painted—Sam: a good dog, 1980–1993. For days Molly lay on the grave and brought dead birds to leave as gifts.

With Sam gone Molly continued on, a bit remote and quiet, but functioning. She raised two more kittens in the dark recesses of the barn's hay manger, and she taught them to hunt and be wary of coyotes. She weathered the winter and by spring she was all cat again. When Margie bought Mick the Australian shepherd puppy we named Blue, Molly was aristocratic and condescending. She hissed and spat. She batted his curious nose and turned into a snarling fury when he wanted to play. She hung back and watched and waited. By fall Blue had grown into a clumsy but interesting teenager, and Molly began to pay some attention to his courting.

By winter Molly must have decided her period of mourning Sam was over, and she took up with Blue. She moved from the barn onto the porch. She slept with him, curled around his neck, or paw-massaged his back. She played more and carried herself with a kittenish air. When Blue and I headed out for a hike, she followed, her tail upright, her ears alert. If Blue occasionally got rough—running her down, bowling her over, mauling her around until her fur was wet and spiky—Molly took it all in stride, like an older woman in love with a younger man. Little by little, the pair became inseparable.

These days Molly waits by the kitchen door each morning for Blue. If he doesn't come out soon enough to suit her, she cries. Each day, meeting, they kiss faces and Molly curls round and round Blue's legs and rubs under his chin. She is eight (seventy-two in cat years) and Blue is three (twenty-one in dog years), yet they have the most balanced, accepting relationship I have ever seen. In their own quiet animal way, they are teachers who make me realize I have a great deal to learn.

Despite the winterlike conditions, the livestock holds up. Any sign of spring has been put on the back burner. No birds sing. No hint of warmth hangs in the air. The willow buds that were beginning to open ten days ago are now caught in semiclosed suspended animation. When I hike after chores, the world huddles remote and still and very cold. Somewhere, far off, an unseen raven croaks. A hawk wings over in a slow, studious way. What can it find to eat on this frozen day? A winterkill? An unwary rabbit? A chilled and unsuspecting chickadee?

I spend the morning typing letters for Arrowhead Ranch and the afternoon balancing checkbooks and paying property taxes. I take the end figures in to Mick. We spend hours penciling out our estimated expenses and predicted income. No matter how we figure, we fall short. We make lists of alternate ways to bring in cash flow: sell land, rent the cabin, lease out grazing, lease out fishing, raise and sell hay, eliminate the cattle, take in pasture horses. We make charts labeled pro and con. Stay and struggle. Sell out and break our hearts.

At dusk it still snows. At 7:00 p.m., fifteen degrees. At 9:00 p.m., five degrees and still falling.

Friday, April 11th

It is minus two degrees at 4:00 a.m., one degree at 6:00 a.m. This frigid grip feels threatening, a kind of choked consciousness that harbors the shadow of illness and death, because new life can only withstand so much cold. Pauncho calmly chews her cud in the barn. Mick returns to bed feeling like a Popsicle against my back. Chore time, edged with misery, numbs fingers and toes. I walk as humpbacked and chilled as the calves. Their snow-free backs are evidence that they have slept in their sheds. The cows, by contrast, wear crusty white mantles. Armored with frost-spiked whiskers and balled, ice-clod-jammed hooves, the horses walk with a mincing gait over to their hay. Overnight the yearlings packed themselves into a shed for the close contact warmth of shared hide and heat, but the bulls stood only in the windbreak screen of clustered willows. Because they are thick headed and thick hided, nothing fazes their slow, plodding natures. Mick mumbles about the weather and confesses he is glad he sold the cows in February. "With this weather, we'd have a pile of dead calves as high as this house."

Late in the day, after Mick has returned from loading hay and working on the cranky, worn-out engine on the Chevy, I head to town for mail and errands. On the wide open flats south of Fairplay, a neighbor's cows and new calves bunch up, rumps to the wind. With a glance I know which calves will be dead by morning. Weather is a wanton mistress and demands her due. This kind of day breeds what ranchers call "death loss."

At the county offices I hear word of South Park Heritage Resource, an organization that hopes to save the remaining ranch lands in South Park from development. This might be a light at the end of the tunnel for the county's agriculture, but it seems a dim light shining in a whole lot of darkness.

Saturday, April 12th

Stars glimmer against the window. I pat Mick on the back and whisper that I will go check his heifer. The kitchen windows are glazed with thick ice, the snowy ground on the way to the barn as hard as iron underfoot. Pauncho curls tightly against the barn's inner wall. Her muzzle dangles frost-covered whiskers, and her eyelashes are coated with crystalline fringe. I tell her she's one smart gal for not calving on a night like this.

On the porch the barn cats plump up like furry balloons, crouched on old pillows and pieces of carpet. Molly is in her cardboard house, wound round herself like a coil of yarn. She squeaks out one tiny meow for Blue, but does not move from her warm nest. The fire built, I check the thermometer: minus twelve.

Mick and I chat about our predicament. Finally, we are able to talk without biting at each other. At one point he says, "No matter what happens to us, I'm a better man because of knowing you." I thank him over and over again all evening. He teases me that my repeater is working, but I just can't help it. Knowing that I have been a beneficial aspect of his life gives me an incredible drive to keep on fighting to survive.

Before bed I glass the sky for Hale-Bopp and find her blazing away just above a thick bank of tumultuous clouds. She is a comfort to me, or as a friend wrote me in a letter, she is "like seeing an angel." Heartened, uplifted, and renewed by Mick's belief in me, I allow the mass of cosmic energy to serve as a beacon in my dark search for self.

Sunday, April 13th

Warmer. Only eight below. Mick goes out at 2:00 a.m. to check Miss Pauncho the Delayer, then comes back to bed. I snuggle in a while longer too, but the day's list of chores knocks at my brain. I wrangle myself out of bed and start laundry and bread dough. When Mick notices that I'm in my Amazon woman attack-and-clean-the-house mode, he says he'll do the chores alone.

In between six loads of laundry, I remake the bed, make dinner rolls and sticky buns that boil over in the oven and burn on the bottom so that the house fills with black smoke. The bread bakes better, and I rush Mick through a noon meal of chipped beef on toast. Mick chooses to work

The ranch house and Mick's handmade salt wagon.
Photo by Laurie Wagner Buyer.

outside in his cold shop rather than face my whirlwind antics. I turn up
the volume on the tape player and listen to Cowboy Celtic as I vacuum,
dust, water plants, then spring-clean the bathroom.

An old turn-of-the-century hand-hewn log homestead, our house
begs for attention. The windows need to be reglazed, the frames stripped
and repainted inside and out. Carpets need to be cleaned or replaced. I
want to strip the fifteen coats of ancient paint off the kitchen cupboards,
door, and windowsills, but have yet to find the time. By afternoon I have
reduced my fanaticism for the day. I figure out if I do one room a week I
can be done with my onslaught of spring-cleaning by June first.

We call Mick's mother. Feeling spunky, she is full of laughter and teasing. At eighty-eight, she uses oxygen most of the time and easily runs out
of puff. She lives alone and still manages to do okay, with some help from
family and friends. She tells me her back is aching, a sign that another

storm is due. I tease her that she should work for the National Weather Service as a forecaster because I'm certain her predictions would be much more accurate than the reports we get out of Denver.

Mick's mother was born Mary Mina Allen in the small railroad town of Como in 1909. She was the second daughter of Florence and Henry Allen, who met in the high-mountain town of Breckenridge when they both were witnesses to a gunfight. Henry, a professional gambler, was twenty-three years older than Florence, but they married and raised their two girls in difficult times. During the peak days of the South Park railroad, Henry successfully built and ran a fancy saloon. He had a reputation as a fair and honest gambler. When the Depression hit and Henry died with kidney disease, Florence stayed on in Como, running a luncheonette, serving hot soup and homemade pies to weary travelers. Mary's older sister, Eila, went away to school in Denver and eventually married Art Johnson, the son of homesteaders, who worked on the railroad as a fireman. Mary stayed in Como until she met John H. "Bill" Buyer at a dance and then, at eighteen, she became a rancher's wife.

Monday, April 14th

I take fifteen minutes for stretching exercises as I listen to the words of Cowboy Celtic's haunting song, "Tempting the Salmon to the Fly." The story about a fly fisherman and his longing for a river keeper's daughter gives me cause to ponder the creature comforts that lure us into loving someone or into following a certain direction in life. Our most elemental needs, certainly, like the physical ones of shelter, warmth, food, and water. Then the more complex mental needs like being stimulated, challenged, having a self-identity, a purpose, a set of goals. Then the strange, rough waters of emotional needs like being loved, appreciated, respected, cared for, nurtured, encouraged, supported, and the needs (though many shy away) to be touched, held, petted and praised, coupled sexually and sensuously in a kind of true belonging. Then the most obscure, seemingly unreachable spiritual needs, like those of understanding our place and purpose in the universe, of comprehending where we fit in and how we are controlled by the intricate and fragile natural world, of believing that somehow the joys and sorrows we experience prepare us for a wiser, more understandable life.

I think of the fly fishermen who come to Arrowhead for the escape it provides them. "Far away, far away, from the noise and the madness . . ." the song says. Most of them are urban dwellers. Some are dynamic, young professionals caught up in the roller coaster ride of raising families, demanding jobs, mortgages, car payments, doctors, dentists, college plans. Some are retired businessmen or retired military. A few are women. All are dedicated to the elusive moments found on stream or lake when all the elements—physical, mental, emotional, spiritual—merge. They become caught up in the timeless thrill of a perfectly cast fly that lures a trout up out of hidden depths or a rushing riffle. There is little discernible difference in the way we cast our hearts out into the world in hopes some mystical, magnificent creature will be lured into thinking we are a delectable tidbit worth taking. Then, after the excitement of the chase, the fight, the catch and surrender, when we are mesmerized by beauty and mystery, how we hate to release what we've come to love back into the world where it belongs. I begin to see the differences between men and women, like the differences between walkers and swimmers, of lungs and gills, of earth and water, of predator and prey, of skill and elusiveness, the inexplicable attraction of beings from opposite worlds.

Mick drives a conservative sixty miles per hour on our way to Salida, and the traffic on the road passes our truck as if we were tied to a post. Why is everyone in such a hurry?

We have our usual round of errands. At the feedstore door a new owner greets us. He apologizes for the lack of inventory. Shelves are bare. The back docks are sparsely covered with only a few sacks of grain and feed. It's unsettling: first the sale barn and now the feedstore. Agriculture seems to be on a steady downhill slide. By some stroke of strange luck, we are able to purchase all the items we need: twenty fifty-pound sacks of calf developer, ten blocks of white salt, a tin of bag balm, a new medium-weight chore coat, and a pair of irrigation boots for Mick. The new owner, a clean-cut young man, is happy he could fill our order and assures us that as soon as his financing goes through he will have a full inventory again. It is silly of me, since it is all out of my control, but I worry about his future. He is so enthusiastic, so determined to serve the customer, to succeed. I hope the cards that he's dealt will be a fair hand.

Tuesday, April 15th

Wind out of the east is unusual. Mick says all winter the wind blew out of the west and now the folks in Kansas are tired of it so they're sending the constant blow back. The brilliant male bluebird that pecked around the yard outside the kitchen window yesterday afternoon has returned. Concerned that he might be breakfast for the cats, I tap on the glass, and he flies high to land on the power line. Like a bit of blue cloth, he flutters there, an ornament, an epiphany reminding me to appreciate the beauty of small things.

Where I walk, the snow has melted away in soggy sheets leaving patches of wet earth tinged with the first tentative hint of green. A killdeer cries. A deer has left small moon-shaped tracks on the damp road edge. Exhilarated by smells released by the warmer air, Blue races ahead of me. As the ground thaws, scents captured earlier by the snow and ice are set free like squirts of heady perfume. He runs, head down, his nose twitching, reading the scented pages of the earth's story.

Dad calls. He sounds raspy-voiced and weary. It takes all of his energy to think and try to talk. Struggling again with mouth sores and a dry throat, he tries to choke down food when he has no desire to eat.

When I hang up the phone, I step outside and walk up the driveway. My own throat tightens and fills with lumps the size of golf balls. I choke back my inability to accept my father's battle when I can do nothing to help. He needs a swordsman at his side and one to cover his back, and all I am able to do is make phone calls, pray, and speak platitudes. This helplessness paralyzes and angers me, stops me on the road. I cannot breathe or see or swallow, so I stand there stupidly trying not to feel anything.

Then I hear geese far away calling with brassy, brazen honks that sound like joyous prayer. I turn to face the cries and see them flying above the distant Arrowhead Ranch lakes, two dark gray specks winging across a light-blue sky. As I watch, they turn, a graceful glide in perfect unison, side by side, and fly my way, calling and answering one another. My eyes lift to watch them soar, wings outspread, right over head, so close and low I see their rubbery paddlelike feet, the downy lightness of their breasts. I turn to follow them with my eyes. They loop a slow spin and return, flying right over me again. Then they wing northeast back toward the open water of the lakes. Whatever comfort is found in wind and wings and in the bracing cries of life, I clasp it close. My eyes dry, my throat clears, my arms relax at my sides as I walk on to the gate, breathing crisp air in great gulps.

Wednesday, April 16th

Mick tells me that I need to go spend time with my folks, if not for them, then for myself.

At noon, we share homemade bread and venison stew. While I hurry with dishes and packing, Mick checks my vehicle, then returns to tell me good-bye before he heads out on the four-wheeler to fix fence. He is anxious to get the meadow pasture ready so he can turn his corralled, stir-crazy yearlings out on grass.

Driving out the ranch road I look in my rearview mirror, but I cannot see any sign of Mick, only the dark timbered smear of Black Mountain, the dry brown ridges, and the strip of blue ribbon that the river creates. Leaving still isn't easy, but it is easier, perhaps because of the old adage "practice makes perfect." Someday, instead of interrupting my life like a big boulder plopped down midstream, I hope my escapes and returns will become part of life's natural flow.

Dad answers the door, looking like a slow-moving shadow, all angles and bones when I hug him. His jaw line is sharp. His shoulder blades stick out like unfeathered wings.

We fill the afternoon and evening with small pleasures: watering the trees in the backyard, admiring the just-emerged pasqueflowers, going to the grocery store, washing my Explorer, enjoying a meal. Mom and I grin and wink at each other when Dad eats spoonful after spoonful of the juice of the stew I brought. His mouth is shrunken, and he has trouble talking, but he is still handsome. I see the boy he once was, as if the cancer has uncovered his younger self. I notice a tinge of gray in his short sideburns and at his temples. He has not lost his hair.

When Dad decides to go to bed, Mom and I sit on the floor on either side of his chair. We all hold hands and whisper the Lord's Prayer.

I ask my mother, "Why did we whisper?" "I don't know why," she says, "we just always do."

Thursday, April 17th

I wake early to call Mick. He tells me a herd of elk hit the north-south line between the DM and Arrowhead Ranch bending a dozen metal posts to the ground. He fixed fence until he wore himself out.

"There's a sign on the A-frame," he says.

"Oh, groan."

The seventy acres north of the ranch is for sale again. This worries us because we are not fenced separate from that piece of subdivision land. We are lucky that the most recent owners do not mind our cows. What if we get ultra-environmental, cow-hater paranoids for new neighbors?

I ask, "Are you okay?"

"Oh, yeah, fine . . . just busy . . . there's so much to do."

"You don't have to do everything in one day."

"Yes, I do. One blink and summer will be here."

Mick recites a plethora of chores: dragging meadows, fencing, irrigating, tearing out beaver dams, moving cattle, branding . . .

"'Bye. I love you," I say, knowing he is anxious to get off the phone and get on with his day.

Watching Dad nibble on part of a papaya, I ask, "Who's driving?"

"You," Dad says.

Driving down to Colorado Springs I serve as an odd chauffeur. Dad marches toward the radiation wing like he's reporting for duty. I run after him and give him a quick hug. He pats my shoulder and smiles.

After getting a cup of cocoa from the waiting room coffee machine, Mom settles in the same chair she has claimed every day for weeks. By now the staff should have placed a name plaque on the pale blue recliner designating it as "Joan's chair."

We talk of her father's death, her mother's death, of whether or not she is afraid that Dad will die. She has a what-will-be, will-be attitude. She has seen Dad through three open-heart surgeries and has learned to handle the unknown by not dealing with it. Mom is staunch and philosophical. She feels the doctors are doing the best they can, and she believes he will get well. When her parents died, her mother, Louise, at age sixty-seven, and her father, Arthur, at age seventy-seven, she had only had brief visits with them for many years. She says, "You are a lucky child to have this time with Dad."

When we leave the hospital, Dad feels well enough to stop for lunch, the first time in ten days that he has been interested in food. We wend our way through the city's noon-hour traffic to Gertrude's in Old Colorado City.

Walking from the restaurant we feel the roasting warm sun. After months of wan sun and cold, the midday rays heal. Dad stops and turns his face into the heat, closing his eyes. His hand reaches out for an awning brace to steady his balance. I touch him on the arm and point to a bench down the street that is in the sunshine. We migrate there, Mom and Dad on one bench, I on the one opposite to them. I watch as they close their eyes and reach out simultaneously for one another's hands.

Mom says, "Let's go home now and sit on the deck where birds and squirrels will entertain us."

A half hour later we place white plastic chairs in a semicircle. Mom and I roll our pants legs up above our knees and I take off my long sleeve shirt, leaving on a tank top. My bra is uncomfortable, so with magician-like moves learned years ago in camp, I wiggle and pull it through my sleeve hole under my armpit. My father laughs, and I grin as I fold the cotton undergarment in thirds and stick it in the waistband of my pants.

I set the table and put out the salad while Mom boils water to make macaroni and cheese and opens a can of tuna fish. It is a meal we ate often as children, especially when Dad was away on temporary duty overseas. Mom asks me to say grace. Though the memorized words form easily in my mind, they don't come out of my mouth very gracefully because I'm out of practice. I keep my eyes open, watching my parents' calm faces until we all say amen.

Friday, April 18th

Another dawn call to Mick. He has been dragging meadows and fixing more fence. He says his itchy rash is disappearing.

"I think that mineral stuff you bought is working," he says.

"Oh good . . . or do you think that when I'm gone you aren't as stressed out?"

"Could be," he teases. "Could be." Mick is a loner who loves being alone, but he also loves knowing I will be coming back.

"When are you coming home?" he asks.

"Saturday, early. Okay?"

Dad drinks mango tea with honey and eats a tiny bowl of Life cereal with strawberries. He leaves the milk untouched in the dish, one red berry floating like a little boat in a calm white sea. He folds the newspaper sections neatly, says, "I wore myself out reading," pats me on the shoulder, goes to the couch, and half sits, half lies, his head pillowed on the arm rest.

I glance at the clock, then peek in at Mom.

"I guess I should get up," she says.

"Back rub?" I ask.

"Sure." She rolls onto her stomach. I trace lazy circles on her bed-warm back, the satin slide of her nightgown smooth under my fingers. She smells of Jontue and soap and that unique fragrance only my mom has. I breathe her in like the scent of fresh flowers.

"I still think of you girls as teenagers," she says. "I was just lying here thinking that you are all in your forties, and I can't believe it."

"I think I'd rather be forty-something than be a teenager again," I say, kneading her shoulders. "I wouldn't want to go through all that again."

"You were a good kid. You all were. Good girls. We're so lucky."

"Well, we're lucky too, to have you and Dad . . . not that Dad hasn't been a pain in the butt sometimes."

We laugh at Dad's old flaws—his terrible temper, his fits of bad behavior, his demands, his critical attitude. We had to learn to love him for who he was, then he finally grew into a wonderful husband and father. We forgive past transgressions as if they never happened.

"He just needed to grow up," I tell Mom.

"I know," she says.

"He just needed time. Like we all do."

Dad drives to the hospital, so I snuggle in the back seat and doze, listening to him chatter to Mom. I am a child again, secure and safe with Dad in control, our lives revolving around him and his decisions. I like letting him set the pace because I'm a better follower than I am a leader. Growing up I never liked my father. I feared him. I respected him. I loved him. I yearned for his approval, but I didn't like him. Quiet and shy, I fell short in his eyes. Boisterous and loud, he was often overbearing, sometimes downright obnoxious. I understand now that he was just a young man burdened with the responsibility of a career and family, trying to find his way through the labyrinth of his own emotions, fears, and insecurity. I grew up believing Dad had all the power, that he controlled our lives because he was meant to. As Mom and we three girls grew into ourselves, struggling to find a place and purpose in the world, Dad was finally able to release his control. It wasn't an easy metamorphosis, but we have all emerged, somewhat wounded certainly, but still strong and able to fly on our own. I wish Karen and Eileen were here with us. Then I laugh. Chances are we would be arguing, pinching, and pushing each other as we did as children, each one demanding, "I get to sit behind Dad!" For years Dad thought the reason we all wanted to sit behind him was because we loved him most, but if the truth be known, when we sat directly behind him we were in the safe spot, the zone where his smacking hand could not reach.

Driving away from the hospital, we sing along with a tape I gave to Dad.

In earlier times our family sang together on long cross-country drives. We were off-key and out of tune, but we raised our collective din to the skies like a pack of coyotes. Who knows what we were trying to celebrate, just some urge springing from the heart, some small effort to bridge the gap between adults and children, acknowledging our connection by proving we knew the words to the same songs like "Mares Eat Oats" and "Over the River and Through the Woods."

I spend part of the night returning phone calls for Arrowhead Ranch. When I join my parents in the living room, they are watching WGN news out of Chicago.

"Want me to massage your feet?" I ask.

Dad nods.

Brittle and dry, Dad's feet are icy. I coat them with cream and knead them hard, then rub his calves. The cold blueness of his skin scares me. It reminds me of the cold mouths of sick calves who are on the verge of dying. I rub and rub and rub, willing warmth and circulation into his skin. He says nothing, just closes his eyes and leans his head back. When I finish, he smiles and pats my head.

"Next?" I ask Mom.

"Sure," she says.

Her feet are alabaster cool, silky to the touch, smooth except for two small calluses on the bottom of each foot below her second toe, the mark of a woman who wore high heels for many years. She has delicate toes, and her trimmed toenails are short and round. Smaller than mine, Mom's feet are slender and narrow, her ankles trim, her calves firm. Her feet feel ageless and unchanging.

Saturday, April 19th

I take the long route home via Fairplay so I can pick up mail. As I near the ranch, my eyes readjust to the countryside. In the past few days the snow has melted and there is a tinge of green across the pastures. The wind howls, and I have to wrestle the gate to keep it from leaping east. The heifer pairs graze along the willows on the pasture near the house. Far across the valley the yearlings pick their way up a steep hillside to the top of the ridge. Mick and Blue sit on the stoop, waiting for me. We trade tidbits of news while we eat lunch. Mick leaves to take the tractor and the harrow up to the Mikels place so he can drag out the winter accumulation of cow manure on the meadows. I'm left with dishes, an overloaded desk, and pervasive silence.

Blue has been waiting patiently for me. We head out in the dark with a three-quarters moon lighting the roadbed. The last soft notes of a robin die away. Far off I hear frogs singing, a harmonious chirping that burps out of the cold wet mud where they have hibernated. I listen while I search the sky for Hale-Bopp. I find her half-hidden behind a sheer curtain of clouds—a milky blur, but still identifiable and reassuring. I like the night. I cherish the air that hovers around my face like the breathy, warm kisses of a first-time lover. I am in love with the firm, hard, rocky road beneath my feet, the smell of sage and damp earth that hangs in the breezeless night. What I don't like is the invading sense that it is all so temporary, impermanent, full of shift and change.

Sunday, April 20th

I have a strange habit of cleaning house on Sundays. It is something I do instead of going to church, a way to end the old week, a way to begin the new one. I start out in a tornado fury to divest the house of flyspecks, cobwebs, dust kittens, and dirty windows.

I mix Spic and Span in a bucket, don rubber gloves, and put classical music on the tape player, a luxury I can enjoy only when I am alone. I put two big books—*The Law and You* and *The Stockman's Handbook*—on top of the step stool to make me tall enough to reach the hall ceiling. As I scrub I think of the hands that plastered the rough walls, covering over in white the smoky hand-hewn and chinked logs of the house's shell. I take down old black-and-white photos and study the faces as I wipe the framed glass: the old Buyer Ranch east of Fairplay, circa 1950; Mick's sister, Arlene, and her cousin, Donna Gardenswartz, sitting by the '37 truck in front of the ranch house where the family brands

VH DM EⅡ

are clearly painted on the shingled roof; Mick and his cousin, Larry Johnson, ages nine and ten, holding up a trout that, even when hoisted aloft, nearly touches the ground; the hay crew, circa 1938, with Mick's grandparents, parents, hired hands, and Mick himself, fresh-faced and all eyes at age seven; Mick's mother, age thirteen, with her Indian blood showing up in her piercing eyes, rich complexion, and high cheekbones; her father, Henry Allen, professional gambler, nattily dressed, suitcase in hand, heading off to Cripple Creek; Henry and his cronies outside the corner saloon in Como, Colorado; and finally, a large gilt-framed double photo dated 1902, by photographer James Arthur, of a woman in long skirts, her hair upswept, standing by a pole fence overlooking a pond. According to family lore, the photograph has great value and should never be sold or given away. Is money hidden under the frame?

I blitzkrieg the bedroom next trying to reach all the hidden nooks and crannies where winter's wormed-away dirt hides. Above Mick's chest of drawers hang recent photos of his children. Above my dresser, a family portrait of Mom, Dad, Karen, Eileen, and me, and one of Dad in his uniform snapping a sharp salute.

All day the wind blows. Mick arrives looking battered and bruised by his hours on the cableless tractor. Blue and I walk downriver to the dump. Green grass sprouts everywhere, so new and short the cows would need, as Mick likes to say, a tobacco sack and a pair of tweezers to get a decent meal. I place my hands palm down on the reemerging growth to feel spring.

Monday, April 21st

All night the wind blows. Snow pellets and sleet hit the window. A loose piece of tin taps out an ominous drumming. Mick does not sleep. He says he is uncomfortable and plagued by a rare headache. On the back of his scalp he wears a jagged scar left from a boyhood escapade. Jumping on his cousin's bed in the Johnson's Como home, he hit his head on the dresser while doing somersaults. No 911 number. No emergency room. No crying and whimpering to his mother because he knew he'd be punished for goofing around. It was better for him to hold his tongue and suffer the hurt in silence as his cousin pressed a wet rag to the bleeding. Stubborn as a jack mule, Mick won't take an aspirin, or put heat or ice on his head. At 3:30 a.m., he gives up tossing around, dresses, and goes out to check Pauncho the Undelivered. Nothing. He crawls back into bed shivering.

"Goddamned nasty out there," he says.

"Mmmmmm," I mumble.

"Hope the calves are hunkered down somewhere dry."

Within minutes I hear Mick snoring, and I'm grateful he has found some rest. Maybe I gave him my sleep because now I'm wide-awake, listening to the wind-borne snow-rain pelt the side of the house.

I go with Mick to fight the wind and feed. Only half of the yearlings have come in. Hardly hungry, the horses wallow their hay around out of habit. The heifers and their calves come out of hiding to meet us on the flats, but we take their hay back into the shelter of the brush to keep it from blowing to Kansas. The calves look dry and sassy. Mick says they holed up in the wagon shed during the worst of the storm. I can tell he is happy with the way they are growing by the way he looks them over without comment. If he was displeased, he'd be saying, "There's one sorry dink," or "That sorry, potbellied son-of-a-bitch won't amount to a hill of beans."

Speckled with green, the earth is damp everywhere I walk. I head west right into the spitting, stinging mouth of the storm. It's not pleasant, but it's wakening, like itty-bitty slaps from God urging me to keep my chin up, hold my head high.

A blackbird calls from a willow, a robin on a fence wire bobs sprightly, a female bluebird flits by, a pair of geese on distant wing is identifiable only by their cries. When I stop at the fenced-off end of the horse pasture to listen to the river run, I hear the pealing screams of gulls. I close my eyes and see the sea, the sand, and the sheer cliffs. I hear waves and smell the ocean's salt tang, the fishy perfume of shells and debris. But when I open my eyes again, all I see is dark pine timber and the lighter, still-barren branches of silvery aspen trees. I see a bald blue sky and, coming over the ridge, a wavering, moving clump of motion, the dancelike flight of a flock of gray-and-white gulls making their way up from Antero Reservoir searching for feed. Despite the cold wind, their cries make the day seem summery, the stiff breeze part of their natural blustery habitat. Last night I heard the frogs; today I hear the gulls. Then two ducks squawk up the river channel, startling me from my reverie.

Mick leaves to go up to the Mikels' to finish dragging meadows. I head over to Arrowhead Ranch for an afternoon of business letters, phone calls, and filing. The wind works itself into a storm, blowing sheets of snow and sleet in from the north. The small trailer that serves as my office rocks like a rowboat on high seas.

The words South Park and wind go together. It has taken me nine years to form some sort of symbiotic relationship with the land and its wind. The country reminds me of the western men I've known: tough, demanding, elementally harsh, unforgiving, stubborn, and difficult to be part of. Yet there are glimpses of true tenderness and heart, a fragility that makes me gasp, realizing that the bluff and bluster of their daily demeanor is a necessary part of their protective outer shell. Mick cannot help being what he is. It's his nature to be tough. But when I see Mick helping a newborn calf or playing with the cat, I think of a frail pale-petaled columbine growing out of timberline rocks.

Mick is bushed by evening, his face pinched and sullen. The headache that started yesterday has hung on tenaciously. The bumpy rounds on the tractor in driving sleet haven't helped. I attempt to kiss him, but he turns his head away.

I try to tuck Mick in bed. Recalcitrant, he turns away from my hands on the covers, but he allows a kiss on his forehead.

"Does your head still hurt?" I ask.

"Yes."

"Shall I get you something for it?"

"No. Who was that on the phone?"

"Mary Ann. She and John are struggling over the idea of adoption, but she thinks they are on the right track."

"You talked a long time."

"I know. It helps me to talk."

"It doesn't solve anything . . . talking."

"No, but it helps."

"I don't have anyone to talk to."

I feel like Mick has slapped me in the face.

"I'll listen," I say.

"I can't talk to you. You don't understand."

"You could if you would try."

"You Wagners always have an answer for everything."

"Mick . . ."

"No, just go away. Go take your bath. I don't have anyone to talk to, no one on my level."

"Aren't I on your level?"

"Not a chance."

Slow moving anger creeps up on me from all sides.

"Mick, this is making me crazy. Making me angry."

"Figures. You always get angry."

"Mick, if you want to talk, I'll listen."

"Never mind. Go away."

I stalk into the bathroom, slam the door, and immediately regret doing it. The peace I had after talking to Mary Ann is gone. In its place is the horror that somewhere along the way in the past fifteen years, Mick and I involuntarily quit being friends. Something has happened, something I didn't want to happen, but it's happening anyway, beyond my control. We had been such good friends in the beginning. We once talked for hours, telling each other everything, even confidential, conspiratorial secrets. Our hearts were open to the wonder of being friends, of caring for each other. Now we can't even say "pass the pepper" without flaring up, bristled like sparring cocks in a bloody ring. Tears slide down my cheeks and plop into the hot bath water. More horrible than our inability to talk to each other is my knowing that I have lost my capacity for kindness. Admitting that I am no longer willing to be kind to Mick hurts me worse than his silence.

I sit on the edge of the bed and search the sky for Hale-Bopp, but cloud cover conceals her visage. It saddens me that she is not there tonight when I need her most. When I creep beneath the covers, Mick rolls away from me. He sleeps intermittently, wakening me often with his restlessness until I finally seek the quiet calmness of the couch.

Tuesday, April 22nd

I leave for Arrowhead Ranch where I will spend the day in the field with my boss, Scott Saunders, Arrowhead permit holder and close friend Gary Nichols, and Leon Kott from the Soil Conservation Service. A handful of others, extension agents, biologists, and engineers, will join us.

I'm in the middle of cleaning the clubhouse when Gary comes in with a bowl full of bugs for me to see, squiggly invertebrates he scraped off rocks in the stream: stoneflies, mayflies, several kinds of caddis. Trout treats. Fish food. The best indicators of a healthy, productive stream. The river, Gary reports, is low and clear and may be the best fishing all year. On his last trip here, he caught fourteen fish and his friend Brad caught twenty-one browns and rainbows, both wild and stocked. It shows how successfully our fish population has wintered-over in the river.

We discuss many topics this afternoon: fauna, flora, the cattle-stocking capacity of the ranch, numbers and dollars versus the environment, how to recoup lost vegetation, where to stabilize eroded banks, how to reestablish willows, what contributes to siltation, the offer of Trout Unlimited to do some volunteer work to improve habitat.

It's cold with a feisty wind that chews through my layered clothes and jacket, leaving me goose-pimpled and shivering. Toward the end of the day, I quit on the last river observation site. In the half-warm truck I collect heat from the windshield-strained sun and rest. The highlight of the day is seeing a flock of great blue herons. Usually I see one lone bird. Occasionally, I see a pair together. But never have I seen nine of the large birds soaring in unison, trailing their legs, their long necks tucked up into their chests. A few of the herons land on the hillside above East Lake, and hop comically through the sage before braving the wind and flying again.

Wednesday, April 23rd

Standing still at twenty-four degrees with a skif of snow and a pearly sky bordering on blue, the day promises to be fair. Mick sits by the potbellied stove, coffee cup in hand, when I slip into the kitchen wearing weariness, my arms open for a hug. "Want pancakes?"

"Sure," he says.

I serve up the flapjacks brown-blond and hot. Mick douses his with thick maple syrup.

I split wood while Mick feeds Nate and Pauncho. He pours pellets for the yearling heifers that have trailed in, and forks hay off the '37 into feed cribs. Then we go together to feed the horses, bulls, and pairs on the old four-wheeler. In anticipation of tomorrow's storm, Mick scoots the bulls out the gate onto the meadow and lures the heifer pairs into the enclosure where the calves, who have grown shaggy and tall, can seek shelter in the shed and pile together for warmth. The haystack on the upper end of the ranch has shrunk to a tail-end fifteen bales. In the equipment shed, a hundred bales of reserved hay from 1995 is stockpiled, and we're glad to have it. If this storm dumps the predicted one to three feet of snow—a class-five blizzard with warnings out for stock losses—it will be a week or more before we see the ground again.

For now, though, the earth is snow-free and damp, painted with the green wash of returning grass. When I walk, flocks of robins spring up everywhere, in last year's old grasses, on sagebrush, in the willows where rising sap colors winter-gray branches with streaks of orange and yellow, in the pines and spruce, on fence posts. Their warbling song fills my ears and cheers me. It must be a migration going through because there certainly isn't anything here for them to eat. They move en masse, flitting in short bursts of flight before they settle and sing again. The wind has died since yesterday and shifted to the east. The divide looms clear and rough-sided, heavy with recent snows up high. All that snow is a warning that flood-stage waters will come again in June. Blue and I are on our return walk when we hear Mick coming on the four-wheeler.

"I'm headed up to the Mikels' to check water. Wanna go?" he asks.

Blue and I double up on the seat behind him, and we roar up the road.

The ditch head gate has been plugged again with chewed willow sticks and debris. Mick has been coming up here nearly every morning

View of the Great Divide looking west from the cabin.
Photo by Laurie Wagner Buyer.

to squabble with the persistent beaver. They built a huge dam and blocked off his ditch, backing up the river into a giant pond. Mick lowered their dam, but left enough for them to have a smaller but adequate pond. He'll turn to traps or the .22 only as a last resort. Left unchecked, the engineering culprits can ruin all the work Mick did last fall rebuilding the head gate and repairing washed-out ditch banks. We see the muddy hole in the riverbank that the beaver call home and spot their slide trails off the steep hillside where they have cut and dragged aspen trees for food and building materials.

Mick puts on his waders and uses a long metal hook to clear the front of the head gate. A rush of water spills through to fill the ditch. He wades across the lower end of the pond and pulls a few selected willow sticks and aspen branches out to allow more water to escape.

Turning for home, we crest the ridge in the timber and Mick spots four cow elk in an open space, their tan hides blending them with tawny winter grasses. Only their buff butts give them away. He calls Blue back and makes him sit on the four-wheeler with us as we watch the cows mill and circle, head for the fence above Tumble Creek, stop, then jump one by one in graceful arcs. The elk are close enough for a sure shot and would be good eating if we needed camp meat.

We stop along the road with stretchers and pliers and staples to repair fence damage—a gate crushed down by elk, and some broken wires and busted posts that are fallout from a county road grader that caught the fence with its blade. All the work that has hidden beneath winter snow now needs to be done.

Late in the day, Mick goes out to feed his heifers and lock up Pauncho the Nervous. Figuring the impending storm may be a bad one, I run into town for the mail. Alive with water, the air is misty, foggy, part rain, part sleet, and part snow. The highway is a sheet of moisture that sprays high in slow dark rainbows whenever a big rig zips past me. The closer I get to Fairplay, the worse the weather. Everyone in town must have thought the same thing I did about the mail. The post office parking lot is packed with cars, trucks, and vans. I'm in and out in several minutes as the storm gathers strength, growing weird colored skies and worse-than-ever-wind. I do not stop for any other reason but head for home, hugging the shoulder of the highway where I can see the dim outline of delineator posts.

Concerned, Mick has been watching for me from the living room window. I have only been gone an hour and a half, but Blue leaps and barks and carries on as if I'd been absent for a week. We eat supper and watch the news while the rain-sleet-snow drama outside plays on.

Just before dark, Mick goes out to put Pauncho-Who's-Holding-Out in the barn and takes Blue for a short walk up the road. He returns worried. "It's gonna be a bad one. By tomorrow we'll be buried."

Mick goes to bed early. I stand at the window and stare into blackness. All I hear are snow pellets stinging the window glass.

Thursday, April 24th

Surrounded by snow, and it still snows hard at dawn when Mick trudges out to check Pauncho the Unpredictable. I volunteer to help with feeding, but Mick says my extra weight on the four-wheeler will make it harder for him to get through the deep snow. He returns hours later weighted with a mantle of snow across his coat's shoulders, his cap totally white, his boots and leggings crusted over.

"Jesus," he says, "this is as bad as '57. Dad always said watch out for a storm around the 25th of April. Calves died like flies that year. We lost sixty. In '38, it came in June when the leaves were out and it broke limbs and trees and clogged up the ditches and flooded over and washed out banks. What a mess! Get me the pistol. If I can make it up-country, I'm going to check the head gates and look for beaver."

While I mix bread dough, I watch the clock, promising myself I will not start to worry until Mick has been gone over an hour. When he comes through the door again, Mick looks totally done in. He is snow from head to toe, so I use the broom to brush him off on the porch.

"I couldn't see a goddamned thing," he says. "I was all over the pasture trying to find the gate. Heifers are fine. Calves sticking to the shed. I drove round and round to tromp out a feed ground for them. Horses and bulls all right. I couldn't make the hill at the cabin, had to back down and hit it two or three goes. Worried myself sick on the county road. Afraid I'd drown out and have to leave the four-wheeler. I couldn't have walked that far in this snow."

All this runs out in a garbled rush. He plops in a chair. I feed the stove another stick of wood and put the kettle on to boil. Moving slowly, Mick strips off his coat and soggy cap and gloves and hangs them near the fire. Next his pants, which are wet from the thighs down. He sits in his long johns and shirt, bent over at the waist, looking old. I put a cup of hot tea with honey in front of him, and he slurps it from the spoon. I build a fire in the living room for him. Within moments of hitting his recliner, he is sound asleep, his head flopped wearily to the side, his arms hanging straight down, hands open, palms up. Blue slumps onto the rug by the stove, and curls into a pile of wet, ripe-smelling fur. I sneak back into the kitchen to stir the soup.

It snows nonstop, piling up deeper and deeper until every visible surface is covered in a shroud of white. As Mick struggles to put on his coat, I ask, "What?"

"Have to go check on Pauncho Villa," he says.

"I'll go. You've been out in it enough. If she's doing anything I'll come back and tell you. If she is okay, I'll go on and walk a little. I need some air." Blue follows with little enthusiasm.

The whole world whirls with snow, falling from the air, swirling on the ground in horizontal waves pushed by a southeast wind. Two steps off the walk Mick shoveled earlier, and I am up to my knees, wallowing. A blown-in drift at the corral means I must kick and foot-shovel the gate to get it open. Pauncho is in the barn, blocking the doorway. She eyes me and snorts—a single hollow blow—and rolls her eyes. She seems calm enough, but her tail is kinked and twitching. She's close to calving, but no action yet.

I high-step out to the road where the snow that melted into the warm dirt bed is not so deep. I wave toward the house and give the okay sign in case Mick watches from the window. I decide to walk the three-tenths of a mile uphill to the gate. Twenty-five steps into the trek, and my heart pounds a ragged beat and my legs cramp. "Ridiculous," I say, "go home." But I march on, trudging, dragging my legs. Twenty-five steps. Stop and blow until my heart rate eases. A line of sage tassels above the snow is my only guide in a sea of white, that and the tops of the dark spruce on the far south ridge. All else is a moving mass of whiteout. Blizzard conditions. Before I'm halfway up the hill my legs burn and I'm soaked through with sweat, my face encased in wet snow, my glasses iced over. I'm breathing like a woman practicing Lamaze for a natural birth, puffing like a steam engine. Blue keeps his nose against the back of my knees. I turn once to look at him. He's wet and miserable. His eyes ask, "Where the hell are we going and why?" My unspoken answer, "Nowhere, no reason, just because."

Twenty-five steps and blow. Finally, I see the gate and push on in one last determined rush . . . twenty-eight . . . twenty-nine . . . thirty! I laugh out loud at my craziness and hug the fence post. The plows have been by on the county road leaving a heavy snow berm and disappearing tracks. My own footprints have already vanished in the constant sift of wind-borne snow. When my heart slows to a dull thud and I can breathe again, I head home, downhill. I can barely see the buildings. It makes me think of stories that abound in the West of people falling down and freezing to death in storms when they were only a hundred yards from their house, or of losing their way between the barn and the cabin where they end up walking in circles until they keel over with exhaustion. Where are all the robins I saw yesterday morning? Did they find shelter? Can they wait out the storm? Somewhere calves are dying like flies.

We listen to the police scanner while we eat. I-70 west is closed. Highway

285 past Conifer is closed with twenty-six inches of snow. Cars are off in ditches. Trucks are high-centered in snow and ice. Denver International Airport has only rain. Downtown Denver, four inches of snow. Lakewood has ten inches. In Colorado Springs, the snow is so heavy and wet it is snapping off trees and downing power lines. Eighteen inches here and still snowing.

Mick rests awhile longer, then goes out to pump water for Nate and to check Pauncho again. He's back in half an hour.

"Well, she had it," he shouts from the kitchen door.

"Any trouble?" I ask coming in from the living room where I'd been napping.

"No. It's a dink. Weighs maybe twenty pounds."

"It'll grow," I say.

"I doubt it. I can't believe I waited all this time for a puny runt calf. I should have sold her."

"She'll be fine. She has a big bag. Lots of milk. It'll grow."

"A damn dink," he says, shaking his head. "I'm gonna go try and plow this snow."

Ponderous, the backhoe moves up and down the road, sometimes belching out clouds of ugly smoke. Mick tries to go feed the heifers with the four-wheeler and buggy, but he cannot get two hundred yards from the barn because the snow rolls up over the headlights. He makes his way back to the house to tell me he's taking the backhoe with five or six bales in the bucket. "It's the only way I can get there," he says.

Mick reports later that there is better than two feet up-country, which does not surprise me, but it is more snow than we have had all winter, more snow in one storm than we've had since we moved here nine years ago. We are used to deep snow. It is something we lived and breathed in Wyoming. But it was never something to play in—skiing, snow boarding, snow machining—it was something we worked in, fought with, argued over, loved because it was part of a hard, familiar landscape that we could not live without, hated because it wore us down to nerveless nubs. Shovels became part of our anatomy. We wallowed every place we went, so that when spring finally came and the snows receded, exposing bare ground, we did not know how to walk. Storms have always shaped our lives.

This evening Mick looks as weary as I've seen him in a long while, yet he absolutely glows, like a bed of coals. His eyes sparkle, he's animated, talkative. He isn't angry about the weather. He rises well to a challenge. Test him and he will endure. Give him the worst, and he will survive. Keenly conditioned to adversity and problems, he thrives on struggle.

Before bedtime, a couple of fleeting openings in the clouds reveals clear skies. The snow that fell for over eighteen hours fades to a light sparkling dust spilling from the darkening sky.

Friday, April 25th

At 4:30 a.m., I'm wide-awake staring at the black window wondering what woke me. Mick's arm curls around me, warm and comforting. Then I hear the sound: plip . . . plip . . . plip, drops of water falling from the long icicles hanging off the roof.

I insist on helping Mick with the chores. Our world is like the winter scene in *Dr. Zhivago*, all sparkly crystals, white as far as the eye can see. While Mick feeds and pumps water I dig a path to the woodpile and search for drift-hidden logs. The heavy snow sticks like concrete to the metal of the shovel. Half the work is shoveling; the other half is knocking excess snow off the scoop. As I beat the butt-end logs with a maul and heavy hammer, I watch Mick wrestle the '37 across the yard. He stops to clean out the gate, squeezes through, gets up a good head of steam, but hits a pothole and is stuck, the truck lurching to the side. He climbs out and digs through the snow. He climbs back in the cab. Black smoke pours from the exhaust, but the old beast breaks through and churns across the pasture to the corral. It takes him a half dozen tries, backing up, bucking forward, but he makes it to the cribs to fork off hay for the yearlings. Unable to climb the steep hill to get home, he backs out the gate and leaves Chev sitting in the snow. Shovel over his shoulder, he begins the long hike home.

I pick carpenter ants from the chewed-out caverns of the log I'm splitting. They are balled together in a black mass, a nest of them, hibernating. I don't want to carry the wood in the house with ants in residence because the warm air will coax them back into life, and they'd be marching everywhere indoors. Some lucky bird will find the glistening tidbits at the foot of the splitting stump. The wood boxes full, I surprise Mick at his backhoe. He leans against it, head down. I'm concerned but he raises his eyes, removes his cap, and swipes the sweat off his forehead.

"Well, I made it." He grins.

"I was watching you."

"Guess there's still some gas in this old boy yet."

"I guess so. You done good, kid," I say borrowing one of his mother's complimentary expressions.

"We'll never make it up-country unless we take this."

He reaches into the cab and turns on the ignition with one hand, and sprays a squirt of starting fluid into the carburetor with the other. The diesel engine whines, and a puff of brown smoke burps out of the vertical exhaust pipe. I stand and scratch Blue's ears as Mick winds up the exterior extension cord for the tank heater and stores it in the shed. He hands me a shovel and points to the loader bucket that is caked with yesterday's plowed snow. I scrape and whack at the set-up mess while he pours a quart of oil in the engine.

"Hay from here," he yells. "Horse barn. Poke down seven bales from the loft."

I nod okay and wade through knee-deep snow over to the barn. Across the corral I can hear Pauncho the Pitiful Mother bellering in the cow barn. Hand over hand, I climb the straight wooden rungs of the ladder up to the loft and shove down seven bales of green hay. I think of the hot sultry August day we brought the load in from the field and stacked it. Now, the loft is dark and cold and reeks of cat piss. Mick brings the backhoe to the door and sets the bales one by one into the bucket, placing them width to length like interlocking pieces of a puzzle so they will stay on.

Pauncho the Pathetic bellers again.

"Her calf?" I ask, shouting to be heard.

"Dead." He pulls himself up into the cab. He turns back, asking with hand signals if I am walking or riding. I make a walking motion with my fingers, and he nods. Blue sits at my feet, expectant.

I follow the rumbling backhoe across the buried pasture, grateful for the tromped trail to walk on. Heavy clouds, every shade of imaginable gray, from milky pearl to nearly black, boil around the top of the divide and pile up in thick banks in the east. The heifers and calves are ravenous. The heifers have long dangling icicles hanging from their tails and bellies, but the calves are dry and frisky. We feed out five bales for them, then two for the bulls. Their shaggy red-and-white hides are nowhere to be seen in the snow-laden willows, but they will wander in sometime and find the feed.

Mick plows back the snow to find clear ground. The horses maul me when I reach the hay pen by the cabin. They nuzzle my hands and my ponytail sticking out the back of my scarf, looking for treats when I have none. If I emptied my coat pockets, all they would find would be hay chaff, a string (which I carry for catching Brandy out in the pasture when I want to ride), a few miscellaneous pieces of flint, and some wadded up Kleenex. I don't even carry a pocketknife. I use Mick's, which goes to show how dependent I am on him. Bored, the horses back off and amble away, except for Brandy, who stays so I can scratch his itchy ears and scrape some of his long, dead winter hair off with my gloved hand.

The sky opens like an eyelid and a bright iris of cloudless blue appears. The clouds shift and jostle, vanishing overhead until sunlight spills through, drenching us in warmth. The snow metamorphoses into a billion scattered diamonds.

I use the heavy broom to brush snow from the vehicles and sweep the melting walk. Worried about the place where the roof leaks on the house, I drag the heavy ladder around through the snow and climb up the steep pitch. I spend half an hour shoveling off huge heavy chunks of snow and knocking three-foot-long icicles down from the eaves.

Mick returns home snow-covered. He carries the five-gallon red water can filled with drinking water from the spring by the cabin.

"I only got stuck three times," he says. "The snow at the cabin is thigh-deep. I even had trouble finding the spring outlet, everything is so buried."

He looks worn down but excited.

"Go rest. I'll fix lunch."

I call out to him when the salad and deer steaks are ready. When he sits by the set place at the table, I walk over and kiss him on the forehead.

"What's that for?" he asks.

"Just because you're you."

Saturday, April 26th

At Arrowhead, the sun bakes the front of the east-facing trailer that serves as my office. There isn't nearly as much snow here as there is at home just three miles upriver. Lacking a snow shovel, I use the dustpan to scrape six inches of snow off the porch steps and walkways. The roof drips on my head as I work, making me laugh.

I straighten the sign-in area and return a call to La Salle Trout Farm. They want to sell us grass carp to help alleviate weed problems in the lakes.

Gary and Valerie arrive a little after 9:30. The sun shifts, giving way to black clouds curling in from the southeast. Gary is exuberant and excited, Valerie more quiet and subdued. Like me, she isn't sure that fishing in the snow is such a good idea, but we sign in, discuss the dismal muddy road conditions, and decide the only travelable road is the relatively flat one leading to the East Lake. They head downriver using four-wheel drive. Dressed in my waders and vest, hauling along my fly rod, I follow.

Rudy, Arrowhead Ranch's caretaker, has plowed away the snow, but the road stays a sea of mud and standing water. The deep ruts suck me here and there, slewing the truck sideways like a kiddy-car track at a carnival. I park several hundred yards from the lake where I can turn the vehicle safely.

My waders immediately collect inches of red-clay mud and I walk Donald Duck style on earthy high heels. With the temperature dropping, I pull up my hood, squirm into an extra coat, and strap on a fanny pack.

Gary and Valerie laugh at the fickle weather, which was supposed to be forty degrees and sunny. Gary helps Val get set up for a float tube. Dressed in fleece pants and waterproof boots, heavy coat, insulated chest waders, and a colorful knit cap, she pulls on a pair of gloves. He ties her feet into wide flippers, gives her instructions on how to step into and hook on the tube. Gingerly she backs down the muddy slope to the water's edge, Gary guiding her until she reaches waist-deep water. She looks like a duck wearing an orange-and-green donut. With her purple coat and cap she hunkers down like an exotic water bird floating on the slapping whitecaps of the lake.

"Are you scared, Val?" I shout.

"Not exactly, but if I spring a leak and fill these waders, I'll sink like a stone to the bottom."

Gary hands her a rod and net. He has hooked her up with a newly tied silver fly called a Zonker. Before launching himself out into the water, he ties a brown woolly bugger on my tippet and instructs me to try long casts, at least ten feet out from shore, and to use short jerks bringing the line in.

I'm already freezing, my fingers stiff, my coat plastered with snow.

I cast sloppily from the west shore, fighting the wind and an already aching shoulder. Flocks of waterfowl circle the lake. Fifty snow geese undulate against the gray sky, dipping and swirling, changing flight patterns in a rhythmic balletlike way. They sink low enough for me to see the black edges on their wing tips. They survey the lake, but seeing us, they shy away and head south toward Antero Reservoir. Several pair of Canada geese honk from the north banks, and a flock of ducks flap over the ridge, wings whistling. They too turn away, rising up and disappearing into the snowy south sky. Braver and noisier, gulls circle in squalling disarray. They spin tight aerial configurations and land near the east shore. The echoing cries of sea and summer sound bizarre here where we fish in a snowstorm.

Valerie's rod tip arcs. She has a strike and her tube spins as she works the trout.

"Yeah, Val," I holler.

We shout back and forth across the waves. She has a twelve-inch fish that is neither a brown nor a rainbow. I suggest a Donaldson Steelhead rainbow that we stocked last summer. She reels in and releases her catch.

She yells, "Now I'm having fun!"

I switch shores, putting the snow-laden wind at my back, casting at an awkward angle. I wish I had enough passion for fishing to perfect a cast or work harder to learn the plethora of knots and flies.

Gary catches and releases three large fish, the last a twenty-inch hard-fighting brown. He maneuvers toward shore and hands me his rod so I can help him land the trout. The pull and bend puts pressure against the rod tip, and I grip the butt with both hands.

"Let him run," Gary says as the line sings out. When I feel the brown ease off, I reel in slowly, steadily, backing up, trying to get the fish in close to Gary's net. Adrenaline surges and blood rushes into my fingertips making them tingle.

Five more minutes of complex strategy, the run and retrieve of the line, and Gary finally reaches out to scoop the trout free of the lake. The barbless hook releases easily from the fish's fin. Gary holds the large brown in the water a moment before letting go. In the blink of an eye, the trout disappears into the depths.

"Healthy?" I ask.

Fresh caught fish. Photo by Laurie Wagner Buyer.

"Yes, but thin."

I worry about the fish wintering in this man-made, closed environment, wonder if the fathead minnows and scuds and other invertebrates
we put in the lakes are enough food.

"Froze up," I say to Gary. "You two are tougher than I."

"Dressed warmer is all. Glad you came up."

Beating my way home through mud and thick snow, I barely make out
the road edges where the county plows left a berm yesterday. I reach the
ranch gate trembling and relieved.

After a long nap in which I pull out of a disturbing dream like a trout
rising to a fly, I fix Mick a simple supper. He leaves to plow more snow. Blue
and I pick the packed trail to the cabin. The horses rest on the feed ground
absorbing the last warmth of the day. I brush off the end of a pile of lumber
for a seat. Blue nestles between my legs. Cookie and Candy ease over to
investigate. Blue growls in warning, but I tell him it's okay. Intimidated

Amigo (left) and Brandy. Photos by Laurie Wagner Buyer.

by two tons of black hide and hooves, he slinks back to a safer distance. I'm braver, knowing that a wave of my arm or one harsh command would spook them away. I hold out gloved hands to each. They sniff and snort, lip-nibble my palms, begging for treats. Their eyes are liquid and fathomless, docile as a doe deer's. They are all bluff, bluster, and bigness, but gentle to the core. I scratch their chins. I blow into Candy's velvet nose, and she half rears in mock terror then returns, snorting. They soon tire of me and turn to one another, head to tail, to scratch backs. What starts out as mild nuzzles along each other's withers turns harder and harsher. I can hear the rasp of teeth against hide. Then Cookie bites Candy, tearing off a hunk of hair. They squeal and side kick, acting like typical girls, their torture treatment a sign of caring and jealousy.

All of us hear Mick plowing up the trail, the snap and pop of the crawler's engine, the clanking of the steel tracks. The mares raise their heads and watch, all eyes, ears pricked. Jill and Brandy and Amigo lift their heads from lipping up the remains of their hay. Closer comes the sound. How long will the mares wait until they break and run? Mick hunches forward, concentrating over the controls. A three-foot-high berm rolls off the angled blade, pushing big balls of packed snow to the side. He looks up and nods. Thirty feet away. Twenty. Fifteen—the mares whirl, spooking the others. Blue picks up the rear of the herd, barking and nipping heels.

"Here," I shout, "stop that!"

I rise and wave, trot ahead of Mick on the JD Crawler, to reach the bare ground and walk away from the setting sun. As predicted, the air has grown sharp. Cold rolls up the river valley in icy waves.

When I talk to Dad, his voice is strained and raspy.

"How are you feeling?"

"Not too good. I sleep all the time. My throat hurts way deep."

"Sleeping is good though. Can you eat?"

"I try. Some things don't taste too good. I wish I felt like doing something."

"You will, Dad. You'll get stronger again."

"I want to get the surgery over with. I want them to schedule it now."

"I know, but you need to gain some weight, get stronger."

He sighs and mumbles something.

"I'm sorry, Dad. What?"

"Do you want to talk to your mother?"

"Sure."

"JOAN!" he hollers, sounding like a bullfrog.

That part of Dad hasn't changed. He's still a great yeller.

"Hi, my Laurie," Mom says.

"Hi, Mom. How are you holding up?"

"Fine. Being bossy. We both slept most of the day."

"When do you see the doctors again?"

"Tuesday. But if he's not better, we may go in Monday."

"Have you heard from the sisters?"

"Kari Bari called."

I smile at this nickname for my older sister, Karen. When we were young, Karen and Eileen teased me with a taunting refrain: "Laurie Pourie, pudding and pie, kissed the boys and made them cry. When the girls came out to play, Laurie Pourie ran away." This outraged me so much I'd scream back at them: "Karen the Carrot. Karen the Carrot. Eileen the Bean, the rotten Tangerine!"

"I wish Karen and Eileen could both come. We would all keep you company while Dad's in the hospital."

"Oh, Lordy." Mom laughs.

"Just think, we could do 'girls-night-out' every day."

"We'll see," she says. "I ordered three boxes of rainbow-trout candy for you for the Arrowhead clubhouse."

"That was nice. I think of you all the time, but I try not to call too often."

"I know. I understand," she says. "We miss you. Come soon, all right?"

Sunday, April 27th

"Uh oh," he says, coming into the kitchen, "cleaning day."

"Yep. Toast and egg?"

"Sounds good."

Mick thinks I'm overzealous in my pursuit of dirt, cobwebs, and streaked windows, but I was raised in a military family where white-glove inspections were not a joke.

I take my time this morning, stopping to rest and read in between my chores. My day goes well until I burn a frozen pizza at noon. Mick doggedly eats his first piece. I can hear the crunch of burnt crust between his teeth.

"It's good," he says.

"Liar," I say. "Oh, well, a little charcoal is good for your digestion."

"I'm outta here," he says, taking a handful of cookies with him.

I tear apart the dining room, taking photographs and frames full of collected arrowheads from the walls, moving books, plants, and chairs. Then the room is empty except for the large, 1940s carved table that belonged to Mick's grandmother, the oak glass-front cabinet, a heavy leather-covered armchair, a buffet, and the gun cabinet. Large and austere, the room boasts hand-hewn, chinked-log walls on two sides, pine-wood paneling on the other two. A low plaster ceiling dips to barely six feet on the west side where a huge window looks out on the divide. The afternoon sun pours in like liquid gold, bathing the logs with luxurious tints and hues. I swipe a damp cloth over the rough logs that grab and tear at my cloth as I go. It takes me all day to wash the crystal candy dishes and vases, the bride-and-groom glasses and first-anniversary plate, the two-hundred-year-old olive dish and toothpick holder, a chipped shot glass from Mick's grandfather's saloon, painted plates from Grandmother Allen, a tiny porcelain teacup and saucer from Grandma Buyer. Tucked away in the cabinet are Dave Miller's hand tools: a plane, a scribe, a dehorning tool. Things found around the ranch also find a home here: a whiskbroom handle, a hand-carved peg clothespin, an old rusted hammer head, iron bit rings, a belt buckle, Mick's father's and grandfather's pocket watches, Gram Buyer's cream skimmer, a collection of silver spoons, a woven pine-needle basket, an old U.S. Army flat padlock used on mule packs, the porcelain cookhouse dishes from the old Buyer family ranch.

❧

In the quiet, still evening air, Mick and I walk up the muddy road to the gate. I try to draw him into conversation.

"It's a beautiful place, this ranch," I say.

"The mountains sure got overloaded with snow this go-round," he replies.

"Do you think it is prettier than the O Bar Y?" I ask as we lean side by side on the gate.

"No."

"Is it prettier than the Old Buyer Ranch?"

"By a long shot."

"Don't you think we are lucky to live here?"

"You chatter like a magpie," he says, his polite way of telling me to shut up, so I do.

I reach out for his ungloved hand. He takes mine briefly and squeezes it once before letting go. Not a man to be held or examined, he remains elusive to me.

At the shop he says, "I'll be in soon." I nod and walk back to the house.

All my young years I dreamed of a man who would be strong and silent. It has taken me forty years to discover that strong, silent men are held prisoner in jails of their own stubborn making. I have no key to Mick's inner self. I have no skills to assist him in a planned escape. All I can do is look longingly, lovingly, through his self-constructed protective bars and bring him cookies.

Monday, April 28th

At 5:30 a.m., Mick nudges me nicely. "Time to get up." I moan and roll over, snuggle deeper into the covers. The remembered rush of lovemaking as the sun set, spilling light and warmth onto the bed, comes back to me. I want to stay here caught in that perfect moment of communication and closeness.

"Want me to get up first?" Mick asks.

"Yes," I say and go back to sleep.

When I wake again, I hear the crackle of the fire and radio static, the crunchy cascade of cold cereal being poured into a glass bowl.

"Morning," I mumble, pressing myself to Mick's side where he sits at the small round table.

"Hello, gorgeous," he teases me over my pathetic appearance in silk turtleneck and undies, my eyes puffy slits, my hair stuck out every which-a-way.

"Did you sleep?" Mick asks.

"Yes, but every bone in my body aches."

"I wonder why?"

"Because I moved furniture all afternoon," I say as I stick out my tongue and scoot off to the bathroom wishing we had this kind of camaraderie every day.

The sun battles clouds in the east. Gray sky skirmishes with blue. Unsettled and restless, the weather doesn't know what it wants to do. An army of robins hops across bare patches in the yard. A couple of killdeer scream out in the meadow. Mick tells me the backhoe has a main-seal oil leak. I see $3,000 to $5,000 disappear before my eyes. Equipment repair on all the old run-down stuff plagues us. I blink back unbidden tears over all the household repairs I dream of doing.

In a mixture of snow slop and mud we try to find the driest, cleanest spots to feed. Parked by the spring pipe outside the gate, Mick and I look the cattle over with critical eyes. One rangy heifer looks all bones and angles, but she sports a big bag, and a healthy calf tags her heels.

"That red one looks thin," I say.

"She's a calf out of my favorite Simmental cow."

"Is she pulled down because she's milking so good?"

"Yeah, just like her mother."

The power of another spring settles around us, soft as a whisper, a wish, remembered promises.

"We've been through a lot together in fifteen years, Mick."

"Yes," he says.

A huge, empty silence hangs between us, but I say nothing more.

"This is my last year," he says.

I glance up to see the joke twitching on his lips, but he is serious, his demeanor staunch and sage. Handsomely worn, the skin of his face is polished and burnished red brown from the stronger sun. Dark glasses shade his eyes, but he is not looking at me. He looks cross-country to the plains far away from the high peaks that surround us. He leans against the four-wheeler frame toying with one glove.

"I can't do it anymore," he says. "Not the physical work. I could still cripple by with that. It's just the mental work, the worry, and the stress. I just can't do it anymore."

"I know" is all I can think to say. When he adds nothing further, I say, "I'll help you. Whatever you need to do."

I do not try to hug him or touch him or console him. I know better. He prefers being alone with his own suffering.

We stand for a long time. I pass a willow branch through my fingers, feeling the suspended buds that have been waiting well over a month for enough warmth and sun to open.

Mick shoves up and straddles the four-wheeler, pushes the starter button.

"Want a ride?" he says over the roar.

"No, I'll walk." He pulls away. I stand and watch his back until it disappears.

A meadowlark trills notes as sweet and soft as homemade ice cream. The song breaks my heart and then mends it back. The bird sings over and over until I am crushed and healed a hundred times. Mick's words melt from my mind.

In town I hear the local paper ran an article about my poetry. Everyone is happy for my small success. For the first time in my life, I'm part of a community. I would be hard-pressed to tear up the tender but tenacious roots that have been trying to take hold over the last nine years in this valley. If I'm ripped away from this place, will my roots refuse to be transplanted? Will I shrivel up and die?

I creep home on the wet highway, battling blowing snow and the white-out whirl of unwelcome thoughts. No matter what—ranch sale, divorce—I have to find a way to stay. I need a familiar landscape to survive. I want the same view out my window every morning for the rest of my life.

Tuesday, April 29th

The weather vacillates like a vane in the wind, switching directions and changing speeds. Spring keeps poking her head between the clouds hoping to discover winter retreating, instead finding the continued roar and howl of wind-borne snow flurries off the divide.

I arrive at Arrowhead Ranch early to straighten the clubhouse and prepare to meet a prospective permit holder. The furnace in my trailer office chugs and blows like a steam ship, but does little to stem the icy rush of air that sneaks in at every window and door crack. It is an unkind day, not the best for trying to show the value of belonging to a fly fishing resort. But my tour guest, Ron, is a hardy soul. We visit cabins, pushing our way against gusts of wind and hanging on to open doors. We scout the lakes, fighting in four-wheel drive on muddy roads, in places skidding along deep boggy ruts. To me, after months and months of no-escape winter, the landscape looks dull and dreary, still brown, the colors washed out by wan sun. Ron, however, soaks up the view of what I see every day as if it were the world's most fascinating place. For people who live and work in cities, who get their outdoor experiences in small bites whenever they are able to sneak away for a week-long float trip or a day's fishing, the aura of Arrowhead Ranch and the upper valley where I live is a paradise regardless of the weather.

I leave Ron at the East Lake where a flotilla of ducks paddle circles and dive on the far northeast corner. He casts repeatedly into the open water, says he'll fish until he freezes out. Later, the sign-in sheet shows he caught two browns and twelve rainbows in three lakes using both an olive scud and an olive woolly bugger. He toughed out five hours in the uninspiring wind.

My afternoon revolves around a South Park Heritage seminar hosted by the Colorado State University Extension Service, in which people from the Division of Wildlife, Colorado Open Space, Rocky Mountain Elk Foundation, American Farmland Trust, and the Colorado Cattleman's Land Trust speak to us about conservation easements and possible ways to preserve agricultural lands and the ranching-farming way of life for future generations. I join Dave and Carol Neukirch for a barbecue beef and beans lunch. Gary Nichols, in his position as Park County's Tourism and Economic Development Director, introduces me to the old-time ranch families as well as the new moneyed investors who are seeking an interest in the future of South Park. I'm able to talk briefly with a tax attorney who specializes in agricultural estate planning. The family limited partnership that Mick has arranged with his children seems like little protection against the IRS. I drive home in a snowstorm, feeling sad. If by some miracle Mick manages to hold on to the ranch for his lifetime, the possibility of saving it from sale at his death in order to pay taxes seems impossible. Is it just foolishness to love something with all your heart, work for it, worry over it, sacrifice for it, grow old and weary with it, give up your soul for it, only to lose it in the end to something as stupid and intangible as taxes?

Wednesday, April 30th

Mick leaves alone to feed. Blue trots at his side, ears up with his simple canine single-minded optimism. Beating my way against the relentless wind to the truck, I'm off to Arrowhead again for another tour. The sun lifts the land into a lovelier view, its light pulling deep green and dark brown colors from the trees. From the willows, grayish silver spiked with burnt umber orange radiates against the startling canary yellows of new growth. From the sky erupts an unbelievable blue plumped by summer storm clouds. From the now snow-free pastures and meadows, quilted brown and beige like old hay is now stitched with thin green lines.

My guest, Rob, asks myriad questions, some of which are way beyond my capacity to answer. He is a retired landscape architect and notices things like the lay of the land, the bad drainage problems along roads, the places near the river where undercut banks have succumbed to weathering and sloughed off into the water.

The Trophy Lakes at Arrowhead Ranch with Buffalo Peaks background. Photo by Laurie Wagner Buyer.

A walker like me, Rob often suggests we get out and look at the land. He wants to feel the landscape around him—the wind, the sun, the moist air, the changing weather. At South Lake, some large trout feed aggressively at a shallow backwater where the warmer water has brought on an early hatch. We see the bright rings of their rising, the occasional lift and dip of their heads, or an exposed dorsal fin. Here and there we see the shadowy slide of their shapes in the mirrored water when the light is just right to show them in the small wave chop. At Trophy Lakes, more geese, ducks, and a large black cormorant with his long neck giving away his identity against a blue-sky backdrop. A big brown swirls the shallow water of the west bank, and elk tracks and droppings mar the drying mud surface of the dam. At East Lake the close sight of a small bunch of antelope climbing the sage-spiked ridge blesses us. Curious as domestic goats, they see our vehicle approach and stop to watch us. When we park beneath them, they tiptoe to the edge of the hill and peek down at us, unafraid. Their bodies are a patchwork of tan and white, and the black shine of the buck's horns looks like ebony. On our return drive, a solitary male bluebird flits in front of the truck, an airborne jewel.

I'm pleased when Rob writes out a check to join the resort. I'm within five memberships of meeting my expected goal to bring in the required income needed to keep Arrowhead Ranch running another year.

I spend hours at my desk writing the May first newsletter. The foreign names of flies are fast becoming part of my vocabulary: orange scuds, mayfly nymphs, bead heads, red egg patterns, prince nymph, parachute Adams, San Juan worms. I have lived my life learning new languages. In every different place we moved when I was a child, I had to tune my ear and tongue to dialects and inflections, unknown words, slang, strange sayings, localized meanings and grammar. When I was in my early twenties, in mountain wildlife and backcountry environs, I tasted words like buckskin, braintan, water wolf, cayuse, snowslipper, and chinook. In my late twenties, I turned to the subculture of ranching and learned heifer, steer, singletree, latigo, chaps, hames, britchin, head gate, corner post, hoof nippers, baler, swather, zerks, scours, bangs, red water, black leg, stoved up, work brittle, dink, slink, and the ever present goddamn-son-of-a-bitch. Now, in my early forties, it is the language of anglers, the garbled Greek of outdoorsmen that I must master.

The wind gives up, and the evening feels soft and accepting. Looking out across the valley, tallying the years we've worked, the fences built, the pennies scrimped and saved, the losses suffered, the hidden, almost imperceptible joys along the way, I promise myself again that I will not leave.

Hale-Bopp seems sunk lower in the sky when I search and find her. She's barely above the rotting bunkhouse roof. I whisper to her. I touch the lips of the old lady on the wall beside my bed. When I nestle up against Mick's warm flank, I say my childhood prayers. I will pray to any god, to any power, to any source of goodness and wisdom through all the eons of time and memory, if one of them, or all of them combined, will just give me the strength to go on.

MAY

❧

Thursday, May 1st

The brief warm surge sank to twenty degrees. With the refrigerator empty I decide to head to Salida for supplies. Mick says, "I'll take you. I've been feeling cooped up." His admission of cabin fever is rare. We head out in a stiff wind under milky gray skies. All along the highway to Trout Creek Pass we see new cattle brought in for grazing—mama cows with little calves and yearlings. Mick shakes his head. "There isn't enough grass left on those worn-out pastures to feed a sick rabbit, let alone hundreds of head of cattle." With the cold winter we have had, there won't be any new grass coming for a month or more. The land of ten thousand haystacks looks more like desert than oasis.

"What really pisses me off," Mick says, gripping the steering wheel, "is that the cattle get the bad rap when it's the dummies who lease the land who are the idiots."

Even the Arkansas Valley, usually vibrant and green this time of year, looks held back and stunted. Sap rises in the willow trees, however, and the branches flame with color against the washed-out sky.

We pull into the feedstore and cannot speak: the equipment is gone, the hay is gone, all the panels and feeders are gone. The door is locked, the windows boarded over. A sign says: At the request of Salida Feed, please contact Mountain Protein and Supply in Poncha Springs for feed. A ton-and-a-half hauler with a huge trailer on behind sits on the scales with a big for-sale sign stuck on it. Mick and I sit in the truck and stare.

"Guess it's a good thing all we needed was dog food," Mick says as we pull away. For nine years we have frequented this store, paying a higher price for the convenience and accessibility. Mick is worried, quiet, and sad. His day has been anything but relaxing or fun.

"Doesn't it bother you?" he asks.

"I can't let it bother me. I can't worry about things so beyond my control. I've got all I can handle worrying about you and the ranch and Dad."

"Will it reopen?"

"I don't know. How can we know?"

We take our insurance agent, Jill, to lunch. She fills us in with the pieces of gossip. Both the sale barn and the feedstore are supposed to reopen. The San Luis valley operators, who planted ten thousand acres in potatoes last year and lost their shirts, are now going back to alfalfa hay. That should bring hay prices down. Cattle prices are up. All the losses in the Dakotas and the flooded Midwest may mean the market will stay up. But how many producers have we lost? How many will never recover from the slump? Jill runs her cattle by farming them out to other ranchers and is looking for grass for fifteen heifers and a bull. We know of nothing to lease in South Park. I tease her, saying she needs to marry a rich rancher. Mick looks at me as if I've said the dumbest thing on earth and asks, "Is there such a thing?"

We say nothing on the hour's drive home. Where will Mick go, who will he be, if he has no cattle, no ranch, no space with which to insulate himself from the world at large?

Back home, Mick leaves immediately to do chores as I unload the truck. Everywhere we went today was snow-free. Here, still white, little drifts stuck in the vehicle tracks show that it snowed again while we were away.

Caught up in winter's web, Mick takes Blue for an evening walk. He returns rubbing his hands, trembling. "It's a cold son-of-a-bitch. Do you think it will ever warm up?"

Friday, May 2nd

The creeping cold sets spring back with a wallop. We dole out the hay to the hungry animals. I cannot stop shivering.

UPS leaves a package up at the ranch gate. From Bill Murray's eldest daughter, Jo Anna, the box contains goodies from Wolfermann's Bakery. Christmas in May. She has saved me the task of baking this week.

Bill and Jo Murray are clients of mine at Arrowhead Ranch. Avid fly fishermen from Austin, Texas, they take the sport seriously and spend most of the summer stalking elusive trout in our lakes and stream. Bill, the most magnanimous person I have ever known, and Jo, protective and nurturing matriarch of their large family, are close friends. Like fairy godparents they have adopted Mick and me.

Crawling into bed I search the sky again for Hale-Bopp, but she is gone, moved outside of my field of vision. I miss her. I miss knowing she is blazing away, lighting a path. I trust that she is still out there hidden from me. Even when I cannot see her luminous glow, she gives me hope, reminds me of cosmic powers beyond my ken.

Saturday, May 3rd

Restless, I walk to Arrowhead Ranch to greet the first guests of the season staying at the Ridge Cabin. Blue pouts because I will not allow him to follow me. The expression on his face is the look of a child told to go to his room. The crusted snow holds me aloft. Where I walk on exposed earth, my foot forms to the malleable contours of softening dirt. The wind at my back pushes me, nudging me toward the rising sun. On the river meadow, twenty grazing bulls raise their heads and eye me. A Watusi with horns that span a stretch larger than his body looks sanguine. I stumble over a

Bill and Jo Murray, Laurie and Mick, Joan and Frank (Mom and Dad).
Photo by Laurie Wagner Buyer.

stone and he lowers his head, tipping his horns. I stop and do not move. He
paws the earth, throwing big clods over his back and dusting the air with
dirty debris. I hold my breath, not even blinking, until he gives up thinking
I'm anything dangerous and goes back to grazing.

Along the river willows I meet our guest Gary Whitlock out early
trying for trout. The stream purls, ice free and running wild. We chat
of everyday things—the winter, the weather, the need for stealth in approaching a hole and dropping a fly inconspicuously against the undercut lip of a dark bank. When I turn to hike on, he turns back to his task,
fly rod poised, ready to cast.

At a Trout Unlimited Banquet in Poncha Springs, I browse the auc-
tion offerings and listen to the whirl of activity surrounding the watery,
cold world of trout, but my mind is on our river and our land and what
we can do to survive.

Coming home late to the ranch, I stand at the gate on the county road
and stargaze, then count the invasive lights of new homes dotting the

ridges across the valley. So much to lose. So much to miss. Along the timberline near Jack's Camp, a cow calls for her calf, then a night heron offers his occult cry as it flies unseen across the velvet sky.

Sunday, May 4th

Sundays are the way I mark our rural life, the pattern of weeks that stretch into months that stretch into seasons that stretch into years.

We don't need a kitchen fire but I build one out of force of habit. The sun rises lazily, kissing everything with languorous light. Winter slipped behind the curtain of sunrise, never even taking a bow for playing the part of the extraordinary villain who manipulated our lives and caused such furor over the past eight months. Suddenly, without warning, true spring arrives. Mick releases the cattle to wander the pastures in search of any grass sprigs to be gleaned. Yesterday the hard warm wind cut off the snow cover, melting it like butter into the soft pancakelike surface of the earth. As much as I'd like to be out where a meadowlark chortles beyond the kitchen window, I plot my spring-cleaning course and attack the living room.

Forward motion: dismantle everything. Scoop away buckets of ashes from the wood stove and chips from the woodbox corner. When Mick returns, it looks like a bomb has gone off, blowing everything away from the walls and out into the dining room and the hallway. He shakes his head and turns to escape.

"Whoa! Can you fix these electric sockets?" I ask, pointing to two wall plugs that have never been properly attached and mounted to the zee-brick wall behind the wood stove. "That one knocked me on my butt."

Mick grimaces like I've asked him to eat something he loathes.

"What'd you touch it for?" he asks.

"I was dusting," I say.

He snorts like a surprised buck deer.

"Mick, couldn't you just fix it somehow? Tape it back against the wall. Take it out. It could start a fire."

"That plug would never start a fire."

"Well, just do it because it would make me feel better."

"You are so fuddy-duddy, Mrs. Clean."

"I know. My great failing."

I huff out to the kitchen, and he stomps behind me, mimicking my pique with exaggerated motions.

"Why are you so cruel to me?"

"I'm not," he says.

"You are. I'm just asking you to help me with something I don't know how to do myself."

I dump my sixth bucket of dirty Spic-and-Span water down the sink drain.

"Okay," he says, "I'll fix it."

The next hour we work in the same room, stoically concentrating on our own tasks. I scrub the ceiling and walls and dismantle the fan and lights to clean them.

Mick sprawls out on the bricks to get eye level with the wall plug. He drills and carves and cusses under his breath. The job is more complicated that I thought, and I'm embarrassed that I asked for his help when he has other work to do.

"I didn't mean to rope you into something so difficult. I'm sorry."

Silence.

"Why are you angry now?" I ask.

"I'm not angry. Hell! Where's my screwdriver?" He pushes tools around until he locates it.

"If the plug will work, we can put a lamp by your chair so you can see to read."

"I don't need a lamp," he says.

"Well, we can plug in your scanner so you can listen to local scoop and scandal."

Mick gives me a glare that says, "Please shut up."

So I vacuum, letting the roar and the suction of dirt off the carpet replace my desire to scream. Primal scream. Female frustration scream. A scream to end all screams. A scream so loud and long and soul-emptying that when the last echo dies off the timbered ridges, one would know some great presence had called out in warning and passed on by.

Folding clothes at the kitchen table, I hear Mick putting his tools away. I peek in the door and see the plug "Mickey Buyered," fixed cowboy style, nothing fancy, nothing professional, but fixed.

"You are a good man." I kiss him on the forehead while he sits on the bricks, wrapping the cord around his drill.

"You are an infuriating woman."

"Aren't you the lucky one to be married to me?"

His grunt sounds like a bullfrog.

"How about lunch?"

Mick's eyes light up. My peace offering is a hamburger and French fries. His is a hug from behind while I clean up the dishes.

"I'm gonna drive around the loop," he says.

"Okay."

"Wanna go?"

Surrounded by mess, I sigh. Tomorrow I have to go to work over at Arrowhead.

"Honey, I can't."

"I thought about driving up Hoosier Pass." He looks wistful. A Sunday drive sounds like a cure-all. How long it has been since we just took a trip to see the country? But, if I don't finish putting the living room back together, our lives will be in an uproar for a week.

"I can't go," I say. His expression tells me he is afraid of going alone.

"Go on. You'll be fine. Take Blue. It will do you both good to get off the ranch."

"You won't go?"

"I can't."

Hours tick by. I rehang photos on the wall: Mick driving a team with the Marlboro men riding saddle horses in a white forgotten Wyoming landscape; nine bull moose trailing out of a haystack midwinter; Mick and Tom Palmer going across the sixty-five-foot expanse of the Green River bridge driving a six-up team with the Wind River Mountains looming as backdrop; the elk herd at Black Butte that Mick fed for seventeen years for the Department of Game and Fish and in the distance the buildings of the O Bar Y Ranch with the Sawtooth Mountains rising to the sky; Mick fending off a charging bull moose with a snow shovel while his dog, Tammy, races in to help protect him where they are surrounded by six feet of snow so that only the tops of the haystack fence posts stick out; Mick driving a team of blacks in a rainstorm, the snowscape surrounding him like fog, his yellow slicker and orange rubber gloves standing out from the whites and grays and browns and blacks of the photograph like they were hand painted; a Hereford cow standing in the June snow against bare willows baby-sitting seven newborn calves; Mick driving four-up—three blacks and a gray—through belly-deep snow; and, lastly, a huge print of the O Bar Y in early summer with the meadows green, the cows spread out grazing, the hulk of an old beaver-slide hay stacker in the foreground, the white massive bulk of the Sawtooths behind. The stories of Mick's life captured and held forever.

When Mick returns, I've put things back in place so he can sit in his chair and watch the news.

"What did you see?" I ask.

"New houses. One at the forks. One at Ansleys. New roads. Traffic. Five feet of snow on Hoosier."

"Did you have fun?"

"No. But Blue had a big time. Never made a peep. He just looked and looked and looked."

"I'm glad you're home."

"Me too," he says, flipping channels. "They're closing in. I don't think I can stay here and watch it happen. I don't think I can stay here anymore and see it all change."

We walk together, our small family, Mick, Laurie, Blue, Molly. The air is sweet, saturated with spring fragrances, with sage, earth, manure. The wind springs up out of the west so that we walk askew, faces averted from the chill. Blue bounces from gopher hole to gopher hole. The heifers and calves eye us as we walk the dirt road. Whatever wonder gives birth to spring is with us. I hear the ground give underfoot, hear the moisture suck and settle into the dry interstices underneath our feet, hear the frogs far out in their boggy slough bottoms. I stop to listen.

"What is it?" Mick asks.

"Nothing," I say. "Nothing."

But I hear it, soft as a baby breathing in sleep, the land coming back to life, stirring, restless, awakening.

Monday, May 5th

As mother-of-pearl light blooms at the window, I realize that I no longer fear my father's cancer, I have no power to change his fate, no more than

I have the power to change my own. I hear the rasp of grating change in each hard syllable Dad speaks. I have grown fond of that hoarse man. Because of his disease, he is gentler now. At 156 pounds, down from his usual 180, he is all angles and bones softened by the growing humanity in his eyes. No longer spunky, high-speed, effervescent energy, he has become tenacious and steady, idling at a comfortable cruising speed that gives him perspective to see the road in front of him, where each curve of the highway leads. I am so proud of Dad's acute love for life, but also for his willingness to embrace his destination.

Overnight the earth turns green, a frail, suggestive, hesitant color, but green. Only dirt-riddled snowdrifts remain around the barns and outbuildings and up on the shaded north-slope ridges.

Midmorning finds me at the confluence of the highway and the county road faced with the flotsam and jetsam of careless highway cruisers: beer bottles, pop cans, baling twine, papers, tires, boards, wire, hubcaps, nails. The sun beats down, hot on my bent head, as I scan the littered landscape and slowly fill two thirty-gallon trash bags. The larger junk I shove and heave and load into the back of the truck. Traffic whizzes by at breakneck speed.

By noon I cannot wedge one more crushed can into my load. I drive through Arrowhead on the now dusty dirt road to the back of the ranch where a dump has been established in the deep, mined-out gorge of an old irrigation system. My sacks of trash cascade down the junk-sided ravine: boards, tires, rotted fence posts follow. I'm overwhelmed by the garbage man creates and how we wallow in our waste products. We are not sensible consumers, and we are certainly insensible about our trash. Yet, even here, on the edge of a dump, the earth blooms. A bit of rabbit brush clings to the claylike soil. A flock of gulls whirl and scream overhead, chipmunks play chase through ranks of half-burned tires, and old swallow-nest holes dot the heaped mounds of yellow earth. The sky stretches overhead like a cool silk sheet so opalescent it is neither blue nor white. Horses pick their way across a winter-peeled pasture toward the green line of a beaver channel near the river. They bend their necks to drink and crop the new, water-soaked slough grass. Not even a breath of breeze moves the still air. I wipe the sweat from my forehead with a grimy sleeve, then drive home.

Mick has been dragging all morning, spreading winter's manure across the rocky pastures.

I scrub up at the sink and throw together chipped beef on toast.

"Good," Mick says. "Thank you. Gotta go."

After supper Mick and I ride double on the four-wheeler to the cabin to fill the five-gallon can from the spring so we'll have drinking water. My garden is still wrapped in layers of aquatic weeds that I forked from Arrowhead's lakes and dried to use as mulch. I pull away the wiry mats to reveal the first lime green shoots of the chives, the pink bulbous growth of rhubarb plants, the yellow-tinged curl of horseradish leaves. Earthworms writhe and weave back down into the dark earth.

We walk west. Warm air swirls around us. My armpits ooze sweat. It feels funny to have warm hands and feet. We wend our way uphill to the bench above the spring source, saying little. We absorb the evening. I am intensely happy and it surprises me that this emotion comes unsuspected, like something alien and alone. An unseen snipe flies and dives, the whistling air in its wings *ooohing*. Robins twitter their coming-night songs. Far off in the willows, the horses spot us and come looking for cubed candies. Shedding off, they grow slick and shiny on the tiny bites of green grass they find springing up along the protected willows. Memories sprout up everywhere: the fence posts we set the first summer, the wires we strung, the staples pounded with such fervor. Across the fence on the little lot Mick bought for me, a piece of the river runs between high red banks. Here, ungrazed, the grass is long and brown-gold, specked with old cow pies and fresh elk droppings. An ouzel flits and dips along the wet rocks of the stream.

Heading home we spot a porcupine crossing the pasture. I search for a stout stick and hand it to Mick.

"Keep Blue back," he says and trots awkwardly through the sage to do battle.

Mick picks up the carcass by a quill-free foot and finds a large badger hole to stuff the prickly critter into. I join him in burying the sizable body. We cover it with enough dirt so that the dog or horses or cattle won't get a snoot full of quills. It pains us to kill any animal that is not eaten or utilized in some way, but porcupines have injured our animals and girdled so many young trees that we try to do some management on their increasing population. If they are outside the ranch boundaries, we leave them unharmed. If they cross the line to pastures where cattle and horses accost them, then we dispatch them with a blow to the head and bury them. We have spent too many bloody hours pulling quills out of the mouths, noses, foreheads, and legs of cattle to be totally free of the live-and-let-live mindset. Blue stays on a knob of high ground watching. When we walk on, he follows, glancing over his shoulder at the small mound of red earth that marks the porcupine's grave.

I glass and glass the night sky searching every star for Hale-Bopp's brightness. She is gone. Maybe she's beyond and below the divide. Maybe she's behind the rise of bunkhouse and tall spruce trees. No matter how long I look from the bedroom window I cannot see her shining.

Tuesday, May 6th

Thirty degrees at dawn swells to over sixty by midafternoon to create a see-the-grass-grow day. I ooze out of bed feeling like primordial slime. I ache all over and I'm dead tired. I send Mick off to do chores with a half-hearted kiss.

Mick has been using his ancient Massey-Ferguson 50 tractor to scrape away old hay and manure from the corrals. I open the yard gate for him and he trundles by with a nine-foot English harrow. He waves his thanks.

Our tiny yard is covered with wood chips, dog bones, and old grass, so I begin with rake and shovel at the far end, creating artistic piles of debris. The wind dances up out of the west and substantial gusts play havoc with my artwork. My face and hair and hands turn gritty with dust. My skin tightens and pulls, feeling prunelike in the heat. I take a break to drink a glass of juice, slather on some sunscreen, then get back on the job, wheeling loads of wood chips, rocks, and yard rakings to a sunken hole against the river pasture fence.

I pull the mats of mulch off my flowerbeds to reveal the yellow-green of new growth starved for light. Delphiniums, poppies, violets, rhubarb, chives, all have survived the months of cold. I use great care uncovering them and feel the plants yawn and stretch, reaching out and up for sun.

Mick and I eat our supper sandwiches silently, both too tired to talk. Renewed, we hike the eighty acres across from the ranch house, picking our way through sage. Where the snow has gone off, the earth's crust is already dried up and cracked. We raise dust just walking. We see signs of where the heifers walked when the ground was muddy, their tracks paired up like twin crescent moons. Here, too, are the tracks and droppings of elk. We scout for flint, but find none. Near a grayed and weathered post, the old phone wires stretch along the ground east to west.

I see a glisten of blue beneath the sage and find a perfect insulator still wired on the twisted groove of wooden post top. Mick, with gloves on, untwists the wires and wood and presents me with the jewel.

As we come down off the hill, the air still warm, the low light edged with gold, the mountain peaks loaded with snow, I ask Mick, "If we could figure out a way to stay here, would you be content to grow old working the ranch?"

"Winters in Wyoming are more exciting," he says.

His cryptic answer makes me drop the conversation.

At home I say an early good night to Mick and ease between the sheets. Luxurious softness surrounds me as I sink into piled up pillows, cant my novel to the late light coming in the window. The phone rings. A client from Arrowhead Ranch asks for reservations.

I settle in again, squirm my butt back into the familiar hollow, tilt my head back to ease the ache in my shoulders. The phone rings.

My sister Karen tells me Charlie is very into his cowboy boots and shirt, jeans, and hat, and that for months he has been begging for a brace of pistols. When Charlie receives the money I sent for his February birthday, he pleads for a set of pearl-handled six-shooters at K-Mart. Once home, Karen instructs her son about never pointing a gun at anyone for any reason and cautions him about using his guns properly.

"The first thing he did," she says, "was point the pistol right in my face and say 'bang, bang, you're dead!' I took those guns and threw them away. Charlie bawled his eyes out, but enough is enough. He told me he didn't care, that when he goes to Aunt Laurie's ranch, she will give him real guns to use."

"Oh great," I say.

When I finally hang up the phone, an hour has passed.

"Good heavens," Mick asks coming to bed, "what in the world did you talk about?"

"Girl stuff," I say.

The phone rings again.

"Jesus Christ!" Mick says.

Carol calls to discuss her housekeeping schedule at Arrowhead Ranch.

I lie for a long time suspended between wakefulness and sleep. The scenes and sounds outside the window change each moment: clouds, starlight, frog song, and the far-off wail of a coyote. I roll over to snug myself against Mick's side. I try to match my breathing to his, try to find his evenness to calm my restless mind. I finally sleep, but dreams wear me out. When I rise at 4:30 a.m., I'm tired.

Wednesday, May 7th

I build a small compact fire to comfort me and soothe something soul deep that is far away from the physical warmth. I write while I drink chamomile tea sweetened with honey. When I spoon the thick gold from a green-glazed pottery jar, I vision the bees' work and summer days rich with the scent of alfalfa, clover, and wild flowers. Whose hands handled the hives and extracted the essence of insects for me to enjoy?

Mick is out early doing chores. He pokes his head in the kitchen door to tell me he's taking the tractor to get the log footbridge out of the river before it rises with run-off.

An hour later he is back.

"I buried it," he says.

"The tractor?"

"Just the front end," he says, grinning. "Went over the pipe in the meadow, and the mud just gave way under me. High-centered on the pipe. God, it's a bog hole."

"Need help?"

"No, I'll take the cat. You know me. I always get myself out. Found the abutment log downriver. Will try to get that too."

"Sure you don't need help? I could have my duds on in seconds."

"Nope. See you."

He takes a banana and leaves.

Midmorning he is back again.

"Get it?" I ask.

"Stuck three more times. I crossed downcountry, but the whole meadow is quivering like jelly. Nothing but a big bog hole. Hard to believe it's only the snowmelt. We'll have grass until hell's no more over there if it would just warm up."

"Were you able to get the logs reset?"

"Yeah, but I went to walk across them to push over the butt ends, and I heard something crack. I got off fast. Put a chain on the ends to pull them onto the bank and when the other ends hit the river, they cracked in half. Couldn't believe it. Rotten as hell. So no bridge now."

I serve braised pork chops, yams sweetened with brown sugar and butter, brussels sprouts with lemon and herb seasoning, slaw made of cabbage, peas, and carrots. Cowboy coffee cake for dessert.

"Gotta go. Work to do." Mick is ready to leave as soon as his fork hits his empty plate.

"I'm going to Arrowhead this afternoon. Where will you be?"

"Upper Mikels', pulling dams, if I can get there."

Light as a cloud, a blue heron lifts from the riverbank and floats upstream. I see her rise then land, rise then land, then fly dozens of times before I lose sight of her smoky gray-blue color in the thick willows. Ground squirrels scurry from hole to hole. Flickers, one of our best spring indicators, have returned. Several dart in front of me, the orange fire-flash of their wings and distinctive flight pattern alerting me to who they are. I round a corner and see a Hereford bull grazing on short lush grass between willow bushes where the ground is protected and warm. He is so intent on grazing, he neither sees nor hears me even when I whistle to give him warning. After months of hay, the grass must taste like manna to him. He is slick red and shiny, his massive white curly-haired head topped by thick down-turned horns.

Blue sleeps against the side of the house, oblivious to my approach when I return home. Mick stands at the kitchen sink drinking a glass of water in long gulps.

"Did you survive?" I ask.

"Tough duty. Pulled two dams. No snow or mud going up. Dry as a bone on the east slope where I fixed the fence. Some asshole hauled in a load of aspen wood at that site on Tumble Creek. They tore the hell out of the road getting in. Cut deep ruts. Left all the gates open. I swear . . ."

Mick shakes his head. "I wonder if it's that same son-of-a-bitch who was there last year."

Unidentified campers got caught in a bad rain-snowstorm last Memorial Day, and when they couldn't drive out the sticky gumbo hills on the Forest Service road, they dismantled the ranch gates and came on through, cutting axle-deep ruts in places, sliding off the two-track road and gouging holes in the slough bottom, then tore down the corrals to get poles to put under their wheels for traction to get unstuck.

"Why is it," he says, "that any jerk with a four-wheel drive thinks he can go anywhere, tear up the country, leave his damage and trash. I'd like to find out where they live in Denver and camp out in their backyard and leave my trash."

Dad calls. "Hey! Laur! Your sister sent me a juicer. I won't use the damn thing. You want it?"

"You should try it. Carrot juice is a heal-all."

He doesn't say "yech," but I can hear it anyway.

Blue and I go west into the wind, skirting the slough where frogs belt out a beauteous song. Sprigs of green rise beneath each bush. Lichen and silver sage and grass all come alive in the shelter of the knee-high brush.

Nearing the county road, I spy something white. It has been too warm for it to be remaining snow. An empty plastic engine-oil bottle. Quaker State. Green lid. I pick it up. Five steps farther I see another white eye-catcher stuck against stiff sage branches: a disposable and dirty baby diaper. Blue sniffs, exploring the foreign scent. "Nasty!" I warn him and pick it up by a tab and carry it gingerly. I puzzle over the kind of person who would open the window on a moving car and fling a dirty diaper onto the ground. Someone with the IQ of pond scum. Along the way I also pick up a length of rusty barbwire, and a twine drug off the feed ground by a heifer's foot. Laden I pass by the burn barrel to unload my finds before going back indoors.

Mick drifts toward bed. I settle in an easy chair and drape myself with an afghan. Blue circles a spot in the carpet, tramping down a bed. He spins one way and then the other. Finally, he plops down with a huge sigh and curls himself head to tail and sleeps. If I stir, he opens one eye. If I settle, he closes his eyes and sleeps again. The house seems oddly quiet; then I realize that no fire crackles in the wood stove.

Thursday, May 8th

The early hours speak in soft, unhurried tones. My mind shifts from dreams to reality, my body begins to stir, a slow process, each nerve ending rediscovering connections to make me open my eyes, stretch, move a leg, an arm, roll over, walk. Sensation reborn every day: skin against sheet, dim light against eyes, hair through fingers. Awakening.

Mick has already built a fire. I ask him what he has to do today. He begins a litany of chores.

I laugh. "Whoa, I didn't mean what you had to do for the next month. I just mean for today."

"That is for today," he says, half serious, half teasing.

Our work gears are rusty. We've been in low range chugging through winter for months. Though not a forty-hour, eight-to-five workweek, ranching has its own rigidity. There are no days off, not even weekends. No sick leave. No benefits. No vacations. No retirement plan. No perks. No health insurance. No camaraderie of fellow workers. No gold watch at the end of fifty years. If you're lucky, you manage to hang on to the home place and pass it on to your children.

Blue barks, herding the cattle around while Mick feeds. When Mick returns, I fix him a snack. He rests a few moments, checking out the weather channel to see if the major storms knocking the New Mexico-Texas area are pushing north. Our sky refills with menacing clouds, the air damp and chill. Mick hits the road to go up-country for the never-ending and thankless task of pulling out dams.

Before lunch I mix up a pan of fruit bars full of dried apricots, pears, prunes, raisins, and walnuts. The smell of cooking fruit and brown sugar fills the kitchen. When the bars cool, I sift powdered sugar over them, decorating each lump and hump in the gold-brown confection like God's hand diverting snow squalls over hills and ridges. I pop a small bar in my mouth and let the sugar melt before savoring the sweet flavors.

Leaving as soon as he has eaten dinner, Mick returns to the Mikels' to tear out more beaver dams. The backed-up pond water has engulfed his head gates and ditches. It's such a laborious, backbreaking, cold, miserable task. When I first went to work for Mick, I chided him for killing beaver. He did not argue with me. He simply gave me the task of tearing out the dams, day after day, until I tired of the job and took the .22 in hand.

In the early afternoon, I start out with a halter in hand, my pocket full of crunchies, to find my horse.

Brandy grazes grass shoots hidden in the sage on the hill. He stands and stares, but he will not come to me. I walk to him, talking. He reaches out and takes two cubes from my hand, then lifts his neck and curls his nose upward, teeth bared, an equine grin, a snarly-looking smile. He hangs back on the halter rope, not exactly balky, but sluggish. He does not want to leave his buddies.

After tying Brandy to a trailer hitch, I search the little storage shed for my shoeing tools: rasp, nippers, hoof knife, hoof pick. I bend over double asking Brandy for his left front foot. He hesitates, then complies, lifting his leg with a gargantuan sigh that says, "I hate this."

I pound his hoof with the side of the nippers, knocking out a compressed hunk of mud and manure. Using the pick I dig out the rest of the dirt stuck in the crevices of the sole, around the squishy pliable frog, alongside the bars and bulbs of his heel. When his foot is clean, I begin the arduous trimming. I gouge here and there, chopping off hunks as best I can, leaving the heels high, dubbing off his long toes. Going beneath the hard and scaly exposed sole, I use the curved knife to slice the softer, whiter, more easily cut layers. Then I rasp the bottom of the hoof smooth and level.

Within five minutes I am soaked wet with sweat and my legs quiver like Jell-O. Fifteen years ago I could shoe my horse alone. Now it takes every ounce of energy I have just to trim one hoof.

I move to his right front and ask for his foot. Brandy rears, fighting the halter, jerking back, a thousand pounds of spooked horse against a solid trailer. I jump out of the way, then stand still, whispering, "Whoa! What's the matter, son?"

He has wrenched his neck and stands shaking, blowing, snorting, his eyes rolling, staring at the trailer. A cardboard box has fallen in the commotion. I close the door so Brandy will not imagine any other boogers in the dark hole.

Halfway through the trimming he blows again. "Are you really scared or just pissed because I have you tied?"

Eyes wide, ears at attention, he blows a rolling snort through quivering nostrils.

"Okay, now, one more try."

As I release his foot, Brandy blows a third time, breaking the hook on his lead rope. He flies over backward. Spinning away, he stands still, shakes his head, then lowers his neck to munch on the new green grass by the wood block.

I grit my teeth to keep from cussing. He stands placidly until I approach on his right side, then shies. Is he going blind in his right eye? I use extra care as I comb out his mane and tail, the sorrel-gold hairs glisten in the sun like strings of melted pennies. I curry his dry, flaky coat, and handfuls of old hair float to the ground. I collect the piles and wad them all together to form a ball the size of a grapefruit, then place it in the prickly wild-rose patch where the birds will find building material for their nests.

Cautious bringing pad and saddle to Brandy, I lead him through the first two gates, tighten his cinch, checking it twice before I put my toe into the stirrup and swing into the saddle. Nervous, he sidesteps, then stops and stands until I readjust my weight, and we move off. Tense beneath me he walks, his head swiveling to catch sight of anything that moves. He spots cattle trailing along the pasture fence a quarter mile away and stops to stare.

"Okay," I say. "Just the heifers." He moves on and I ease him into a shuffling jog trot. A half mile downriver we stop to open a gate to go into Arrowhead Ranch. I tighten his cinch another notch. He has lost weight, enough so I can see his backbone and ribs. Brandy too is getting old.

"If you're thinking about dumping me," I say, "please pick someplace soft."

We wend through the willows to the river where several anglers gear up to fish the stream. Brandy hears the zzzztttt of line being pulled from a reel. Then someone opens a car door, and a warning bell spooks him into a prancing dance.

"Stop!" I whisper and slap him on the shoulder. "It's only people."

Brandy's heart pounds beneath the saddle, and I stop on a flat spot in the shade of a pine to let him blow. After a winter in virtual solitude, everything scares him.

At the Homestead Cabin I find Rudy fixing the plumbing.

"How're you, Rudy?"

"Okay. Okay. Had me a fight with two dogs. Seen 'em? They was chasin' horses in the corral. A Chow and a Malamute thing. I got 'em run off."

"Get your gun next time."

"Hell, I hate to shoot some kid's dog."

"Can't help that. These are probably the same ones who were running stock at Neukirch's."

"I called them folks at the highway. Ain't theirs. But that lady said those dogs had been at her place running her horses."

"Rudy, shoot them."

"You are a hardhearted woman," he teases. "Working with you is a hard job."

"Don't I know it? I'll ride round the back way and check the inflows to the lakes." I wave good-bye and ride away.

Underfoot, the ground glistens green. Brandy moves smoothly from trot to lope to walk. Ducks splash up off a river pool, quacking. Ground squirrels scurry across our path. A V-line of geese honk over, heading for the lakes. Though the wind blows cold, I untie my scarf, unpin my hair, and gig Brandy into an all-out gallop across a flat stretch of meadow. Such small freedom makes me dream of riding on and never looking back.

Friday, May 9th

The clouds that gathered yesterday collected in groups to wrap dawn in a damp overcoat. It smells like rain. My friend Dianna arrives with oatmeal-cranberry-sunflower seed cookies as a gift. We shuffle coats and packs and gear, deciding what to take on our hike. At the river we help one another climb through a four-strand barbwire fence and stop to listen to an ouzel giving a single bird concert in the culvert that takes the river water under the county road. We spot the first fragile wild flowers hidden beneath some brush and smell the damp perfume of pine needles in dense timber. Then in the meadows tiny white flowers bloom through the old grass like stars fallen from the sky. For two and a half hours we tramp and talk. The easy camaraderie of women makes me wonder why women and men cannot converse in the same light-hearted way.

With supper dishes done, I ask Mick if he wants to go to the cabin with me for water and a walk.

On the way up-country, I work hard at conversation, asking Mick about his day, asking if there is anything I can do to help him. He does not want to talk. I try another ploy to draw him out.

"Let's make love tonight."

"No." His voice is soft, but as surprising as a slap.

"I have too many things on my mind," he says in apology, "too many problems. Too many worries."

I shove my hurt deep down inside where it throbs like a giant toothache. When we reach the cabin, Mick says, "Let's get out of the wind."

We enter quietly, as if we were going into a church. My heart crumbles and my mouth feels full of dust, my throat parched. Mick climbs the stairs to the loft. I get the broom from behind the bathroom door and begin to sweep up the dead flies littering the linoleum, letting the simple task loosen the tightness in my chest.

"I didn't bring you here to work," Mick says as he comes back downstairs. "I'll go fill the jug," he says and walks out.

I pile the desiccated flies and dust in a corner by the sunroom door and leave the broom leaning there. At the spring water rushes from a black plastic pipe. The jug spurts full, and Mick replaces the cap, snugs it tight, and lugs the water can to the four-wheeler and secures it to the front bumper with a bungee cord.

"Want a ride?"

"No thanks. I'll walk."

"How about Blue-boy?" Mick asks.

Blue wags his stub tail, but makes no move to jump up on the four-wheeler.

"Okay. Walk with Mama."

"Mick, why can't we ever talk to each other?"

"Nothing to say, I guess." He drives away.

How different this evening walk, fraught with conflict, compared to the comfort of hiking and talking with Dianna in the morning.

"I don't get it," I confide to Blue. "I just don't get it."

He listens and licks my hand.

Saturday, May 10th

Before first light I creep from the house so I won't wake Mick. I shush Blue and close the kitchen door slowly. The moon and stars worship in the western sky, but the east glows with brightening silver that backlights the trees and silhouettes the heifers who rise from their bed ground in the willows and fan out to feed. Heavy frost sparkles off the ground and the fence poles. It hurts to breathe the knife-edged breeze out of the northwest so I turn east into the sunrise and give the wind my back and hooded head. Blue comes and goes like a ghost animal, racing past in a milky blur, disappearing in the gloom, then reappearing, startling me. I follow the two-rut track downriver, walking quickly to get blood singing in my veins and send warmth to my stiffening fingers and toes.

Below the eon-crafted bank, the river runs like a dull pewter ribbon twined in the hair of tall willows. A pair of geese materializes as dark cutouts on the water. One climbs the bank, flaps wings with no sound, and settles to preen. Far off, the Trophy Lakes at Arrowhead glow side by side, twin mirrors of burnished silver, unruffled by wind from this long distance. A robin offers new notes. A chickadee presents repeating peeps. Bit by bit, like an orchestra tuning up, the birds greet the day.

Back at the house, I ignore my inner wife voice that says I should do my domestic chores. Instead, I sit and write. Papers spread out around me at the table like decorative fans. Mick comes and goes on his rounds of chores. We talk the little talk of trying to be friends again. Work at Arrowhead Ranch and a trip to Buena Vista with Carol for clubhouse and cleaning supplies eats away my afternoon.

Late, just before dark, Mick, Blue, and I walk up the driveway to the county road. We chat in an amicable way. With every kind word we exchange, I forgive an unkindness. Crossing the road onto the national forest, we each pick a worn trail on a two-rut track and walk side by side. Mick spots a tick on my sock, and I stop to pick it off, crushing it between my thumbnail and forefinger. I walk with more care, trying not to brush the sage, ducking under low branches, watching where I place my feet, reminding myself to give Blue a tick check when we get home.

At a division fence separating the forest from Mick's private deeded ground, we follow a game trail up the line and there in the damp duff overshadowed by budding aspen we discover the first pasqueflowers. Overwhelmed by the delicate beauty, the lavender petals, bright yellow centers, fuzzy stems and leaves, I cup my hands around one, not quite touching, but wanting to be close to something so resilient and vulnerable. How such ephemeral things survive long hard winters confounds me.

We walk steadily uphill. I watch Mick's upright back, his flat, lean butt, and his trim long legs. He is another creation beyond my ken.

On and on we tramp through aspen and pine, making our way along a tumbledown fence with pitch pine posts and rusty wire, across the dirt road, through the gate, and home. A coyote's wail way to the east stops us. Soon the bitches will den up with their pups. Soon the education of the young ones will begin: where to run and hide, how to hunt, when to tip back heads and sing full-throated, with complete abandonment. If only I could be as wily and tough, as adaptable and accepting as a coyote.

Sunday, May 11th

Mother's Day dawns cool but clear. Mick is subdued about my leaving again, so I also remain quiet.

Along Highway 9, I see a hundred or more buffalo grubbing the land in search of nonexistent grass. In Hartsel many pickups park at the restaurant and store. At Wilkerson Pass an unusual-looking, newly completed earth-ship house boasts a "for sale" sign. In lower, warmer Lake George, the country speaks spring. Green grass grows everywhere. The aspens proffer new leaves to the sun. Florissant still seems sleepy, and the curvy canyon road contains few cars. Divide is a different story. Early traffic headed for the gambling in Cripple Creek piles up at the town's lone stoplight. Woodland Park, too, bustles with cars, RVs, campers, trucks, people.

Dad says he's been eating well, sleeping well, and even driving. He played poker Wednesday night with the boys, attended a VFW meeting on Thursday, went out for drinks at the Thunderhead, took Mom out for dinner at Crystola, and raked some pine straw in the yard until he tired. His weight is holding at 156.

Dad battles the traffic to Cripple Creek. At the casino's buffet luncheon we toast Dad's peachy glow with complimentary champagne. He plays the dollar slots and loses a hundred bucks. Then, as if orchestrated by the gods, he wins a hundred and twenty dollars. I scold him into keeping what he lost, but he insists on gambling the twenty dollars in quarters before we go. Gambler Frank reminds me of a sweet-starved child staring at candy in the window of a confection shop.

When we stop at the store to rent a video, the sleet we fought coming out of the mountains turns to snow. A young woman soliciting for supplies for the Community Cupboard flags Dad. When he returns outside the store, he piles supplies into her cart and stuffs a handful of bills into the donation can. Tears blossom and spill down my cheeks. Mom holds my hand.

After supper and the movie, Mom turns on the outside lights that illuminate the backyard, the buried deck, the falling snow. We stand together, arms around each other, watching the world turn whiter. We say unspoken prayers.

We find Dad propped up in bed, many pillows under his head because he cannot sleep lying down. He looks like a sphinx, solemn and wise as an ancient Egyptian. I kiss him on the chest and rub his shoulders as he says, "Ummmm," over and over.

I kiss Mom, then seek my own bed. I listen intently. When the furnace and humidifier and refrigerator click off, I hear snow falling on the roof and kissing the windowpanes. Winter returns.

Monday, May 12th

I slip from the cocoon of sleep and walk half-awake to part the curtains and view the white wonderland. The house sleeps. I slide back under the covers and squirm until I find the warm place my body had been. I do not sleep again, but my eyelids droop and close, only to flutter open so I can stare at the ticking clock beside me.

As I talk to Mick on the telephone, I stare out Dad's den window. "Four inches easy, maybe five, but the streets are wet and bare."

"Nothing here," he reports, "wind and a skif."

"Still battling the beaver?"

"Hell, yes. The sons-of-bitches!"

"Catch any?"

"Only a foot, and I hate that. I hate having to trap them or kill them."

"I know, but you've got to do something."

"I know. It's them or me. They may win."

I walk uphill, around the block, savoring the sight of snow stoles on all the trees. On County Road I pass the yard where Sunshine, the burro, once lived. Dad and I loved bringing her carrots and horse treats. Foundered and sore-footed, her feet had grown out like eighteenth-century shoes. She could hardly stand, but she would bray when we called to her and hobble over to the fence, taking our offerings with velvet lips. When we walked on, she would bray again, begging our return. Sunshine is gone now. Someone tore down the shed where she sheltered and encased the yard in chain link fence. Farther on, large lots with big ponderosa pines once pastured several horses that had a wooden stable and an antique claw-footed bathtub for a watering trough. The horses are gone now. The trees felled, the earth bulldozed, and now concrete foundations wait for two new houses. When I reach the road's end and turn to retrace my steps, softening snow plops off the trees.

We drive down the pass and out to Peterson Air Force Base where Mom and Dad get prescriptions refilled. Going through the gates on the military base feels both like a homecoming and strange territory to me. An Air Force base boasts a neat cleanliness that doesn't exist elsewhere. People, in and out of uniform, look sharply well dressed. Children act well behaved and respectful. Part of me misses the order and sense of security I feel when I return to the long-frayed roots of being an Air Force brat.

Running late, Dad speeds across town to Penrose Hospital. We rush into his surgeon's office only to find out that the doctor has been called into emergency surgery. Distraught, Dad sighs. He wanted to get this appointment over with. We chat with the receptionist and leave her a copy of the list of questions we had for the doctor. Dad asks her what the doctor has scheduled on the 27th of May. She says, "Nothing."

"Good," Dad says, "Pencil me in. Tell Doc that's when I'd like to have the operation."

"You seem determined," she says and writes Frank Wagner in the blank space on the calendar.

After supper at home, Dad starts the dishes while Mom and I gossip over empty supper plates. Dad wants to watch baseball and WGN news, so Mom and I retreat to the family room to watch *If These Walls Could Talk*, a drama of women faced with unwanted pregnancies.

As I rewind the film, Mom says, "I'm so lucky I had three normal pregnancies and three normal children, and never had to face the problem of an unwanted child. I wanted all my babies. You girls were all planned."

"You think we were normal?" I ask, laughing.

"Well, all three of you were when you were born. I don't know about now."

I cannot sleep. I'm too cool. Too warm. My pillow is too soft, too lumpy. My back aches. My stomach churns. Life and death. Life and death. My miscarriages haunt me. So does my hysterectomy. So does the knowing that I will have no children to be with me when I'm old. Dilemmas. Sorrow. So few joys. So little celebration. My last thought as I fall asleep is that I'm glad I had no children. Seeing sons and daughters hurt or struggling or suffering would be more than I could bear.

Tuesday, May 13th

I slip into my parents' bedroom. Mom says, "I hear you, Little Mouse."

"I came to say good-bye."

"Already?"

"Yes. I gotta go."

"I was going to get up and have coffee with you."

"No. Stay put. Snuggle in."

I bend down to hug her and breathe in her warm fragrance. There is no other scent like that of my mother.

"You smell good," I tell her.

"I do? Thanks."

Tousle-haired and bleary-eyed, Mom's hands feel frail but silken in mine.

"Love you. I'll call."

"Okay, Sweet Pea. Drive carefully."

Dad waves from the doorway and I blow him kisses as I drive down the street into the bright morning.

I have only been gone from the ranch two and a half days, but it feels like four months. During lunch Mick and I talk nonstop like new lovers. We have missed each other and say so. He rests while I do the dishes, then he is off to work again.

We walk together after a makeshift supper of macaroni and cheese. No barbs tonight. No digs. We act gentle with one another, and my love for Mick smolders again. We hit a north-south fence line and follow it south, commenting on dead wood, elk tracks, and a few brave wild flowers. The wind is unforgiving, our double coats and gloves a sad necessity. The land we cross to reach home is not Mick's.

"Someday there will be a house here," he says.

"I know."

"I won't be able to swallow that."

"Do you have a choice?"

"Maybe they will build up high where the road access is easy, and we won't see them."

"Maybe."

The eighty acres of poor, cracked soil with a bit of grass, some decent timber, and some sage rolls flat on the west side. A huge arroyo cuts through the land. Two car corpses lie half-buried in silt, the ZD license plates of Park County still visible. One a Dodge, one a Chevy, circa 1940s. We make up a story about bank robbers in Fairplay who escaped this way and ran aground. "There is probably five million dollars buried in those cars," I say.

Mick laughs. "Probably five million pack rat turds."

Our coupled laughter echoes like rain pouring out of a summer sky. We have been so long without laughter, so parched, so thirsty for joy. We do not talk much more. We do not touch or hold hands.

I pick up an old wire, some metal, a piece of a bumper, and a shock absorber that I find strewn across the pasture. Mick opens the gate for me and I toss the junk onto the edge of the dump above the river.

When I slide into bed, seeking my place beside Mick, he rolls over in his sleep and wraps his arm around me. I cringe for a moment, afraid of loving such an uncertain future. I breathe into relaxation and whisper my old childhood prayers. I blink at the dark sky outside the window, but all I see are a few ordinary stars. Hale-Bopp is no more.

Wednesday, May 14th

With a fleeting promise of rain later in the day, low clouds hug the mountains.

"How cold is it?" Mick asks.

"Twenty-six."

"Pretty chilly. Won't grow much grass at this rate."

"Tired of feeding?"

"Damn weary of it all right now."

"The grass will come."

"Think so?"

"Are you off to wage war again?" I ask.

"Again."

"Maybe you should call the DOW and ask them to remove their recalcitrant beaver from your ditches."

"Yeah, sure," Mick says as if contact with government officials would be worse than dealing with the dam builders himself.

"They're just doing their thing," he says, meaning, of course, the beaver, not the DOW.

"I know. Can I help?"

"Today?"

"Well, not today. I have to go with Scott to the hatchery at Hagen's."

"See."

"I know. I'm sorry I'm so busy. I can't help it. It's my job. They pay me. I have to be there."

He says nothing.

I work away from home so we can afford to stay on the ranch. One third of my salary goes to pay the exorbitant cost of health insurance. One third of it goes to help with the monthly bills. And I try to invest the other third in savings. Instead of explaining, I drop the subject, preferring silence to the stubborn tugging over this old bone of contention.

On the drive to Buena Vista, Scott and I talk nonstop about ideas for Arrowhead Ranch. We shuffle suggestions like a deck of cards. Playing our hands against one another. Discarding ideas that won't help our immediate situation. Holding on to those that will.

Hagen's Western Fishery sits below a rugged hill on the banks of the Arkansas River, which rushes headlong through rock-walled and boulder-strewn canyons. Spring-fed trout-rearing ponds are bordered by green lushness with a sprinkling of wild flowers. Blackbirds hover and flit around the pool edges, some of which are covered with netting to prevent burglary by osprey, owls, herons, and raccoons. Scott and I descend a steep, pebbled trail and walk along the roadway between the aerated ponds and the roar of the river. Humidity hangs in the air like the dampness in an after-shower bathroom.

Hal Hagen waits in his office armed with folders of projects he has done with Aquatic Alternatives, the arm of his business that concentrates on riparian habitat. Hal has provided fish for stocking Arrowhead's stream and lakes since the fly-fishing resort opened in the early 1990s. Passionate about fish and his own opinions, he has a renegade reputation in the field. I like that about him, like the wildness that surfaces when he expounds upon his ideas about the environment, ecosystems, and the artful business of raising and stocking fish.

After introductions, the conversation drifts toward holistic resource management, a concept I'm familiar with, one that Hal has worked with for years, one that Scott is just embracing. The semantics go over my head, so I wander over to watch the river water dashing headlong into midstream boulders and the rocky banks. Getting higher with runoff, the Arkansas already hosts colorful rafts crammed full of adventure seekers that plunge past in a steady parade. Oblivious to the intrusion in her world, a female mallard paddles for the far bank. Since she has no power to change the course of human interference, she accepts it. Her calmness calms me.

Hours pass. The conversation never slows. It just changes direction as we meander past each pond: browns, rainbows, golds, Donaldson steelhead rainbows, Snake River cutthroat hybrids, brood stock, fry, fingerlings, proportionate feeds, aquatic weed mass, spawning channels. What can and can't be done? What population can Arrowhead waters support successfully? What happens when hatchery-reared fish are stocked on top of a wild population?

Mick and I share a simple supper, then he is off on the four-wheeler to work again. Near dark, Blue and I head west hoping to run into Mick coming home from the upper ranch. Black-streaked low clouds battle a hard wind. A few sprinkles sting my face. Mere shapes against the pale green earth, the horses graze far to the west. The heifers and calves spill off a hill across the pasture bucking and kicking. The storm blows in, and a brief wet sheet slaps me from behind. The calves scurry like quail into a shed, crawling under wagons, squeezing between walls and wheels to find shelter as the heifers bunch up alongside in the thick willows.

Mick never comes. Blue and I make a fast dash for the house. I settle on the couch to watch for Mick out the living room windows. Blue waits for him on the stoop. Soon we see the lights of the four-wheeler bouncing up the road. I stand at the window waving while Blue dances circles.

Cold and tired, Mick goes straight to bed. A whoosh of sleet and wind hits the house. We could use a good hard storm to soak up the already dry earth. But when I join Mick, there is no subtle pattering on the windowpanes. Only an odd quiet and the song of the frogs that I believe are calling on the gods for moisture. The world turning green won't stay that way long without rain.

Thursday, May 15th

On my chilly predawn walk to the east fence, the air smells damp, but when I kick the earth, dust floats up to tickle my nose. The hay at the cabin stack yard is gone. Mick turns Nate out onto the meadow with the yearling heifers, and marks the event on the calendar with bold pencil strokes: BULL OUT. Today he will shuffle his Hereford bulls around, putting Mucho Money out with the two-year-old heifers and Beaucoup Bucks in the corral with Pauncho. I named the fancy bulls after Mick paid a pretty penny for them at the National Western Stock Show. Beaucoup Bucks the Bully was injured last breeding season and is no longer functional. He, along with Pauncho of the dinky dead calf, will go to the sale yard soon.

A breeze bucks cold-backed off the mountains. When I arrive at Arrowhead Ranch, I visit with our guest, Regina West, who stays in the bunkhouse with her dog, Breck. Regina recently lost her husband and has come back to enjoy the solitude and fishing they both loved. We talk about the strange ways of life and death, aging and acceptance, then she leaves for the lakes.

I tackle bookwork, type letters, and return calls. Expecting Regina to be back for lunch, I check my watch often. As hours tick by, I become concerned. Just as I prepare to go find her, she returns flushed and excited. She had not had much luck all morning and could not coax anything into taking her fly. When she decided to give up, she noticed swallows swirling over the lower end of the Upper Trophy Lake. She investigated and numerous big trout were feeding just below the surface.

"I threw everything in my tackle box at them. I almost gave up then decided to try a Stauffer's Midge. On my second cast, I had a beautiful twenty-one-inch brown. Oh, lovely."

"Good for you."

"Now, if I don't catch anything else the rest of the day, I'll still be happy."

Regina gives me the description of the fly pattern she used to tack up on the clubhouse bulletin board. A flock of swallows dart and drop in swoops around the bunkhouse eaves trying to decide whether or not to call this place home. Their chirruping cries bring real spring to mind, for swallows seldom come before the end of frosty days because they need enough warmth and sun for insects to hatch, enough rain to have mud to daub their nests.

All day Mick cleaned ditches and cut sods to get the irrigation turned on. I fix our supper, and when the dishes are done, we walk up the road to the Forest Service land and skirt a hillside through the thick pines to reach a subdivision road. The entire ridge south of the ranch has been chopped into thirty-five-acre parcels. For many years we hiked through here with little sign of other people. Now there are camp trailers parked in the trees. Deep scarring ruts mark the road where I used to come and gather shaggy-mane mushrooms. Growing here in profusion, the knobby-headed fungus pushed up through the red dirt and shale like resurrected alien beings. Now, with the trailers and people, we feel uneasy, as if we are strangers in a strange land. We hurry away and cross back onto the ranch, crawling over the barbed wire fence where the elk have knocked loose the two top staples.

Across the valley, at a home under construction, a dog howls. We stop to stare and listen to the unwelcome foreign sound. Apparently chained and lonely, the dog bays sad and mournful like a hound. Though it does us no good to worry about his plea for attention, we do. Then the song of frogs takes over the evening like an asked-for blessing.

Friday, May 16th

I munch on a toasted apple-strudel muffin as I head to town. Several hundred yards from the highway fence, a herd of cow elk stands or lies in a bunched circle. In the middle of the day, in the middle of an open flat, is unusual behavior for elk. With more and more building in remote sites, the elk have few hidden places left to go. It troubles me to see them so exposed, vulnerable, and unconcerned.

After running errands and buying my annual fishing license at the hardware store, I drive home searching the flat for the elk. They have not moved, but seem content to stay clustered in the sun.

"How was your morning?" I ask Mick.

"I finally got him. Caught him. Shot him. Sad to say, but had to be done."

"Did Blue behave?"

"He was the perfect gentleman. I told him to sit and stay, and he did."

"Problems?"

"I had to tear out all the dams again. I've been up there fourteen days in a row."

"Tired of it, aren't you?"

"Yep. Sick and tired."

We are quiet a moment, then Mick adds, "I dusted off my saddle and loaded it on the buggy. Meet you outside."

We load my saddle, bridle, spurs, halter, and pad onto the trailer with his, and I add my shoeing box and Brandy's E-Z boots, hoof pick, curry-comb, and brushes.

We bump across the pasture, Blue barking alongside until I shush him. We park by the hay-lot shed. "Not a bale left," Mick says. "All that was left was a pack rat's nest and the rat, and the black cat got him."

"He did? Good."

Then I ask, "Can you stretch the remaining big bales of hay?"

"Yes. We're gonna make it. There's enough grass now so the horses and yearlings can get by. I still have to feed the pairs awhile longer."

"Feel good to be nearly done?"

"You bet."

"Is winter really over?" I ask.

"Not quite. But I'm getting more used to the idea."

We unhook the two-wheel buggy from the four-wheeler and go in search of the horses.

Haltered and in hand, the horses follow me to the four-wheeler where

I sit on back to lead them while Mick drives. A minor ruckus breaks out with the mares, and for a moment, we are in the middle of squealing, shying, kicking horseflesh. "Whoa," Mick and I holler.

"What was that all about?" I ask.

"Candy's horsing."

"Well, when she wants attention, she gets it."

Amigo and Brandy trot behind the four-wheeler with tiny puffs of dust drifting up from their feet. I parcel out the rope slack according to how close or far away they stay.

At the cabin Mick drops me off so I can lead the horses through the boggy trail shortcut while he must drive around the long way. As I cross the spring creek, the rumble of hooves causes Brandy and Amigo to shy and wheel around. I hold the lead ropes tight saying "whoa, whoa, whoa!"

Candy and Cookie race full tilt down the road bucking every couple of leaps. Even old Jill is galloping hard to keep up. Brandy and Amigo rear, trying to pull free and join the melee.

"Whoa. Enough is enough."

I manage to hang onto them, the ropes hot in my hands, and coax them the other fifty feet to the shed where Mick waits shaking his head.

"They sound like a freight train. I've never seen those mares run like that. Did you see Candy buck?"

The mares plow to a stop by the stack yard, snorting and blowing. I give Amigo to Mick and tie Brandy to a stout corner post. Candy comes over to investigate as we curry and saddle. Brandy is her boyfriend, even though he looks like a little peanut next to her draft horse bulk. She lips his hips and squeals. I shoo her away, but she comes right back, arching her tail and pissing, her vulva twitching.

"She's horsin' all right," Mick says.

"Well, why doesn't she go horse somewhere else? She's a wreck waiting to happen."

We check cinches, swing into our saddles and ride southwest. Mick still looks like he was born on a horse. I stop so Brandy can get a drink of icy water at the spring pipe.

Taking turns to open gates, we wend our way through tall willows and cross the river on rocky bars. The water is up and discolored by runoff, but still only knee-deep on the horses. We skirt a hillside, staying low out of the wind, then cross the river again, this time on a dirt-filled road over a giant culvert. The water soars through the pipe into a waterfall, then into a deep pool. I look for trout, but see no shadows darting away. We ride up a rock-studded ridge, then down into a grassy bottom where the old homestead buildings nestle. In this protected spot, it is green. The willows are still leafless, but here and there fuzzy grayness pinpoints the first pussy willow blossoms. The beaver have worked this stretch of river hard. It is lined with dams every several hundred feet, and the ponds glisten in the sunlight. Here, where the dams create no problems for irrigating the hay, Mick gives the beaver peace to create their own watery world.

We ride on, making our way through the locked gate onto the national forest, then through a closed wire gate and across Rough and Tumble Creek, which runs high and roily with mud. Brandy lowers his head and sniffs the water, then snorts twice before putting a foot in the current. No campers cluster around the creek this early in the season and I like that we are the only humans around.

As we climb up out of the creek bottom, Mick lurches to one side in his saddle.

"Mick, what's wrong?"

"My guts hurt."

"Want to get off?"

"No."

We ride a while longer following game trails in the hillside sage.

"Mick, what is it?"

"I don't know. Hurts like hell."

I stop and dismount. "Come on. Get off."

He's shaky and white when he steps off his horse.

"Where does it hurt?"

He pushes in on his lower left abdomen. My first guess is a flare up of his diverticulitis. My second is an old hernia he never had fixed.

As we volley diagnoses back and forth, the color gradually seeps back into his face.

"Better," he says.

"Can you walk?"

"Sure."

We walk side by side, stepping through the brush leading our horses.

"What happened?"

"Don't know. It just started hurting."

"Did you lift anything heavy this morning?"

"Sure. Sod. At least a million of 'em."

"Well, see!"

He gives me a dark, shut up, do-not-nag-me eyeballing.

"I'm not going to scold you," I apologize. "I'm just saying that's probably what it is."

"I'm getting old, Laur."

"Can't be helped."

"Can't do the work anymore."

"I know." His admission tightens around my throat like a noose.

"Let's ride," he says.

"Can you?"

"Hell, yes. Unless I just lay myself out for the coyotes tonight."

"Is it better?"

"Yeah, I'm okay."

He swings up and trots away, then slows to a walk until I catch up.

"Sorry I'm ruining your day," he says.

"You're not. I'm just happy you wanted to come with me to see the country."

We talk idly, sometimes dismounting so Mick can ease his pain. Through thick stands of tall ponderosas, we climb up the backbone of the ridge south of the ranch. The horses' hooves crunch through the dry needles and pinecones. A half dozen of the giant trees within easy reach of one another are dead. Their needles turned brown, they look like desert skeletons. Some kind of beetle? Maybe the drought? Porcupine damage mars small trees where the bark eaters have gnawed off upper branches, girdling them, and causing them to die. Tiny white asterlike flowers bloom close to the ground clutching the soil. Miniature pink blossoms perch on pincushion cactus.

On top of Bull Elk Hill we dismount to survey the 360-degree view. Behind us to the northwest is Cow Elk Meadow, a little grassy opening surrounded on one side by aspen groves and on two sides by thick black timber. After our discovery of a cow elk that had been mauled by a bear, I had Mick remove her ivory teeth from the upper jaw so I could make them into a necklace for his mother. Though every scrap of flesh and hair and hide has long since succumbed to scavengers and the elements, her scattered, whitened bones remain. To the southwest is Tumble Creek and Jones Hill, a heavily timbered ridge slated for clear-cut logging. To the direct south lies the wide-open flat vista of Long Park that houses two little lakes. When Mick was a boy, the ponds held spring-fed water all summer long. Now one lake is bone-dry. The other has a thin layer of muddy snow melt in the bottom. To the east rises the far-off mirage of Pikes Peak, which shimmers white against blue skies and the dark blue of lower lying mountains. To the northeast, the Trophy Lakes at Arrowhead Ranch shine like cut-glass decorations in the gold-brown pasture bottoms. From here we have an eagle's eye view, and no fishermen line the shores this afternoon. To the north, just a little glimpse of red and shiny silver, we squint to see our ranch buildings and the shadowed hulk of Black Mountain rising above them. We stand side by side and stare at the still pristine beauty. We ache to see the country changing because of the influx of people, buildings, construction, and development. We are selfish to want it as our personal domain. But loyal and dedicated caretakers choke on the prospect of change. Every new person tips the balance against nature. Every new home means a loss of vital habitat. Increased traffic means disruption of established migration routes. Slow invasion gnaws at our unhappy hearts, eats away at our roots.

"Better look while you can," Mick says. "It won't last. It will get worse faster than we can imagine."

"I know. I wish I could be angry, but I can't. All I feel is sadness."

We make our way down off the ridge through pine and aspen, past the gully where we cut our Christmas trees and get our firewood. Wet snow in April bent over innumerable aspens creating a Chinese puzzle of deadfall. The live trees have bitsy buds, still brown; a few more warm days, and they will unfurl and expose the pale green center of their leaves. Then the grove will grow a canopy that will grace the ground with shade and shelter. A lonely, secret spot, like a child's fairyland, this is my favorite place to find wild flowers.

At the ranch entrance I get off and open the steel gate, leading Brandy through. Our horses are soft, and the ride has sheened them with sweat. Their nostrils flare in and out like little bellows. They are old, and the first ride of the year has tired them. Mick sets out across the pasture toward the cabin, but I trot Brandy down to the ranch house to retrieve the wormer I bought for him. He whinnies like a lost colt. I chide him with the ends of the reins, tickling his ears and neck, trying to make him pay attention to the road in front of him instead of craning his neck to see where Amigo went. I tie him Western-movie style to the pole fence, run to the house, spurs clanking, grab the wormer, run back, unwind the reins, vault into the saddle, and trot off posthaste to the gate, beating Mick and the ambling Amigo by fifty feet.

"That was fast. What the hell was I doing? Sleeping, I guess. What'd you do, run?"

"No, trot." I laugh, slipping off to get the gate.

We unsaddle in silence, intent on our work. Brandy hates being wormed, and it isn't my best-loved task either. Mick sits on a plank bench and watches, trying not to grin at my doctor's demeanor.

I unwrap the plastic covering on the wormer tube and slip it and the cap into my pocket. I set the plunger for Brandy's correct weight, then squeeze until the white viscous paste shows at the tip. I hide the tube behind my back and walk up to Brandy, untie him with my left hand, then inch my way up the halter rope until I have a hold just under his chin. When the tube reaches his lip, he flings his head up and backs away. I follow, trying to keep my temper. Once. Twice. Three times. Four. On the fifth attempt, his head up in the clouds and me on tiptoe, I manage a bull's eye into his mouth and push the plunger. Brandy rolls his eyes and drops his head, mashing his teeth and squishing his tongue around the gooey stuff. I feel sorry for him, as I would for a kid given bad-tasting medicine. His canted eye says, "I hate you!"

Mick laughs. I grin, take two crunchies out of my pocket, and hand them to Brandy, palm open. He lips them up. He spits one out, but chews the other.

"There's your lollipop for being a good boy."

I turn him loose, and he joins Amigo to roll in the soft dry dirt in front of the shed.

Most of the evening I sit at my desk in the bedroom and write. Mick, having caught a second wind, is outdoors working on more of his many tasks, the kind that never seem to get done no matter how often he does them. He comes in about seven. I holler hello to him, but keep myself closeted in for another hour until my conscience pricks me saying I should be out in the living room devoting time to Mick.

"Well! Who's this?" he asks. "I didn't even know I had a wife."

"You do. She's just busy." My argument alarm goes off and tells me I'm bordering on bitchy, so I put imaginary duct tape on my mouth.

Mick is quiet. The TV drones on and on about Mark Furman and O. J. Simpson's bloody socks. Blue comes over and sticks his nose in my lap looking for a pat. When he goes to his bed in the corner of the kitchen, I follow him, kneel down, and kiss his scaly, sunburned nose.

"Night, night, sleep tight; don't let the bed bugs bite."

His blue eye opens. Unblinking, it reminds me of Moby Dick and the solemn mask of nature that hides the wise answers to all the puzzling questions of life.

Saturday, May 17th

Molly follows Blue and me downriver in the half darkness of before dawn. I don't realize she is part of my entourage until I reach the high point of land by the dump. I keep hearing an odd crying that I try to identify as a night bird before I figure out it is Molly struggling to keep up.

"Well, Little Miss Short Legs," I say.

I can hardly see her. Her gray coat blends in with the pale light that steals shadows from the sage, but her four white paws stand out like tiny reflectors from the dark ground. It looks like four disembodied cat feet are wandering the pasture in a ghostly search for self.

Visible now along its entire reach, the river has risen enough to be seen through the willows as a sashay of brightness. The soft pink blush of sun under a rim of clouds in the east promises a clear day.

Coming home, Molly lags farther and farther behind. I wait at a gate, squatting on my haunches, calling her, "Come on, Slowpoke, I'm in a hurry today." When she trots close, panting, I pick her up, place her in the cradle of my arms and continue on.

She rides like the queen of cats, balancing herself on my shoulder and arm, her tail flipping past my nose as she looks at the landscape from her high vantage point. How weird it would be to live only six inches from the ground without the benefit of height and the far view.

Mick leaves to feed the stock and load Pauncho and Beaucoup Bucks in the trailer. We are on the road by seven bound for the sale yard in Monte Vista.

Trees are leafed out in the Arkansas River Valley. The sudden green hurts my eyes and I squint at spring, the brilliance so firelike that it seems dangerous. High and rising, the river boils gray and white over black-wet boulders and sloshes against dark banks. Rafting companies are already in full swing, their parking lots full of cars and scantily clad tourists. We of the long pants, long sleeves, and multiple layers to withstand the cold never get used to seeing exposed arms, legs, and midriffs. When we do shed our long johns and pack boots in May, we feel naked until July when we begin to feel comfortable in just jeans, shirt, and light jacket as normal attire.

Climbing over Poncha Pass, we take the west side of the San Luis valley through Saguache. I doze on and off in my usual vehicle motion-enhanced sleep. Mick comments on the number of pivot irrigation systems, the fields planted with alfalfa an incredible green against the unwatered stretches of desert, which are dull gray and patched with white alkali deposits. Cattle dot the huge open reaches of landscape. We hear rumors that this valley, like ours, battles water issues and subdivisions, struggles to survive.

Searching for the turnoff to the stockyards, Mick drives past equipment dealerships, truck sales, co-ops, and potato warehouses. Chock-full of farmers and ranchers, this agricultural area seems a far cry from South Park, which has surrendered to recreation, tourism, and development.

We see the sign and pull into a graveled lot flanked by corrals, pens, and alleys. Bellering fills the air. Mick follows signs with arrows that say "cattle," and we line up behind two other trailers ready to unload. It has taken us two and a half hours to get here, but we are grateful we still have a place to sell our stock. As we wait, we watch men on foot and horseback working the pens. Cattle move every which way, calling. Blue squeaks, shivering in the back seat; he wants to get out and help work. I shush him and scratch his ears.

Mick pulls forward. Before he is fully out of the truck, a hand opens the trailer gate and turns Beaucoup Bucks and Pauncho-Bound-For-The-Burger-Factory into an alley. Another hand squirts glue onto a back tag and slaps one high up on each animal's hip. In seconds the cattle are pushed through a gate and are gone, indiscernible in the ocean of other stock.

Mick exchanges pleasantries with the woman filling out paperwork at a wooden stand built into the corral. He writes his DM brand in a blank space and signs his name, John R. Buyer.

"When will I get the check?" he asks.

"By Wednesday," she replies.

Mick checks his trailer gate and starts the truck. We pull away, and another truck and trailer pulls in behind us. There is now a line of six outfits and more vehicles are turning in off the highway. We make a wide bend around the lot, park, and get out to stretch. Mick snaps on Blue's lead and walks him over along a fence line. I sneak into the stock trailer to pee in private. When I exit the tailgate, Mick and Blue are waiting. Blue wiggles all over.

"Mama," Mick says for him, "I saw a dead lamb over there, but Daddy wouldn't let me bring it along for you."

I laugh. "Thank goodness. It probably stinks to high heaven."

We stand in the warm sun, leaning on the truck, Blue lapping water from his dish on the flatbed.

"Ready to go?" Mick asks.

"Are you sure you don't want to stay for the sale?" I ask.

"No. Let's go home."

Pulling into Salida around noon, we find enough space on a side street by McDonald's to park the truck and trailer. I go in and buy Mick his usual two cheeseburgers, fries, and Coke. We savor the sun, soaking it up like lizards on flat rocks. Mick feeds fries to Blue. Birds hop around the parking lot. Leafed out, the trees burn brilliant green. The grass, newly mown, smells sweet and is even greener. The sky is a bluer blue than I've seen for months. A breeze ruffles through the open windows, stirring napkins on the dash, messing my hair.

Mick pulls into the ranch and stops long enough to let Blue and me out to walk down the driveway to the house.

"What you gonna do?" Mick asks as he unloads a case of oil from the back of the truck.

"Clean house. Do laundry," I say.

He gives me a look that says, "I thought you just did that."

"What about you?" I ask.

"Clean corrals, haul manure."

"Sounds exciting," I tease.

Two hours later Mick comes in to rest. I'm dusting the living room, wearing sweats and an apron, my hair pulled back in a messy ponytail. Sitting in his recliner, he opens his arms to me. Feeling shy, I go over and kneel on the floor to hug him.

He kisses the top of my head. My cheek. My ear. Then tips my chin up and finds my lips.

I still have the dust rag in hand.

"I'm all dirty," I say.

"Don't care," he says and kisses me again. He lifts me under my arms and takes me by the hand into the bedroom.

"The bed's all stripped," I explain. "The sheets are in the dryer."

"Don't care." He grins while trying to figure out how to untie my apron.

"Get that thing off," he says.

"I won't undress unless you do."

He groans, but sits on the edge of the bed to pull off his boots. He smells strong like the warm earthy corral. His hands are sunburned and rough, but his touch is gentle. The sun streaming in the window feels like satin on my skin.

I want to ease the tension I feel inside, but I cannot think of anything astute or romantic to say. Instead I concentrate on the sound of Mick's heart beating near my ear, rhythmic and sure.

When he dresses again, I watch. From my curled position on the bed, he's tall, straight, indestructible, and powerful. I cannot imagine a time without him no matter how tough things get, no matter how much anger and sadness stands between us.

He leans down and kisses my naked shoulder.

"Want a blanket?" he asks.

"No, I'm fine. I'll get up in a minute."

"I love you." He leaves the room, closing the door softly.

I hear him leave the house. I know he's going back to work. I should get up to finish my chores, but I lie for a long time looking out the window at a world that has given itself over to incomprehensible green.

Sunday, May 18th

Morning breaks open clean washed and alive. At thirty-four degrees, the river runs higher, its voice deeper. The silver ribbon running through the willows swells wider, wind torn and wild gray. Pearly with the sheen of dawn light, it exudes moisture. Birds cheep from trees, and I walk fast to get back to the house by 5:30 a.m.

Mick tells me he saw an antelope on our pasture, an unusual sight since they normally don't come this far up into the timber.

At noon Mick and I share a loaf of bread still warm from the oven. Mick eyes the peach pie, but I shake my head saying, "No, it's for company."

The sunny day is studded with increasing clouds and gusty wind. The kids arrive. John has brought his three snow machines to store for the summer, and he'll take back his pop-up camper and watercraft, which have been stored all winter under a big pine tree in the yard, back to Denver.

Mary Ann enters the kitchen carrying a bouquet of fresh sunflowers and baby's breath. We hustle to put on our hiking stuff, tell the guys farewell, tell the dogs to stay, then take off for a seven-mile loop. We reach home footsore, weary, and wind blown. The guys have worked on equipment all afternoon, airing up tires on the trailer, checking brake lights and wiring.

John and Mary Ann are thinking about buying an eighty-acre piece of land from Mick so he will have some income, enough to quit running pairs year round and get out of the heavy work of winter feeding. It grows late, but we walk. Blue runs and plays with Dottie. The frogs begin their serenade. The sky, fighting off a storm all day, succumbs to black clouds and a brisk wind. In the pines and aspens I point out the first wild peas pushing up through the soil, their green stems paunchy with unopened leaves. In a few weeks their yellow flowers will bloom so profusely that the woods will be staked with golden banners. Aspen trunks have been chewed where elk foraged for bark all winter when the snow drifted too deep for them to browse. Their tracks and droppings are everywhere.

We stop in a patch of pine trees so Mick can show John and Mary Ann Jack's Camp. The light is fading now so it is hard to see, but John kneels down and runs his fingers over the carved-out letters in the weathered log. Mary Ann finds a small rusty pail with its bail handle still intact. She wants it for her patio flowers.

John teases her, "You're not taking that hunk of junk back to put on my patio."

"Yes, I am. And it's not junk, it's antique."

The last quarter mile back to the house we fight the cold wind. A subtle but noticeable change comes to John and Mary Ann. They have discovered a new intimacy with the land. An infant infatuation, but I pray it will continue to grow.

Monday, May 19th

Damp-smelling clouds of white air drift about the river and hug the mountains to the east. I walk west listening to snipes' winged flight and wakening robins. Mick feeds and travels up-country to check his yearlings and look over irrigation on the Mikels place. The river rises and an old beaver dam upstream kicks the current into the ditches and spreads water over the thirsty meadows. Mick works miracles with a shovel and some mud. He is as industrious, dedicated, and engineer-minded as the beaver, and his ongoing love-hate relationship with them is over fifty years old. When he returns for lunch, he tells me the first aspens have leaved out. A pale green haze that looks like off-color smoke lies against the dark green of spruce and pine.

In the afternoon I take on the role of an obsessive junk man. I park the rattle-trap blue Dodge pickup I use for Arrowhead Ranch at the division fence between our properties and load old fence posts, boards, rusted tin, decayed roofing, a piece of discarded tennis shoe, stove pipe, tin cans, and wads of tangled barbed wire.

I meet Rudy running the backhoe on the river road. Headed to the big oxbow in the stream where we lost the road last year, he plans to berm loads of dirt all along the banks to preserve the fill. He has been breaching beaver dams all morning in an effort to keep the river in its natural course. The water is up fifteen inches.

At the dump I unload my collected trash and catch sight of a dead calf half-hidden in old hay and baling twine. One dried eye stares up at me. The gold-and-white splotched head points north. The tiny fly wisp tail aims south. In death the calf gives cosmic directions. No flies buzz about the not yet bloated corpse. The dead calf becomes a thing of beauty, the prettiest thing by far in the gully of dead appliances, broken bedsprings, plastic sacks of garbage, and decades worth of cans, bottles, and tires. Given an ignominious burial, the calf has made me stop and ponder. The brief meditation has significant merit and that seems eulogy enough.

I spend the rest of the waning day at my clubhouse desk returning phone calls and shuffling papers before heading home to fix supper.

Monte arrives on his four-wheeler exhausted, freshly sunburned, and dirty from moving cattle horseback all day. As he gobbles pie and ice cream, we hash over the pros and cons of life at Arrowhead Ranch. I leave the guys to talk ranching and cattle, work ethic, and city intruders.

A nearly full moon graces the darkening sky by the time I take Blue up the road for a walk. We watch the heifer pairs and the Hereford bull grazing in the fading light. The peaceful tiredness that comes after a day of hard work seeps into my limbs. Leaning on the ranch gate, I watch the brightening light of the moon. Blue sits at my feet. I put my hand on his head, wishing I could read his mind to know if canine thoughts come anywhere close to mine.

Tuesday, May 20th

I sleep a sleep of restless dreams and wake up out of sorts, stiff in the shoulders and neck, with seized ankles that will not bend.

"What will you do today while I'm gone?" I ask Mick.

"Finish organizing the stuff for branding. Corrals to clean. Got to get the calf table set up, and I still need to go get the irons and propane."

"I'll come back early tomorrow so I can help you."

"Okay."

"If I leave Woodland Park at dawn, I can be back by seven."

To pass the time on the road, I listen to Michael Martin Murphey reading *The Log of a Cowboy* by Andy Adams. Stampedes. Rustlers. Wild river crossings. Indian encounters. The long, hard, slow, fifteen-to-twenty-mile-a-day rate of moving cattle from Texas to Montana. As I zip along the paved highway at fifty-five miles per hour, the amount of change that has occurred in the past 110 years seems overwhelming. Only a few shaggy buffalo bulls and the gold-and-white antelope on Glentivar flats seem part of that older time. That and the still unmolested high peaks I drive toward.

Dad looks better. He has gained back five of the twenty-five pounds he lost since his chemo and radiation sessions ended. Eileen calls, thrilled to tell us she has rented an apartment for Karen and Charlie only four blocks from her own home. Karen plans to arrive back in the Chicago area after more than a decade in Hawaii. Eileen plans to fly in on the evening of Dad's surgery and leave the following Saturday.

We head down Ute Pass to see a succession of Dad's doctors.

"Your dad's going to be just fine," the radiation oncologist tells me.

"We'll hope there is no sign of cancer at all in that esophagus," the chemotherapy physician says.

"If that nagging pain goes away after the surgery," the surgeon says, "then we will know that it has been the esophagus that was giving him the trouble. If the pain doesn't go away, then . . ." he shrugs. "It may be a small blocked artery in the heart that they missed."

We are not home very long when Mick calls. Since he never telephones, I'm immediately concerned.

"Well, I went ahead and did it," he says.

"What's that?"

"Branded the calves."

"You did!"

"The weather report said three days of rain, and I got worried about waiting because I want to move them on to better pasture. I saw the pairs close in, so I gathered, sorted, branded, and dehorned. Only about half had horns. Took me a few hours."

"Well, good for you." I know Mick worked hard to get the chore done but I'm keenly disappointed to miss the annual rite of passage from spring to summer.

Dad is working in the yard in the sprinkling rain when I hang up the phone. He comes in gasping, holding his chest.

"Dad! Same pain?"

"Yeah. It's going away now."

"Sit down. Your shirt's all wet. Is there something that needs to be done?"

"Yes. Garbage man comes tomorrow."

"Go rest. Watch the news. I can do that chore, okay?"

"Okay, Boss," he teases me.

Mom and I fill two large cans and eight big plastic sacks with pine straw, pinecones, and dead grass that have been raked into piles. The rain has stopped, and the air wafts sticky-sweet with the smell of earth and dirt and pine. I point out emerging flowers—sun-loving pussy toes, rhubarb, hens-and-chicks, tiny fairy candelabra. In the flowerbeds, bulbs planted last fall poke out of the dark soil. When we stack the full bags for pickup in the morning, Mom gestures toward the muddy ditch where a car-flattened squirrel lies dead.

"Poor little guy," Mom says.

"Sad. Do you want me to put him in the trash?"

"No. Just leave him. I'll feel better if he's in the open air rather than stuffed in darkness."

Wednesday, May 21st

A damp dawning. The color and intensity of the light stealing through the butterfly-embossed curtains in my room tells the time. Mom comes into the kitchen in a blue-green fuzzy robe, as snugly as a toy bear when I hug her good-bye. Dad leaves his paper to wave at me from the porch as I drive away. Their house is beginning to feel like a second home.

Rush-hour traffic chokes Bluebird Hill as I head out of Woodland Park. In the canyon a lone cow elk grazes and snaps her head up whenever a vehicle zooms past. Her wariness and ragged hide tells me she has a calf stashed in the close-by brush. On the flats the other side of Wilkerson Pass, five shedding buffalo bulls fan out with small bunches of antelope. The dusty, green-tinted landscape begs for rain.

I swing through Fairplay to get the mail and talk with the county assessor about our frightening property tax valuation increase: $931,000 to $1.2 million in two years.

I stop at Arrowhead to check in with Carol. She jabs the shovel she's been using into a chunk of sod she places in front of the clubhouse. One of their cows lay down in a boggy spot and got stuck. Unable to rise, the heifer bloated and died, leaving her week-old calf an orphan.

"Dave found the little bugger starving and brought him home to the corral. I talked to the puny guy and told him it wasn't his fault his mother was stupid."

"We had one get in a ditch last fall. Mick found her dead. She just rolled over and died, all four feet straight up in the air."

"Sometimes ranching just sucks," Carol says. "Worst thing, we can't even eat her."

The loss of a $500 cow puts a huge hole in their budget, but all I have to offer in sympathy is a hug.

The day stays gray and cool. Mick leaves to go check irrigation and clean more ditches. I build a fire in the kitchen stove to ward off the chill, then sit at the table and write. Twice I hear the frantic buzz of a hummingbird darting past the windows, but I cannot catch a glimpse of the tiny fast-paced creature.

When Mick comes back, he naps in his chair. When the phone rings I rush to answer so the noise won't wake him. About 4:00 p.m. I hear the TV click on, so I go in to see him still sleepy-eyed.

"Did you have a good rest?"

"I wasn't sleeping," he says.

"Oh. Maybe you were just resting your eyes."

"That's it," he says, smiling.

I stretch over him for a kiss, and he snares me in a bear hug.

After supper we strike out for a walk. The eastern sky is a roiling mass of huge thunderheads.

"Boy, who's getting it?" I ask.

"Looks like around Hartsel."

"Any chance for us?"

"Maybe, but it is moving south to north along the front range. Watch the clouds."

Moving fast, the storm cell's sheer blackness spells hard rain or hail. Here we only have wind and a damp chilliness. We make it only as far as the gate and return shivering.

I build a fire in the living room and Mick watches TV while I write letters and answer the phone a half dozen times: Carol calling to report she has the sod all laid; my first publisher encouraging me to do a show he's hosting; Arrowhead clients needing reservations for accommodations. Each time I return to the living room, Mick grows more sullen.

"What's wrong?" I ask.

"You leaving again?"

When I don't respond he adds, "To one of those stupid bullshit conventions."

"Mick, I should do this one. They offered me $600 for four days and an evening show. That's nearly as much as I make at Arrowhead ranch in a month."

Silent, he stares at Bryan White singing on Prime Time Country.

"That kid ain't country," he snaps. "He ought to sing in New York City."

I let the conversation lapse. Mick goes to bed. I take a long soaking bath in gardenia-scented crystals and put on my silk long johns. Rain patter on the window cheers me. I climb into bed and snuggle into Mick's flank.

"Good night. I love you," I say.

He does not answer because he is angry again, angry at me, angry at the world. I cannot let it bother me. I stay close to him, hoping our combined body heat will thaw out the icicle that sticks in his heart.

Thursday, May 22nd

On the dark porch I put on coats and scarf and gloves then step outside. The first rain kisses my face. My lips, dry and flaky, open to the moisture. I tilt my head back, begging for more. The sprinkle is not much more than a drizzle, but I hear the drops hitting my coat and falling in sensuous plops from the roof. It is barely light enough to make out the wet fences. Mud sticks to the bottoms of my boots.

When the sun bursts over the eastern hills, the earth looks a hundred times greener. Mick listens to the morning news. Some eastern plains towns got four inches of rain. Flooding is predicted in many places. The sweet music of the rain sings "grass, grass, grass."

Rain and more rain. Concerned about the calves, Mick leaves to check on them. He is glad he got the branding done before the storm hit. I organize my thoughts and schedule the things I must do before Dad's surgery.

A slow steady drizzle falls. It rains and rains.

Midmorning I put away my pad and pen, wrap on an apron and stir shortening, sugar, vanilla, eggs, flour, soda, salt, oats, and chocolate chips together. I spoon sticky gobs of dough on greased sheets and bake until the rounds turn golden brown. The oven warms the chilly day and sweet treats to fill the empty cookie jar. And it continues to rain.

I wake Mick for lunch. He stretches and yawns like a long lean cat. I offer a hand to help him rise and he follows me into the kitchen. Washing his hands, he looks over the growing pile of cookies.

"No," I say, reading his mind. "After dinner."

Like a scolded child, he gives me a cockeyed grin, sits and eats.

At Arrowhead Ranch rain spills off the clubhouse and makes tin-roof music. I do paperwork and visit with hardy, dripping anglers who have braved the storm to fish the lakes.

Later, after supper, Mick, Blue, and I hike downriver to look over the stream where major damage occurred last year at the Arrowhead road. In places the water laps over low edges, but so far the banks hold. Water fans out everywhere like silver lace in the old brown grass. We head home across soggy meadows where new grass spikes inches high. Within minutes our boots are soaked through. No complaints: wet feet means feed for cattle and horses.

Friday, May 23rd

When I pull into the clubhouse, Carol is watering the new-laid sod. We carry garbage cans marked "Please recycle aluminum cans" to every cabin, then take the pickup to the Ridge Road to load big rocks to outline Carol's proposed flowerbeds. We work in tandem, grunting and moaning, laughing and cussing the hard work. Back at the office I tackle piled-up bookwork as I listen to Carol talking to the rocks as she places them: "Now stand up there. No you're too big. You go over there. Well, just go ahead and fall over then." Like living things in her hands, each rock must have its proper place.

I find Mick tightening the twine on a big bale of hay loaded on his '37 Chevy when I pull in the yard. He tells me another neighbor contacted him about doing a grazing lease in order to retain agricultural tax status on his subdivision lot. "Boy," he says, "don't you just love the way people hate cows until they find out that cattle on the land reduces their taxes."

Saturday, May 24th

Even my bones feel bruised this morning. They feel purple and green. Still I roll from bed determined to walk up Copper Ridge to offer up prayers for my father. The thermometer sticks on thirty-two degrees. Topped by frozen tears, each blade of grass glistens. Screeching killdeer dart out of the sage. Shasta daisies blossom, as do the tiny purple snapdragon-heads of milk vetch, and the first gray-green, orange-tinged spears of Indian paintbrush.

On the ridgetop I sit on a stump looking across a great distance to Buffalo Peaks, and when I pray I do not ask for my father's life. I ask only that he will not suffer, or if he must suffer, that he is granted the strength to endure. I cannot ask for anything for myself. No thoughts or words come to express my emptiness. I just ask to be given the will to go on.

Back home Mick waits for me. I have been gone an hour and a half, and the day is fully lighted.

"I was getting worried. Where did you go?" he asks.

"Up on the ridge by the fire pit."

"You . . . oh, I see." Unable to even mention my father's illness, he turns away.

"Are you off to the Mikels?"

"Yep."

"I'll type up your cattle leases for you."

Mick leaves on the four-wheeler with Blue perched behind.

I work on the grazing leases for eighty acres to the southeast of us and seventy acres to the north of us. The people who own these marginal lands have us fix the fences and allow the cattle to forage and bed down on their lots. In exchange they receive an ag-tax status instead of having to pay much higher residential costs.

Mick comes home in the best mood I've seen him in for months. Spring gave him a shot in the arm.

"How'd it go?" I ask.

"Made some progress. I'm in good shape. Water enough. Beaver more or less under control, leaving things alone for now. We may get some hay yet."

"Good! You have your choice of leftovers or leftovers for lunch."

"Leftovers are fine," Mick says signing the paperwork I have laid out on the table for him.

Memorial Day traffic burdens the highway and Fairplay is very crowded. At the Y-intersection leaving town, I wait impatiently while twenty-five cars pass by before I can get on the road. I keep the truck at sixty-five, but cars, trucks, trailers, and campers pass me as if I'm not moving. Hugging the white line I hope I won't have to take to the ditch. Where are they all coming from? Where are they all going?

Rain-soaked clients wander in and out of the clubhouse breaking up my work routine with sporadic conversation. All afternoon wind-driven rain comes and goes as well. So much for camping in the high country on Memorial Day.

By dusk, though the rain has moved on and the sky has cleared, even the wind has died down. Before full dark Mick and I walk through the pasture looking at sinkholes, threading our way through the sage, commenting on the grass, the cattle, the summer ahead.

"Did you ever figure out which way the future leans?" I ask.

"No. Just taking it one day at a time and playing everything by ear."

"Guess that's all you can do."

"It isn't easy," he says.

"I know. I just wondered if we'd be hanging on for a while yet."

"Sure. No choice, is there?"

"Oh, I think there are lots of choices, but choices mean change."

"Too bad I can't go on the same way forever. I've been at it fifty years."

"I want you to be happy, Mick."

"Happy? What's that?"

"Happy. You know. Relax. Have fun. Enjoy life. Ease up and don't work so hard."

"Oh yeah. I've heard about that. Guess I never learned how."

"Can you start now?"

"I doubt it."

I take hold of his gloved hand in an attempt to draw him closer, to let him know I'm near, on his side, ready to help him however I can. He squeezes my fingers, then lets go, bending to pet Blue who trots at his heels. I stuff my hands in my pockets.

The bridge between us crumbles, falling away in bits and pieces. I'm at a loss as to how to do repairs. Perhaps I can't. All things have a life span.

All things age and die. Maybe it is time for me to stop patching and let the center disintegrate. The past few years have been hard work, but I'm learning to walk alone. With eyes wide open, arms out for balance, one foot in front of the other, I avoid looking at the rush of dangerous water beneath me. One distraction could cause a serious fall. Mick never learned to swim, but he has no fear of the water. He has always walked a confident, straight, and narrow trail. He has always walked alone.

Sunday, May 25th

I wake early but stay in bed, unmoving, watching the light come again out of the dark sky. For a long while Mick remains motionless, breathing evenly in sleep. Then he stirs, stretching himself into semiwakefulness. He reaches out and pulls me against his curved body, and I squirm deeper into the musky warmth of the bed covers. He breathes against the back of my neck and on my shoulder where the spirit air stirs my hair slightly. His left hand slowly roams down the length of my silk-clad leg, up my thigh, curves around my butt, reaches along my back until I stretch into his quiet lovemaking.

When he speaks his voice is dry and hoarse. "Want me to get up first?"

"Yes. I'm lazy." I can't move. The bed rolls with the shift of his weight, then I listen to the morning sounds of the house: crumpling paper, the opening and closing of the door to let Blue out, the coffeepot, the radio, the soft scrunch and shuffle of boots being put on, the walking to the window in the living room to check the temperature, the opening and closing of the door as Blue comes back in, and Mick speaking baby talk to him.

Later, when I wash at the bathroom sink, the face that looks back at me from the mirror has the oldest eyes I've ever seen.

Still Mick grins at me when I join him. "Cold, huh?"

"Um, huh," he says over a mouthful of gingersnaps, "thirty."

"Brrrr. Are we ever gonna get summer?"

"Maybe. Two days in July."

"Geez, this country just won't warm up."

"Worse than Wyoming?"

"Maybe. Seems like, anyway."

Intent on ditches and water and beaver and cows, Mick leaves early. I leave a note taped to the porch window: "Mom and Dad. I'm downriver at Arrowhead. Make selves at home."

Along the river bottom I survey clumps of willows, searching for those with the greenest, hardiest shoots. I use a pocketknife to cut each quarter-inch branch, then lay them on the ground in a growing pile. When I have as many as I can carry, I head for the stream, balance on the drop-off bank, and stick each shoot several inches into the stones and mud at the water's edge. Off-color and running wild, the current splashes headlong into banks and gravel bars, knowing its destination.

Aching and miserable, I finally give up the task and hike home into the wind. I throw in a load of laundry and do a half-fast house cleaning. Mick comes in looking frozen to the bone.

"Whenever I come in you're vacuuming," he says.

"See anything?" I turn off the noisy machine.

"No beaver. Traps sprung, but only a few sticks placed halfheartedly in the dam so maybe I spooked him off."

"Really?" I smile. Mick shakes his head.

"Well, for now. I know he'll be back sometime. I reset the traps. And I saw fifteen cow elk."

"Any calves?"

"Not yet. They're getting ready though. They looked scruffy. Shedding time. Not spooky. They just stood there and watched me."

"Wish I'd seen them," I say, then go back to work.

Mom and Dad arrive with a tub of fried chicken and a bouquet of flowers. Dad has gained back ten pounds and cheerfully talks sports and weather with Mick. If Dad worries about his upcoming surgery, he doesn't say anything. Because it is too cold to walk, I suggest a drive up-country to see how far we can get up Weston Pass before hitting the snow line.

Mick and Dad take pilot and copilot seats. Mom and I snug into the narrow back seat as passengers. Blue takes up guard duty on the flatbed.

It has been months since I've driven up this way, and I'm surprised at the number of new homes, fences, for-sale signs, and power lines. Mick points out each change in the valley. Traffic and holiday campers cram the forest campgrounds.

The old stage road, which has been widened for modern vehicles, rides rough as a washboard. Mick drives super slow, which gives us the opportunity to soak in the spectacular scenery. Feeling like a tourist, I let my eyes absorb every nuance of tree and stream, sky and rock. At the Rich Creek trailhead, old snowdrifts clot the trees and as we climb higher the snow deepens, filling ravines and covering the steep peaks.

Mick points out a place where he camped over fifty years ago when an old log cabin still stood beside the headwaters of the South Fork of the South Platte.

"We had a fire in that old stove and caught the bed on fire," he says, laughing. "My cousins and I were just kids. It snowed two feet." He points out the white bulk of a distant peak. "I was on top of that thing a long time ago."

"What in the world were you doing up there?" Mom asks.

"Hunting timberline bucks. Went up one side and down the other. I was younger then."

"I bet," Mom says.

At the top of the pass, past the ruins of the Ruby mine, a giant snow-drift blocks the road. Four-wheel drives have been grinding up the hill-side to go around the drift, tearing up the delicate tundra, cutting deep ruts in the fragile soil. Mick turns around next to the shell of a cabin gone down with age and neglect. From here the view of Buffalo Peaks and South Park inspires awe with long, long vistas filled with timber and sky.

Our downhill journey takes much less time. Back at the ranch house Mick says good-bye with a forthrightness that is difficult for him. "I'm not much good at praying, Frank, but I'll be pulling for you."

"One and the same thing, Mick," Dad says. "I appreciate it."

"Good-bye dear," Mom teases Mick, hugging him.

"Good-bye. Good-bye," he says. "Let me know if you need anything."

After Mom and Dad's car disappears, I make myself walk and pass the miles by studying new plant growth along the way. Wild roses on the ditch bank are leafed out, as are the gooseberries with their little Donald Duck feet–shaped leaves. Wild peas bloom along the south banks where the sun strikes hottest, their yellow flowers like dots of butter against the green leaves. Monte has turned on the irrigation and water spills in silver runnels across the meadows. Thick grass has turned the landscape into a lush pelt. Everything is enjoyable except the wind; the constant wind, the brash, harsh, insistent, ever-present, and disquieting wind.

On the lip of an approaching storm, I cut our tiny yard with the push mower and to use the weed eater along the flowerbeds. My plants are growing. Even a few violets from last year have returned. One pansy blooms pale yellow, as ephemeral and light as butterfly wings. Blue lies on the wooden walkway and watches. Mick taps on the window, waves, and then joins me.

The storm gathers, pulling in wicked-looking clouds around the divide. A few hard pellets of ice-snow spit down. As we sit on the stoop, I brush Blue, pulling the tangled mats of dead winter hair from his legs and belly. Mick and I engage in the idle mutterings of a couple caught up in the limbo of lost worlds. Then we walk uphill to the ranch gate. Mick touches the post and sings out, "All ye, all ye, all come free!"

"What's that from?" I ask.

"Kick the can. Maybe hide-and-seek. I don't know. We played it when we were kids."

"What happens to us, Mick? What happens to all our hopes and dreams and the things we want so badly as children?"

"Beats me."

"Did you dream of being something in particular when you were young?"

"What do you mean?"

"Like a policeman, or a fireman . . . or a lawyer," I add as a joke.

"No."

"How about a cowboy?"

"No. Guess I already was one."

"When you played cowboys and Indians, which were you?"

"I was an Indian," he says.

"I was a cowboy."

"You couldn't be a cowboy—you were a girl."

"But I could pretend. I still want to be a cowboy."

"Not now. You're too busy herding fish and playing poetry."

"Oh, you never know. I could grow up and surprise you."

"I thought you already were grown up."

"Not yet. I've gotten older is all. I hope I never grow up. At least not all the way."

"I was born old," he says.

"Were you?"

"Yes, born old, but one hundred years too late."

"Would you have been happier in the 1800s?"

"Hell, yes. I'd have fit in better."

"No TV. No phone. No fancy four-wheel drive one-ton truck."

"That's okay by me," he says.

"Just a horse, a bedroll, beans, and biscuits."

"Sounds fine."

"No ranch, no wife, no children, no responsibilities, no ties, no insurance."

"Now you're talking."

"Are you really that unhappy, Mick?"

"No, but I wish my life had been different."

"If you had to live it over again, what would you change?"

"Nothing. I guess I'd just be dumb enough to do it all over again the same way."

"And end up in the same leaky boat with no paddles trying to get upstream?"

"I guess."

"Well, a leaky boat's better than no boat, especially when you don't swim."

"Guess I'll sink like a stone then."

"I could teach you to dog paddle."

"No use. I'm too old."

We have talked ourselves out and stroll home in silence.

Cold and anxious to be warm we head for bed. I miss Hale-Bopp's guiding presence as much as I know I'll miss my dad when he dies.

Monday, May 26th

The sky wears the steely gray of a frigid morning. Frost and a scant quarter inch of crystal-like snow cover the landscape wherever there is grass or brush or trees. Only the warmer dirt road has escaped the white brush of returned winter. Halfway to the county road the barest kiss of new sun touches my shoulders. I turn back to look. An orange-red ball sticks between the two granaries like it was placed there by a giant's playful hand.

"Cold!" I place my icy fingers against Mick's cheek.

"Twenty-two."

"Gee. I'm glad I covered my flowers."

Before he leaves for his day's work, Mick brings my Explorer around. He hugs me and wishes me luck.

"What time do you want your daily call?" I ask.

"Six a.m."

"You got it. I love you."

He waits a moment, looking at me. "I love you too," he finally says.

I wait and watch until he and Blue disappear from sight on the four-wheeler, then I load my car. Before I leave, I put a note on Mick's pillow: *I love you more than words can say.* And I place one by his usual place at the kitchen table: *Honey, please cover my plants again if it gets really cold. Thanks for everything. xxxxx Love, L.*

I remove the burlap bags from my flowers. They look shocked and forlorn, but still green enough to be alive.

I drive the road I've come to know so well, and fear never makes a move into my field of vision. Familiarity has given rise to acceptance, if not courage, or comfort, or joy. The curves and turns and passes disappear behind me like a procession of scenic wonders in the rearview mirror.

Mom and Dad's house looks as serene as a sitting hen. The yard is green, the bricks brown and green and stately, the wood blending in with the pines and spruce. An American flag flutters from its perch on the porch.

Early afternoon we leave for the hospital and are caught in the post-holiday crush of traffic on U.S. 24 down Ute Pass. I haven't been in a traffic jam since I left the Chicago area over twenty years ago. A black Corvette sidles alongside us. Another car rear-ends the low-slung beauty with a gigantic crash.

"Don't stop," Dad says. "Tap the brakes to warn the other cars coming behind."

At the hospital emergency room check-in they have Dad's paperwork and plastic ID bracelet ready. We wend our way through the look-alike hallways to Room 927. The view faces east onto the helipad and the Flight For Life helicopter. Trees stretch over the streets of the city. A plains settlement, Colorado Springs was once treeless. Settlers imported every bit of visible green. Trees were tended, nurtured, and encouraged until they changed the face of the landscape.

Dad on Memorial Day just before his surgery.
Photo by Laurie Wagner Buyer.

Dad teases his pretty cheerful nurse, and she takes it all in stride. He is given a gown to put on, and I tie the strings in back for him. Together we battle the expected list of a thousand questions on the medical history and a brief discussion on the surgical prep. Dad must drink a gallon of fluids. Mom and I laugh at the five-year-old-child faces he makes as he tries to chug-a-lug a small glass of the stuff every fifteen minutes. Hours tick by. Dad watches the Bulls game on TV. Mom and I read. We hate to leave, but Dad assures us he is okay.

Back home Mom and I walk around the block to enjoy the evening sunshine and birdsong. A chilly breeze blunders off the peak, making us hurry the last half block to get back indoors.

I'm tucked in bed, unbelievably tired, when I hear the phone ring and then Mom talking to Dad. An hour later I hear her talking again. In the morning I ask her who called so late.

"Dad," she says. "He said we forgot to say prayers so he called back so we could say them together over the phone."

Tuesday, May 27th

What can be said about a hospital waiting room? Mom and I do not talk. We bury our faces in books. I write a bit, think a lot. At nine, a surgical nurse comes to tell us they have just gotten started. A little after eleven another nurse comes by to let us know Dad is doing fine; the doctor had removed the esophagus and was stitching Dad's stomach to the small stub of esophagus at the top of his throat. At noon Mom and I eat sandwiches we brought from home. We watch our fellow waiters, each of them in his or her personal little world of worry. Another nurse comes by and tells us Dad is out of surgery, and we can come see him in forty-five minutes.

The rest of the afternoon Mom and I take half-hour stands by Dad's bed as he slips in and out of consciousness in ICU. He holds my hand in a death grip that reminds me of a baby clutching an adult finger. With a ventilator down his throat, a feeding tube down his nose, a urinary catheter and tubes and drain bags out his chest, he isn't a pretty sight. He can blink his eyes and nod his head. When he wants something, we play the twenty questions game as he nods yes or no. Electronic equipment blinks and bleeps with alien accuracy, but I go by my own tried-and-true country indicators of life: his color is good, his breathing even, his forehead cool, and when the nurse empties the catheter bag, his urine is pale and clear so there's no infection.

Mom tells Dad we must leave. He shakes his head no and holds her hand hard. When she explains that we must go get Eileen at the airport, he understands, shakes his head yes and waves us out the door with a limp backhand sweep.

We beat the rush-hour traffic and make it across town to the airport. Eileen's flight arrives. The three of us create a flurry of unstoppable chatter. Back at the hospital, Eileen's face goes white when she sees Dad hooked up and helpless. She garners some courage and takes his hand.

As the evening wears on we take turns at Dad's side, listening carefully to whatever the nurses can share with us. They say Dad is going to be fine.

When they take the ventilator out, Dad seems more relaxed and calm breathing on his own. The night nurse encourages us to go home and sleep. She tells us they will call if Dad makes any change for the worse.

Wednesday, May 28th

I call the hospital early. Dad's nurse says he is talking and trying to tease her.

We wait on the ninth floor, flowers from friends in hand, craning our necks down the long hall trying to see when Dad comes off the elevator. When we spot him in a wheelchair with a covey of nurses and aides, we rush forward, but they wave us back, asking us to give them ten minutes to get him settled.

When Dad sees the lovely pot of yellow mums we brought, he tells us in a croaking voice to give them to someone who doesn't have any family or friends with them. We hang around with Dad one at a time, each of us taking turns so we will not over-tire him with our constant chatter. Throughout the long afternoon we pace up and down the hallway, sit in the waiting room, or lean against the wall in Dad's room. Finally Dad gives us the "go away" sign. We cover him with kisses until his eyes say, "Leave me alone."

Thursday, May 29th

When I reach the ranch, the valley is green as far as the eye can see and cattle dot the hillsides like small dark exclamation marks. I am very tired, but I go with Mick to fix fence just to be with him outside, walking the earth.

The aspens, with frail new leaves, tremble. Mick finds a five-point elk antler up in the pine timber on the ridge above the Mikels and a chunky piece of petrified wood on an open hillside where the wind and rain have scoured away the topsoil. I carry the rocklike wood in my hand, and I can feel its heavy history.

Storms roll in, and we work in the rain. They roll away, and we steam in the brief sun, then freeze when the wind kicks up, pitching a fit. On our way home we see a man parked on the side of the road, the tailgate of his utility vehicle open, his lunch bottles and papers strewn all over the ground as he fishes the river, casting his line over the barbed wire fence that hosts a large no-trespassing sign. We stop for a second. The man waves. Mick says, "The son-of-a-bitch." I say, "Go on. It isn't worth the effort to try and explain that he's trespassing when the sign is right in front of his eyes."

I call Mom as soon as I get in the door, stripping off my wet clothes as I talk. The surgeon has seen Dad. No evidence of cancer in the esophagus. No tumors. A very good prognosis, Dad's doing well. She and Eileen had a good nonstop talking kind of a day.

Stretched out on the couch I try to read, but my brain races as relief battles worry. Finally, I give up the attempt to relax and take a shower. I study my face in the steamy mirror. It seems a miracle that I am alive, that Dad is still alive. In bed, I hear rain hitting the window. I am too tired to even pray.

Friday, May 30th

Waking first, Mick builds a fire to ward off the chill of a wet morning. I stumble around in a sleepy fog. The sun comes out bouncing light off of every swollen raindrop. Before leaving to check his irrigation, Mick lays me down on the couch and loves me until my legs and arms are limp, until my mind goes blank with pleasure.

All morning I fuss with deskwork and answer the telephone. The water commissioner calls to find out what ditches we are running. Arrowhead clients call to book reservations and ask about the weather.

When noon rolls around I fix Mick deer steak and boiled potatoes, then we head back out on the fence again. The day warms, a perfect temperature to be outside working. A porcupine waddles through the sage, and I holler at Blue to leave him be. Everywhere, trees are down on the fence line. It looks like a huge godlike sneeze blew them down overnight. No storms today, but clouds build again in threatening disarray. Tumble Creek is up, the water darkened with silt.

On our return we decide to drive via Bear Gulch, a ten-mile trek on old logging roads. Dead trees haunt the edges of thick pine and fir. We mark locations for the firewood we will need next fall. Rolling across Long Park, we stop at the stock tanks on Forest Service land, surprised to see that they are full and running water. The leaseholder will be putting cattle back on the allotment this summer.

Eileen calls me in the middle of the evening. Dad was able to get up and walk a bit, and an aide helped him take a shower. He was talking with enough gumption to tell Mom and Eileen "Get out—you're bugging me!" We laugh because any sign of temper shows that Dad is on the mend.

Mick and I play with Blue, throwing his ball across the living room, hiding his ring toy, giving him his daily tick check and a puppy dog massage. He eats up the affection like he's been starving. Smart and sensitive, he knows everything that goes on around him. He mopes while I worry about Dad and Mick worries about ranch chores. Weariness hangs around us like a cloud. Before bed, the three of us sit together. Mick in his chair, me on the floor between his legs, and Blue nestled in my lap.

Saturday, May 31st

I walk under scattered clouds gilded with gold and purple light. Two cow elk and two spikes mosey through the sage heading for the aspen trees. I scold Blue "no" and he sits with his nose twitching.

I work at Arrowhead. The sun streams through the windows making the room so warm I have to open both for a cooling cross breeze. I savor this first honeyed taste and smell of summer. Outside Carol scolds the dandelions that have sprung up all over her lawn. "You nasty little creatures. I'll show you. Tomorrow I'll bring my weed spray." The globs of egg-yolk yellow sprinkled through the green grass glow like golden starbursts on a quilt of emerald eiderdown.

Mick is home when I return. He has had a bad day. I fix him a sandwich and he eats standing by the door. Then he is gone again. The river is up, out of its banks, and beginning to wash out his head gates and dams. I offer to go along, but he waves me away.

I take a bath and read in bed, listening to the frogs serenading the approaching night through the open window. It is past dark when Mick comes in and collapses on the bed. I help him pull off his boots and fold his clothes. Within minutes he is snoring lightly. So tired, feeling battered, bruised, and buried alive with undefined worries, I toss and turn but cannot sleep.

Sunday, June 1st

The river runs very high, its song deeper and threatening. I walk to clear the cobwebs out of my mind and see the first silvery specter-faced loco plant near the dump. Birds call, repeating melodies barely heard above the roar of water.

At breakfast Mick and I are both silent. He leaves immediately to fight the serious problem on the stream. I head back to Woodland Park to take Eileen to the airport, and then take Mom to the hospital to see Dad.

Glentivar Flats stretch wide and greening, and the rolling ribbon of highway unfolds before me. Traffic is heavy: trucks with trailers, boats, campers, RVs, Sunday recreationists heading to the high country. I am one of only a few cars headed east toward the front-range city. Four hot-air balloons hang suspended against the wide sky, their man-made brilliant colors contrasting with the distant deep greens, pale grays, burnt browns, and unfathomable blacks of the Colorado landscape.

Images flash in my mind like still photos stolen from a camera. Shot one: Mick stands on a beaver dam thigh deep in rushing brown water struggling to pull the debris of another washed-out dam over and down into the swirl below. Head gates flood and ditch banks wash away. He calls to me, his voice urgent, but I cannot hear him over the deafening roar of the river.

Shot two: Clad in a funny-print hospital gown, his exposed butt as small and round as a boy's, my father stands unsteadily in front of a large bright mirror, struggling to shave as I hold the loops of his oxygen hose. Gingerly, he places four quivering fingers over the stapled five-inch incision on his neck, then grimaces, twisting his cheeks and lips and chin in circuslike stretches to reach his stubbly whiskers.

Shot three: At the ninth floor hospital window, my mother looks out at Pikes Peak, still snow-spotted, surrounded by the roil of thunderheads and lightning flashes. Unafraid of heights or storm or the approaching night, a pigeon struts along the window ledge.

My attention jerks back to the left side of the highway where an antelope races the traffic, hugging the high wire fence. He is far off, but approaching quickly. The buck pounds the ground as fast as his legs will carry him. He wearies. His head droops. His mouth gapes wide. As he gasps for each breath, steamy puffs escape above his curved ebony horns.

The borrow ditch is deep, the fence high. Vehicles spill past going sixty-five and seventy. He runs and runs.

The antelope reappears in my rearview mirror, still running. The buff-colored patch of his rump wavers and rises as he dips downhill, races back up. I want to pull over, stop the traffic, cut the fence. I want some sort of benevolent magic to draw the fear from his protruding eyes. In the moment it takes me to blink, he disappears from view. I press my foot on the accelerator.

The antelope's spirit runs within me. My father's blood rushes in my veins. Trapped by wire and asphalt and a world that outraces even the fastest sprinter alive, my heart pounds. My lungs ache as breaths come hard and fast. Tears cloud my vision. Yet somewhere the horizon will grow equal to my eye, the ground will level out, and at a low spot in the fence I will wheel and leap and be free.

EPILOGUE

ᴥ

Woodland Park, Colorado, Spring 2007

Seven months after I stopped writing in my journal, on Pearl Harbor Day, December 7, 1997, my father died of cancer at home with my mother, my sisters, and me by his side. We buried him with full military honors on a bitter cold, snowy day at Fort Logan National Cemetery in Denver. I carried out Dad's last wish for me by earning an MFA in Writing from Goddard College in 2001.

With constant cajoling, I convinced Mick to consider a conservation easement for his land. In the fall of 2001, after several years of difficult negotiation, he sold the DM development rights to Colorado Open Lands. Now legally protected from subdivision, the ranch remains a perpetual haven for wildlife and agriculture.

Scott Saunders worked with the Nature Conservancy to preserve the river corridor on the Arrowhead Ranch Fly Fishing Resort. In December 2006, Scott sold the property in its entirety. Now called the Winding River Ranch, the private land is no longer open to outsiders for fishing.

Though Mick and I rebuilt his cow herd, a kidney disease diagnosis in 2001 forced him to sell all his cattle in the fall of 2002. His ranch legacy and the DM brand will pass on to his children and grandchildren. John

Laurie with Blue and Mick in front of the old bunkhouse.
Photo by Laurie Wagner Buyer.

and Mary Ann adopted a girl, Jenny. Melody and Dan gave Savanah a brother, Sid.

While I managed to help Mick save the ranch, I failed to save our marriage. After twenty years of living and working together, Mick sued me for divorce and I signed the papers on Valentine's Day 2003.

The socioeconomic climate in South Park continues to change. The old lifeway of ranching consistently falls by the wayside in favor of tourism, recreation, and development. For example, the 36.25 acres that I paid $22,500 for in 1989 (and deeded over to the Buyer Family Partnership in 2001 as part of the conservation easement criteria) was valued by a local realtor in 2006 at $240,000.

Mick still lives on the ranch with Blue, Brandy, the cats, and the draft horse mares.

Now a full-time writer, I share my mother's house when I am not on the road.

FURTHER READING

Buffalo Peaks Wilderness: www.coloradowilderness.com

Colorado Cattleman's Association: www.coloradocattle.org

Colorado Farm Bureau: www.colofb.com

Colorado Open Lands: www.coloradoopenlands.org

Colorado Trout Unlimited: www.cotrout.org

Comet Hale-Bopp: www.halebopp.info

Great Outdoors Colorado: www.goco.org

Laurie Wagner Buyer: www.lauriewagnerbuyer.com

Park Country, Colorado: www.parkco.us

Pike National Forest: www.fs.fed.us/r2/psicc/pp/

Rocky Mountain Elk Foundation: www.rmef.org

Salida and Buena Vista Area Fishing: www.coloradoheadwaters.com

South Park Fly Fishing: www.southparktrout.com

Trout Unlimited: www.tu.org

A NOTE FROM THE AUTHOR

᪣

I did not know when I started writing journal notes
to share with a friend on February 15, 1997, that my father would be diag-
nosed with cancer, that Mick and I would have an impossible season, that
the weather would be so bitter, or that my writing career would make a
leap into recognition and acceptance. All I knew was that I was struggling with my life, my loves, my writing, and my self-identity. By the end
of May, I had filled sixteen legal pads with diary entries. I don't know why
I stopped writing when I did. Something about my encounter with the
antelope on the highway told me that the story, at least that part of my
story, was finished.

That same summer my friends Bill and Jo Murray came to visit. When
Jo asked me what I'd been working on, I brought out a box filled with the

legal pads. Shocked, she said, "You can't leave all that writing in a box. What if the house burned down? You need a computer." Her statement catapulted me into the twentieth century. Bill and Jo bought me a computer and Scott Saunders taught me how to use it. Up until that point I had done all my writing longhand and then typed final drafts on an IBM Selectric typewriter.

I spent the winter and spring of 1998 putting the manuscript, my first major piece of prose, on the computer. Surprised to find that I had over three hundred pages of text, I thought the story could be a book. The title *Spring's Edge* came to me because the imagery hangs on the idea of winter turning into spring, of that hope we all harbor that new life always comes.

Typed and saved on a disk, I sent the story to Melinda Harvey at Grey Horse Press in Lubbock, Texas. Melinda, the self-proclaimed "grammar Nazi," printed out the story and red-inked it to her heart's content. I made corrections and sent the story out to friends for comments. Regina West, Bill and Jo Murray, Jan Williams, Mickey and Jim Wallace, Paulette Jiles, Nancy Curtis, and Dale Walker all read the manuscript. I owe each of them a world of thanks.

I believed in *Spring's Edge* and the notion that the common everyday events on a ranch, in a marriage, in a family, in a rural, agricultural culture struggling to survive would speak to people. In December of 1998, I applied for a $4,000 literature artist fellowship with the Colorado Council on the Arts and sent part of *Spring's Edge* as my writing sample. In January 1999 my manuscript won an award. One of the panelists commented that the merit of the work lay in the fact that it "gave meaning to 'ordinary' experience, [that it was] luminous [and] thoroughly enjoyable reading."

During 1999, I worked on *Spring's Edge* again whenever I could find the time. I did not change anything major in the manuscript, but I honed and polished each sentence. I submitted the story to four publishers and received four rejections. However, each press told me that they appreciated reading *Spring's Edge* and encouraged me to keep sending it out.

In July of 2000, at my graduate residency at Goddard College in Vermont, I saw the Story Line Press advertisement for the Beryl Markham Prize for Creative Non-Fiction in *Poets and Writers* magazine. I had always admired Beryl Markham, her life, and her writing, so I copied the ad. When I got home I put the contest entry aside thinking that I had nothing to enter that would qualify as creative non-fiction. Then I remembered *Spring's Edge* sitting on a shelf gathering dust. I wrote a cover letter and sent the manuscript off the end of July. One winter evening, six months later, I had a call from publisher Robert McDowell telling me I'd won the Beryl Markham Prize for Creative Non-Fiction. Surprised and delighted, I was pleased that someone saw, in my life and in my work, something memorable and worth reading, something that would endure long after the moments of emotion, beauty, purity, and clarity that stirred me to write were gone.

After many unmet promises and five years of waiting for Story Line Press to publish *Spring's Edge*, I realized that the financially strapped publisher was unable to honor the contract we'd signed. Concerned that I might lose the rights to the memoir if Story Line filed for bankruptcy, I asked Robert McDowell to return the rights to me. He did so with heart-felt apologies.

At a Western Writers of America conference in 2005, I pitched *Spring's Edge* to Luther Wilson at the University of New Mexico Press. The story survived a rigorous evaluation from the required readers and editorial boards. In January 2007, ten years after writing the story, I signed another contract. I spent that spring making the revisions required by outside readers and cut 44,000 words to bring the manuscript to an acceptable size.

I am indebted to Luther Wilson for believing in this book and to Dawn Wink, fellow rancher and writer, for her careful reading and encouragement. Finally, endless appreciation to my beloved other, W. C. Jameson, for reminding me every day to trust my poetic sensibility and to hold fast to the rhythms of the natural world.